THE
FUTURE
OF (ALMOST)
EVERYTHING

How our world will change
over the next 100 years

SECOND EDITION

PATRICK DIXON

P

PROFILE BOOKS

This edition expanded and updated in 2019

First published in Great Britain in 2015 by
Profile Books Ltd
3 Holford Yard
Bevin Way
London WC1X 9HD
www.profilebooks.com

A CIP catalogue record for this book is available from
the British Library.

ISBN 978 1 78816 234 0
eISBN 978 1 78283 181 5

Text design by sue@lambledesign.demon.co.uk

Typeset in Dante by MacGuru Ltd

Printed and bound in Great Britain by
CPI Group (UK) Ltd, Croydon CR0 4YY

Mixed Sources
Product group from well-managed
forests and other controlled sources
www.fsc.org Cert no. TT-COC-002227
© 1996 Forest Stewardship Council

Contents

Introduction

The truth about the future

Over the next 20 years, our world will be shaken by a series of seismic events and inventions, overtaking governments, corporations and our personal lives. We are hurtling at astonishing speed into a future that few understand, with massive implications for the future of humanity.

Take hold of the future or the future will take hold of you.

My job is to live in 2050, and to see tomorrow as history.

Since 1996, I have worked with around 400 of the world's largest 2,000 companies in every industry, and with many governments, as a guide to the *truth* about life in years to come. Most of what I predicted has happened, described in 17 books and a thousand keynotes.

Here is what I am telling senior leaders across the world about life up to 2050 and far beyond, based on a proven methodology, including a chapter on life in 2120. As we will see, in the years ahead board debates about the future will not be so much about *trends*, which will often be obvious, but about *timing*, which will be absolutely critical. For example, by when will most new cars sold in Paris be electric powered?

What is really changing – why many other trends will fizzle out

We face the greatest threats to survival in human history, while technology also offers the greatest opportunities ever known to solve these challenges.

Consumer choices are changing radically. Most of today's companies will vanish in 20 years. Who will be the winners and losers? And what actions do leaders need to take?

Future generations will be truly shocked at the scale of our population growth, our destructiveness, our careless waste and toxic pollution. Decisions made in the next two decades will change life on earth for over 10,000 years, as tens of millions more species are wiped out, as carbon dioxide levels continue to rise, and as we continue to alter entire landscapes.

They will also be shocked at the increasingly 'asymmetric' nature of risk: how easily small groups with limited resources were able to hijack entire national agendas, dominate global news, damage economic growth, force changes in corporate policy, or hold entire communities to ransom. So we need to pay close attention now to how such groups will gain future power and what their agendas may be.

On the other hand, many trends will develop rather slowly or predictably, much as they have over the last 30 years. As we will see, most people's daily lives will evolve more gradually in many ways than many assume. Indeed, history shows that the more shocking a prediction is, the more likely to be wrong, so we need to take great care, particularly over media-hyped issues such as Brexit or the longer-term impact of President Trump.

Many 'major trends' that now dominate media attention will fizzle out completely, some very soon. Take the digital revolution for example, parts of which are close to maturity. The growth of e-commerce doubled in the UK from 12–24% of retail in less than 5 years. At that rate, 100% of UK retail spending would be online in just over a decade, which of course will never happen. So the current growth rate will slow and plateau quite soon. The same is true for ownership of smartphones globally, growth of time spent online, and so on.

Either you see your own future as something to prepare for, or something to be shaped by your actions. This book is therefore about being *futuristic* rather than *fatalistic*.

As some of my clients have discovered in the past, you can have the greatest strategy on the planet, and superb leadership, but if the world changes unexpectedly, you just travel even faster in the wrong direction. As I learned in my first career as a cancer doctor looking after the dying, *life is far too short to lose a single day* doing things that are a complete waste of time, or that we don't believe in, so we urgently need to know where we are going.

The greatest risk is institutional blindness

Media headlines are full of sensational, alarmist, confusing, foolish and nonsensical predictions, so where do true *foresight* and *insight* come from? We need to start with common sense, and with open eyes.

Over many years, I have seen time and again that the greatest risk of all to any organisation (and indeed to any forecaster) is institutional blindness. When bankers spend too much time with other bankers, the result is soon a banking crisis. When IT people spend too much time with similar IT people, the result can be major system weakness, poor customer design, or vulnerability to cyberattack. When military commanders spend too much time playing war games with their colleagues, the result can be ...

The scariest audience I have ever addressed

I give up to 60 keynotes a year, in many nations, but the scariest audience I have ever addressed was the Pentagon. My task was to give a trends lecture to 500 senior military leaders, and suggest ways in which they could use their vast military powers to *reduce* international tension, *improve* the image of America, *prevent* future wars and *eliminate* national security threats.

The people in my audience were commanders of a major part of the world's greatest force of warships, fighter planes, submarines, nuclear weapons, cruise missiles, drones, tanks, artillery, troops, military intelligence, and so on.

I wandered around the exhibition hall outside the auditorium, looking for some last-minute inspiration. It was packed with impressive displays of military hardware. Sales teams of global arms companies were explaining to me how to target and kill large numbers of people even more efficiently, with even less effort and risk, using their exotic technologies.

It struck me how last century it all felt. The capability of such hardware was truly shocking, technologies awesome, but owning mega-weapons can never build trust, nor deal with underlying causes of conflict, nor repair the heart of broken nations.

How to trigger a major conflict in seconds

In future, the defining issue for a commander will not be how many missiles, or drones, or other forces he controls. It may be something like whether he should give an order in seconds to shoot a six-year-old girl who is walking towards a US army checkpoint, and who might conceivably be carrying a bomb – and all in full view of live TV newsfeeds.

A child whose death could spark local outrage, widespread civil unrest and further bloodshed, as well as global condemnation. The entire might of a military superpower is completely useless in such a moment.

What worried me most of all as I paced outside that hall was that I had been strongly warned that I was the *first* non-American that had *ever* been allowed to address that regular military assembly. Their policy to date had been that only the voices of American citizens were worth hearing. So it was a privilege to be there, and they were very gracious in their willingness to listen to someone with a different world view. You will find a similar blindness in the war games played by other Ministries of Defence in most other nations.

Trapped in a narrow vision

Any organisation can be affected by a mild form of collective madness – the inability to see the wider context. Each of us reads the world around us through our own set of glasses, which distort our perception and reactions, shaped as these are by our culture, birth-place, history and experiences. Therefore, *the* most important step in accurate Futuring is to be aware of your own limitations: take *off* your own glasses, and create mental space to put on other people's.

A personal journey

My own life journey has taken me to 60 countries. I have talked with leaders of the world's largest corporations and governments; engaged with every industry; met innovators and entrepreneurs; advised the super-wealthy; and worked with the poorest of the poor, in megacity slums, refugee camps and remote rural villages.

Market research can't tell you the future

One of the first truths I learned is that market research is a completely useless, expensive and dangerous guide to anything but the very short-term future. Companies and governments waste much of the $46bn they spend on it a year, asking people how they will behave. But moods can change in hours, in response to new products, social media, atrocities, sporting events, huge scandals or the death of a national hero.

Market research is still important, however. We do need to pay the closest attention to our customers, and how they feel. Listen carefully to what they say, and sort out any problems that they see. But don't *believe* them when it comes to the future.

One word will drive the future

Another truth I learned is this. One single factor will drive the future more than events, economics, innovations, technology, demographics, religion or politics. Leaders often focus on metrics, data, financials, analysis, processes, customers, competitors, investors, public opinion and regulations. All these things matter but there is one central element, which is even more important in shaping tomorrow.

If we wish to explore the future, we need to look at how people are likely to FEEL, as well as what they will THINK. The single word that will drive the future is EMOTION. As we will see in every chapter of this book, emotional reactions are usually far more significant than events themselves. All leadership has to connect with emotion, which is why robots cannot lead.

How far do you need to see?

Whenever I am asked to give a lecture on the future, I always ask the same question: how far ahead do you want me to take you, and into what areas?

If you are a *share trader*, you need only to see 3 milliseconds further than the market to make billions of dollars in high-frequency trading.

If you are a *fashion house*, six months ahead may be far enough. If you are a *bank*, your future horizon is probably no more than five years. If you are a *major insurer*, your view will stretch to a decade or more.

My *pharma* clients need 25-year vision, because it takes them 15 to bring a new drug to market, and patents expire after 25.

Energy companies want to look even further. Not long ago I was talking to a senior executive who had signed contracts a decade earlier to extract oil and gas from under the Caspian Sea. It will take another decade to get those fields operational, with a lifetime of 30 years or more. So on signing, she had to take a 50-year view of future energy prices.

How do you guess the future?

How on earth do you *begin* to guess the average price for a barrel of oil from 2040 to 2050?

Some people say that it is impossible and pointless to try to predict. All we can do is prepare for uncertainty. This is dangerous, naive, foolish and fatalistic nonsense. It all depends, of course, on *what* you are trying to predict.

Yes, it is true that no one can consistently predict short-term swings in market prices or exchange rates, or the result of close-run elections, or the next decisions by erratic or stupid politicians, and we can never be *certain* what tomorrow will bring, but that is not what our journey is all about. It is perfectly logical and vitally important for every decision-maker to have well-reasoned expectations of what he or she thinks is most likely to happen – while also considering alternative scenarios, to manage risks.

Long-term trends are often very predictable

All reliable, long-range forecasting is based on powerful mega-trends that have been driving profound, consistent and therefore relatively predictable change over the last 30 years. Such trends are the basis of every well-constructed corporate strategy and government policy. Here are just a few examples:

- gradually falling rates of growth in world population
- people choosing to marry later, or not at all, leading to fewer children in many communities
- rapid but predictable fall in price of digital technology, telcos and networking
- rapid growth of all kinds of wireless/mobile devices and mobile payments
- shift from traditional retail to online sales, with faster delivery
- connectivity between people, companies and machines
- rapid growth of emerging market economics
- rapid growth of emerging market middle-class consumers
- hundreds of millions of people moving to cities
- large migrations from poor nations to wealthier ones
- better global literacy and more university graduates
- fall in costs of production of most mass-produced items
- rapid increase in global trade (despite protectionism) and intense hunger for travel
- formation of trading blocs, free trade areas, currency zones
- ever-larger global corporations, mergers, consolidations, with shorter, more agile supply chains
- rapid growth of gene screening to predict future health
- growth of biotech therapies including stem cells
- better life expectancy with improved diet and health
- ageing of many populations e.g. EU, Japan, South Korea, China
- baby booms in emerging nations such as India and Nigeria

- feminisation of many societies, with more women at work
- increasing concern about child welfare and abuse
- increasing focus on 'health and safety' at work globally
- increased concern about environment/sustainability/food supply
- destabilisation of nations with huge mineral or energy wealth
- shift from wars between nations to civil conflicts
- wider acceptance of democracy (but mistrust of traditional politicians)
- wider adoption of civil rights, protecting the vulnerable
- higher customer expectations for convenience, comfort, value, service, honesty, reliability, speed – and more complaints when standards fall
- rapid automation of routine tasks, in homes, offices, factories
- growth of Artificial Intelligence and increased potential for state control

I could list hundreds more for your own specific industry or nation. These wider trends have been obvious to most trend analysts like myself for a while, and have been well described over 30 years. They evolve much more slowly than booms and busts, or social fads.

All trends connect to all other trends

All major trends interact and only make sense in the context of all other trends. What is more, your own *personal* future is being shaped by over 7.5 billion other people's futures. That is why it is so illogical and dangerous to focus on a single trend. But, sadly, that is what so many economists, biologists, techno-gurus, military advisors and other specialist 'experts' tend to do, each blindly micro-forecasting within their own speciality.

I am not saying that I haven't also got some things wrong. Anticipating future trends is always a risky and potentially humbling process. If you want to judge for yourself, you will find over 600 YouTube videos, hundreds of presentations and articles and the text of six entire books posted since 1997 on my website, visited by over 17 million different people.*

2040 is closer than we think

You may think this a strange question for a Futurist to ask, someone whose career has been built on making sense of rapid change, but this question is of utmost importance:

How much has really changed in the past 20+ years?

The truth is, that despite all the hype about the speed of change, it would not take long to update a business leader who had recently woken up from a coma that had lasted 20 years – probably less than a couple of hours to cover the most important global and social changes. Let us call him Tom ...

Little would really surprise Tom. What would we tell him about? The dot.com crash and 9/11 attack; wars in Iraq, Afghanistan and Syria linked to Islamic militants; cheaper and more mobile computing; faster web, more e-commerce and rapid growth of social media; cheaper technology and robotics; Asia rising fast; more worries about global warming, and solar panels everywhere; big market crash following a long boom, triggered by a bank lending crisis; corporate banking scandals; rising retirement age and worries about pensions; Russia flexing its muscles again; some worries about viral epidemics; and more autocratic, nationalist leaders in nations like Russia, Turkey, Hungary, China and America.

Pushed to see radical change?

But walk Tom down the streets of any capital city in Europe and he would struggle to see much *radical* change, for example, in fashion, music, day-to-day culture, politics, the hopes and dreams of young people. Things would look pretty much the same, apart from more people looking at smartphone screens far more of the time, and buying more online.

Tom would doubtless point out that many people, like him, were

* http://www.globalchange.com

already using smartphones such as the Nokia 9000 in 1996, with full web browser, email, camera, word processing, notepads and prices halving every 12 months. And he might well tell me that his daughter used to run up to 16 chat screens simultaneously back in 1997. Most of the other things above were also signposted in the 1990s in some way. So what would really feel so radically new to Tom today?

Young and old share very similar lives

There is also far less of a 'generation gap' today, compared with what we saw in many developed nations back in the 1950s to 1970s. Younger and older people listen to similar music, watch the same films, wear similar clothes, travel to similar places, and share quite similar values.

People eat out more, and standards of living have risen. Technology is cheaper. Most homes in Europe and America look very similar to what they did in 2000. Offices are more open plan, and people carry their own computers or mobile devices. But most still commute. And TV news looks the same. Hollywood film plots keep being recycled, albeit with better graphics, and major sporting events still attract huge crowds.

Many things in 2040 will also be remarkably similar

The *truth* is that *daily life* for most people will be very similar in many ways in 2040 to what it is today. In many parts of the world, a three-year-old child will have a life that is very familiar, when they are 18, to people who are 18 today. They will have attended high school, taken exams, and be heading for first jobs or university. Hopes, thoughts and dreams will be similar in many ways to yours at the same age.

They too will look in the mirror and wonder about self-image, and hope one day to meet the right person and settle into a wonderful long-term relationship. They too will seek a happy, comfortable life, and think about 'making a difference', or what government they want, or about a more sustainable world.

And when that new generation become parents themselves, they will have similar worries to previous generations about the well-being of their own children. So please don't make the mistake of thinking that human nature will be any different because of next-generation digital, mobile, robotics, virtual life, wearable devices, gene programming, social connectivity or anything else. You only have to look back at the stories of people's lives written 2,000 years ago to realise that our deeper psychological and physical needs are similar in many ways.

The M generation is more concerned about the long-term future

Yet at the same time, fundamental shifts *are* taking place, shifts that will transform societies, wipe out many multinationals, destroy many governments. And the M generation, whose entire adult lives are being lived in the third millennium, is far more concerned about long-range issues such as sustainability.

History will record a very different kind of world by 2050, with a totally new balance of power, new global cultures, new industrial giants, new forms of government and new social habits.

Six Faces of the Future

I have used a Futuring method over the last two decades: Six Faces of the Future. Each face is important and is a chapter of this book, but the relative strength of each face will depend on who you are and where you live.

It is impossible to keep all six faces in view at once: some are related, others are opposites. Together they form the faces of a cube, which we need to keep turning. Emotion is the force that makes the cube spin. The faces spell the word 'FUTURE'.

Fast – speed of change, Wild Cards, future of digital, AI, robotics

Urban – future urbanisation, demography, health, fashions, fads

Tribal – future nations, cultures, social networks, brands, teams

Universal – future globalisation, retail, e-commerce, trade, manufacturing

Radical – death of politics, rise of radical activism, sustainability

Ethical – values, motivation, leadership, aspiration, spirituality

Fast and Urban are closely related and sit together on one side, while Radical and Ethical are also together on the other. On top is Universal, and beneath, pulling in the opposite direction, is Tribal.

Most executives spend their lives looking at the cube from above, at a world that is Fast, Urban and Universal. However, one twist through 180 degrees presents us with a very different view: a world that is Tribal, Radical and Ethical.

Understanding the tension between these two dominant views is really important. As we will see, a tiny minority who are strongly Radical, Ethical and Tribal can impact a company or nation profoundly. Think of nationalist politicians, anti-migration protestors, Islamic State, or climate change activists, or consider consumers who campaign to stop child labour: they are Radical in thinking, driven by a strong sense of Ethics (you may not agree with these ethics but that is irrelevant), and very Tribal (tight, together, well organised).

For every trend, look for a counter-trend

As we will discover, every trend tends to have its counterpart, which is why media pundits are able at once to describe, for example, trends to greater liberalism and greater conservatism, in parts of the same city or nation.

Drug use soars, with growing calls for decriminalisation, at the same time as a neo-prohibitionist movement seeks to make it all but impossible to smoke a cigarette in a public place.

Hyper-sexualisation of children and young teenagers is still promoted every day in Western media and marketing, at the same time as outrage grows over child abuse and sexual harassment.

Expect to see powerful clashes between opposing trends, and a world increasingly of extremes over the next 100 years, with tendencies to intolerance – as we see in culture clashes between Islam and liberal 'Western' culture, and also within Islam itself. The greatest forces will be unleashed by clashes of *conscience* rather than *culture*, influenced by religious conviction, or lack of it. The truth is that in a pluralistic, multi-track society there are a number of pendulums operating in every city and nation, which is why trend-watching is so fascinating.

All leaders must be Futurists

People often ask me what a Futurist is. But in a sense, all thinking people are Futurists. It is part of the human condition to plan ahead. Futurists are just professional future-thinkers, with a span that reaches across industries and nations.

All leaders have to be Futurists. People only follow leaders with a compelling vision of a better future. Vision has to be founded on reality, based on what we know today, and where we are likely to end up if no action is taken.

Why I am optimistic and not apocalyptic

I am often asked if I am an optimist or a pessimist. I am probably an optimist, despite many future threats and challenges, despite the horrors that small numbers of human beings are capable of.

Over the years, many trend-spotters have given dire, apocalyptic and spectacular warnings about our world running out of food, or water, or space, or about all of humankind being wiped out by major events, or being taken over by robots.

As we will see, the vast majority of such claims are alarmist nonsense. Our world is far more resilient than many fear. Humankind has an astonishing and accelerating capacity for genius and innovation, which will solve many of the world's greatest challenges in ways that are hard to imagine today. In addition, there are many balancing forces within global systems. However, human actions can be totally irreversible – for example, 60% of all animal species on earth 100 years ago are now extinct, in many cases (maybe most cases) as a direct consequence of human activity.

So then, let us turn to the first Face of the Future, which is all about the speed of change, and what that may mean for you.

Chapter 1

FAST

PERSONAL LIVES ARE MEASURED in minutes, major events in seconds. Our world is obsessed with instant information. Digital addiction is already one of the commonest causes of anxiety, depression and complete mental breakdown, particularly among young people.

The average 15- to 25-year-old in the UK now spends an average of 4 hours a day on a mobile, checking for messages every 9 minutes, with time online directly correlated with risk of mental health issues.

But that is nothing compared to the Philippines, where a 2019 survey reported people saying that they spend an average of 10 hours online. In the same survey, users in Brazil said that they spent 9 hours 29 minutes online, in Thailand it was 9 hours 11 minutes, in Cambodia 9 hours, in Indonesia 8 hours 36 minutes, in America 6 hours 31 minutes, and in China 5 hours 52 minutes. The worldwide average is now 6 hours and 42 minutes a day of online activity.

Even if these self-reports are a little higher than reality, this is a completely unsustainable trend with massive social implications, not just impacting emotional well-being. What are we saying? Will young people really want to spend 80 hours a week online by 2030? A growing number of parents are unable to cope with young children who demand at least 8 hours a day of screen time and have lost interest in offline life.

The truth about digital happiness

The whole purpose of digital devices was to make us more happy and fulfilled, save us time, make our lives easier, relieve stress and help us relax. That was the promise, but the reality has often been dramatically different for teenagers, especially when we consider the corrosive impact of social media on their self-image.

Most teenage girls in many nations now feel unable to post images without editing to make themselves look 'more attractive'. Their self-worth often depends on being able to post multiple pictures a day of enviable or interesting experiences. Feelings of self-loathing have become the norm. Self-harm is rocketing in many nations, especially among girls, while suicide rates have also soared. In the UK, 25% of 17- to 19-year-old women have a mental illness, mainly depression or anxiety, and 25% of 14-year-old girls say that they have self-harmed in the last year; 12% of 14-year-old boys have done the same.

Six out of ten American teenagers say they have been bullied or harassed online. Part of this is sexting, where teenagers are pressured into sending smartphone images of the private parts of their bodies, to others – many of which may rapidly become much more public, causing great distress.

Expect future reactions against hyper-digital living

As a result of all this, expect some groups to react strongly against digital life over the next 10 to 20 years. We are already seeing a new generation of hyper-connected parents on America's West Coast who are banning their nannies from going online at any time in the presence of their younger children, who are themselves totally banned from all screen contact. These parents live in fear that the brains of their children will be damaged by too early access to digital stimulation. They are probably correct. Expect far more research evidence by 2025 that children who stare at screens for more than seven hours a day have different brain structures. But the greatest risks may turn out to be emotional, rather than changes to the wiring of young brains.

It's not just the content of what is being watched or

experienced, but the massive jump in luminosity. The latest mobile and TV screens project images that are deliberately processed to be sharper, brighter, more vibrant, more intense, and more visually stimulating than reality itself. When you combine surreal imaging with movement on screen, you create something that is almost irresistibly attractive to the eye. Just try talking to someone while a video is playing just beyond sight, behind them, without losing eye contact.

Some say that daily life for most people has never changed so fast, and we must be close to the limits of human endurance, but, despite all of the above, this is untrue. Large populations have coped surprisingly well with far more dramatic, rapid and convulsive changes at times of natural disaster or regional wars. But one thing is certain: expect a growing market for rapid ways to completely de-stress, whether short breaks, spas, manicures, adrenaline-busting experiences, water sports, saunas, live concerts, and so on.

Strategies overtaken by events

Speed of change will be a huge challenge for all leaders. Strategies of large corporations risk being overtaken by events. Your world can change faster than you can hold a board meeting. Expect growing emphasis on leadership agility, dynamic strategy, back-up plans and risk management.

Most medium-sized or large companies will shrivel and die over the next two to three decades, driven out of business by leaders who are techno-blind and uncomfortable with the speed of radical change. Life will be particularly confusing for people who have spent an entire decade or more in the same industry.

Reaction against constant change

In a constantly changing world, things that do not change will gain value. Expect more listed buildings and preservation orders on bits of towns, government buildings, churches, mosques, temples and monuments.

Ancient trees will be more respected, together with unspoiled moorlands, forests and marine landscapes. Old houses will continue to be prized, for those who can afford to live in them.

Wild Cards: 40-year impact in 20 seconds

Our world is now so joined up that small events can easily trigger giant convulsions, becoming defining moments – such as the collapse of communism and the end of the Cold War 25 years ago, the Brexit vote, or the election of President Trump on a very radical, populist agenda.

A few seconds can change history. An earthquake lasting less than a minute triggered a crack in a Japanese nuclear reactor in Fukushima Daiichi district. As a result, Germany and Japan abandoned nuclear energy, which will impact energy markets for 40 years. Yet, at the same time, the UK and China embarked on a nuclear boom. As I said, emotional reactions to events are often far more important than the events themselves.

The sudden retaking of Crimea by Russia (granted to Ukraine in 1957) was triggered by anxiety that their naval port would be lost to NATO, following the 2014 Ukraine revolution that toppled the President. The invasion led the EU to reduce dependence on Russian gas supplies, inflamed conflicts elsewhere in Ukraine, and started a new Cold War, while sanctions damaged both Russia and the EU.

The global alliance against terror formed after the 9/11 attacks in New York led to two international wars, and will feed anti-American anger across the Middle East, Afghanistan and Pakistan for another decade.

The sudden ban by China in December 2018 on importing waste from Europe and America meant that 110 million tons a year of plastic and paper rubbish had nowhere to go. Chinese recyclers went bust, and global cellulose prices rose 70% almost overnight.

Hundreds of risks

In every large business there are many potentially high-impact risks or Wild Cards. And if you have a list of 400, each with 1% chance of

Examples of major Wild Cards

- viral plague – rapidly spreading, cases in every continent
- Chinese unrest – political/economic instability or meltdown
- North Korean collapse – huge migration and social chaos
- eurozone breakup – after another huge global economic crisis
- sustained cyber-attack – paralysing government, telecom, utilities, transport, banks for several weeks
- major, sustained military action against Israel
- threat to a major city from terrorists with likely nuclear capability or some kind of 'dirty weapon'
- series of attacks similar in impact to 9/11
- solar geomagnetic storms that knock out telcos/IT
- huge volcanic eruption that affects earth temperature
- massive failure of an investment institution, affecting over $4 trillion in assets
- miscalculation by a powerful nation leading to sustained regional conflict
- large meteor strike on a major city – like that which flattened 830 square miles of Russia in 1908, or the one which hit Russia again in 2013, with kinetic energy greater than the atomic bomb dropped on Hiroshima.

happening per year, then you will see on average four major events in every year. But every risk connects to other risks.

Consider this:

How likely is it that 2 people in a group of 10 have the same birthday? Or 2 people in 70?

The answer is: Probability of 2 in 10 people having the same birthday is 10%; 2 in 23 is 50%; 2 in 70 is 100%. Far higher than most would guess. These figures for coincidental risk are based on a well-researched statistical challenge called the Birthday Paradox.

Why benchmarking is so dangerous

Every large corporation is required to manage risks and report on them to shareholders. Unfortunately, as we saw in the 2008 economic crisis, banks can employ hundreds of risk managers, and still be destroyed. Why is this?

Many companies rely on 'benchmarking' – how we are doing, measured against competition or our industry as a whole. However, the whole approach can be highly dangerous, leading an entire industry to march blindly in step together, lemming-like, over the same cliff.

A year or two before the crisis, I gave a lecture to several hundred senior risk managers from the world's largest banks. I told them I was very worried about major banking risks not being properly addressed. Afterwards, I was approached by several risk managers. They said that I was right but they were unable to act. If they advised their boards that they needed to be more cautious, the answer would typically be:

'But as benchmarking shows, we are taking similar risks to the entire industry, and regulators are not objecting. If we take a more cautious line, our financial returns will be lower, analysts will attack us, and our share price will fall.'

Risk managers have to be independently minded, with a broad, rigorous view, informed by trends outside their industry, not institutionally blinded, and with the courage to be literally 'eccentric', to stick out from the crowd, take a different view.

Short-termism will destroy many large corporations

Many global corporations are run from one 12-week period to the next with little regard to the longer term. Business leaders are often drawn down this route by legal requirements to report profitability every quarter.

So, as we have seen in many recent scandals, decisions are influenced by timing: how to delay investment into another quarter so as not to damage ratings, or other ways to massage figures. It can be almost impossible to make large-scale strategic moves, which may deliver profits only in 5 to 10 years' time.

Short-termism has been made even worse by huge annual bonuses paid on the previous year's results. And when you add in other incentives such as share options that may be about to be cashed in, the result can be a suicidal mix. Expect more interference by regulators, forcing listed companies to pay bonuses based on performance over several years.

And of course even great CEOs can be forced rapidly into the wilderness. The average length of tenure in America for a CEO of a large corporation is only 5 years, or 7 years across the EU.

In stark contrast, I often work with huge family-owned corporations – or ones where the family has a controlling interest – and conversations are usually very different. 'Our company was started by my grandfather, and every day I worry about what kind of company I will hand to my grandchildren.'

Such companies often have a strong sense of direction and purpose, command loyalty from staff, and stay in business for decades. And yes, of course, there are downsides to family ownership, including time-expired leaders who refuse to step aside for the next generation, and lack of talent, ambition or interest among younger family members.

I have talked to a number of senior leaders of publicly listed companies who wish that they also were 'privately owned', and who have considered ways to delist. Expect more such conversations, looking to different models of ownership including private equity. Some companies such as Unilever have already stopped producing detailed quarterly reports, in a bid to restore sense and sanity.

Future of the global economy

The first decade and a half of the third millennium was a highly embarrassing time for the academic discipline of economics, and economists generally. So many failed to see the gathering crisis, or to predict accurately how long it would last.

Before the 2008–9 crash I lectured widely on, and wrote about, huge and growing risks from poorly understood global trades in complex financial instruments, and risks from hedge funds. I also warned of future instabilities in global markets, and of deflationary shocks. However, I failed to see how deep the crisis would be, and how long the crisis would last.

Here are the 10 major factors that are likely to shape the global economy over the next decade:

1. **Global economy survived better than many thought.** Thanks to emerging markets, the global economy grew in every year of the crisis except 2009. Growth in China slowed but never below 5–7% a year. A short-term period of lower oil prices will also help growth.

2. **Publicly listed corporations around the world are sitting on $12 trillion cash reserves (excluding financial companies).** That's more than the entire foreign exchange reserves of all nations. Expect large-scale investment over the next 5 to 10 years.

3. **Growth in sovereign wealth funds.** By 2018, sovereign wealth funds of countries like China, Norway, United Arab Emirates, Saudi Arabia and Singapore were worth more than $5.5 trillion, out of a total of $7.4 trillion. China alone owned more than $1.9 trillion, much of which was in US government bonds. Expect rapid diversification into real estate, commodities, mining, infrastructure, health care, logistics, technology companies and a wide range of other sectors, to secure China's future.

4. **Growth in value of privately owned property.** In the UK alone, private real estate is now worth over $6 trillion, with historically low interest rates and inflation. People aged over 65 have seen over $2 trillion of tax-free capital gains since 1980. A significant amount will pass down the generations, or become available using equity release products, over the next 10 to 15 years. Expect the same in a number of other countries.

5. **Central banks will take a more relaxed view of inflation.** Fears of deflation as a result of further shocks will mean that some central banks will err slightly more towards stimulation until they are certain that a robust recovery is underway.

6. **Over 160 million new middle-class consumers** ($15,000– 150,000 income a year) are being created every year by economic

growth, and will drive demand. Some 88% of new middle-class entrants in the next decade will be in Asia: 380 million in India, 350 million in China, 210 million in the rest of Asia, and only 130 million in the whole of the rest of the world.

7. **Booms and busts in huge cycles.** The world's biggest and longest bust in generations will most likely be followed at some point in 5 to 10 years (after trillions spent in stimulus) by one of the world's greatest booms, unless there is a further economic crisis, which postpones the eventual mega-boom and mega-bust. Expect larger and longer economic cycles until 2035.

8. **Further risks of mass defaults on debt.** Despite new regulations, risky financial deals are already growing rapidly again, exploiting gaps in laws, with ever more complex and cunning financial products, sold mainly by shadow banking (clusters of companies carrying out bank-like activities, without being regulated as banks). China will be vulnerable, with over-stimulation of the economy, low borrowing costs, and unsustainable debt – even though government debt is very low compared to many developed nations.

9. **Economic stimulation from next-generation technologies** such as the Internet of Things, Artificial Intelligence, smart homes, smart grids, green tech, biotech, robotics and nanotech are likely to boost the global economy by $80 trillion by 2040. Spending on everything related to green tech and energy saving will itself exceed $50 trillion during the same period.

10. **By 2030, Asia's combined economic output will be greater than that of Europe and America combined.** This single fact will dominate most other trends in this book.

Correcting a 1,000-year cycle

We are witnessing a fundamental re-balancing of wealth across global populations. In the year 1500, India and China represented more than 50% of all global output. By 1900 this had dropped to only 17%, outpaced by industrial revolution in Europe. So the process we are seeing today is part of a 500-year correction in a 1,000-year cycle.

However, the EU and US today still account for 60% of global GDP, 33% of global trade, and 42% of global sales of services.

Unstable and chaotic markets

Expect an even greater backlash against globalisation in some nations, who may feel that they are being weakened by cheap products entering into their countries, or by massive, destabilising currency flows, or other market forces. Over $5.3 trillion of currencies are traded every day, yet nations like the Philippines, Peru, Poland or the UK hold less than $80bn in reserves to defend against speculators. Enough to last only a few days.

More attacks on central banks and currencies

Expect more currency attacks as large investors continue to make (and lose) huge fortunes trying to outguess volatile markets, at times hoping to undermine one central bank after another. We will see similar attacks on commodity prices, short-selling stocks of companies, and on the stability of entire stock exchanges.

Many Asian countries are better protected than they were a decade or more ago, with stronger reserves and alliances, but market power will continue to grow as the process of globalisation steps up a gear, with even greater connectedness.

Virtual cryptocurrencies such as Bitcoin will just become yet more of a target for major speculative attack, with hype and gloom alternating, producing price wobbles that will make and lose billions for those who enjoy gambling on such volatile things.

Future of telcos and IT

A lot of *nonsense* is talked about the future of digital and telcos. Around 4 billion out of 5.5 billion adults already own a smartphone so that market is maturing fast, although with 1.4 billion new sales a year, most people are still changing models every few years. By 2025, over half of all new smartphones are likely to cost less than $70, with prices dropping rapidly, so that some banks and telcos will be giving smartphones away with free contracts (see p. 204).

Vietnam is typical of the next wave of mobile. Wage costs are half those of China, yet 90 million people own over 110 million SIM cards. Millions of people have jumped directly into mobile web without ever owning a land line.

Phone calls are so 'last-century'

One in three people in the UK only make phone calls in order to speak to their parents. They are most likely to send texts to partners and WhatsApp messages to friends. Most people find social media more convenient than talking on the phone, yet most companies are lagging far behind in how they communicate to customers and to their own teams.

How the web will redefine time

The web has made us very impatient – most people in my audiences around the world tell me that they press their browser back button in less than 4 seconds if a web page is slow. That means losing up to 90% of customers in 4 seconds. Even if you don't lose them, it means that they are irritated. And 90% of younger web users in developed nations may press that button in less than 1.5 seconds by 2025. Impatience will be a factor in every business relationship.

The same applies to call centres. Most people hate having to listen to lists of options. Every second matters. Business leaders tell me they consider it a form of personal theft when their time is wasted, and a social crime to install such systems.

Yet in a strange double-think, most of them also tell me that they have installed exactly the same awful systems for their own customers. It is of course a classic case of institutional blindness, since cheap tech now allows us to detect an incoming mobile, work out from Big Data who the person is and why they are likely to be calling, and automatically direct the call to the right person.

Five seconds to double your sales

So how long does it take to find a shop assistant? How long to wait in the checkout? How long to complete an online transaction? How long to respond to an email? How long to wait for a written estimate or return a contract? Expect huge efforts to speed up and simplify customer experience. Every web click loses sales. Every second counts.

Voice to text messages sent instantly as SMS to mobiles, email accounts, and so on will be standard by 2025. WhatsApp, WeChat, SMS, or similar short-length messages will overtake email for personal communications. If you want a lead over your competitors, use more personal messaging.

Telco business models are completely broken

Over 90% of all web traffic will be video by 2025 in many developed nations. It is already the case in the UK that BBC iPlayer, NetFlix and YouTube alone account for more than 60% of the nation's web traffic. A single 2-hour video is equivalent to a hundred million emails, or days of voice calls. So forget charging for voice or anything else – costs are dwarfed by streaming video.

Data on mobiles will increase one thousand-fold in the next 5 years, on 50 billion mobile devices connected to 5G, running at 10gps or higher. That means an entire high-definition movie will download in less than 3 seconds. So telcos will be forced to focus on new kinds of business, for example cloud services for companies.

Mobile payments will hit telcos and banks

We are seeing a huge explosion in mobile payments in emerging markets. One in four adults across Africa are already using mobile money accounts, and Asia payments are booming. The trouble is that a telco may handle 100 million payments a month on its network yet make virtually no money.

In the UK, over 40 million people will be making mobile payments by 2030. However, these innovations will be held back by customer confusion, caution and habit. Look, for example, at the very slow take-up of contactless card payments in America, and the fact that online sales in Germany are only 35% of that in the UK, per person, each year – mainly because of worries about online security.

A billion wearable devices

By 2025, one billion people are likely to be wearing smart devices such as wristbands recording motion, or smart watches that integrate with mobiles. By the same year, at least 50 million potentially significant medical events, mainly related to heart irregularities, will be detected globally each year using smart wrist devices.

Convergence is the enemy of innovation

Convergence means that every smartphone looks and feels almost the same. Every operating system works in a similar way. Convergence is the *opposite* of innovation. All *true* innovation is by definition about doing things differently in order to serve customers better.

Convergence means that the only way to make your product stand out is on price, since everything else is so similar, and that means a desperate spiral to the bottom on profitability.

So expect hundreds of new entrants into the world of telcos over the next few years, all copying things that work well already, and few survivors. Expect huge pressures on profits of today's telco giants as a result. As I predicted, the pace of true innovation in smartphones is already slowing down, as they become optimised within limits imposed by the size of fingers, pockets, and the resolution of the eye.

Simplicity will be a survival issue

Customers will be increasingly intolerant of complex products, and simplicity will be a core requirement for every successful digital company and telco.

All mobile devices are over-delivering on complex features that are rarely used. It is a scandal that many devices and IT systems are still sold full of bugs, incompatibilities and failures that would put manufacturers in prison if they were making cars or planes.

I am often asked by IT companies or telcos to gaze into the future – but often my message is very different. Go away urgently and sort out the mess in your existing products: make them work properly, and support customers better, before you launch further innovations.

The truth is that the pace of real techno-innovation remains painfully slow.

For some years I have subscribed to a large-circulation European magazine called *T3*. Every issue is supposed to be packed with the latest gadgets and techno-breakthroughs. But there is hardly enough real news to fill an issue every 3 months, let alone every 4 weeks.

New ways to feed your brain

The connection between brain and mobile device remains clumsy and slow. For example, reading speeds are no faster than they were – actually in many cases they have fallen, since it is faster to speed-read a large printed document than one on screen. And typing speeds are slower on mobile devices.

Expect intense efforts to find ways to get instant data without looking at a screen in your pocket or on your wrist. Many people (including me) have been very sceptical about clunky prototypes like Google Glass, but we do need to completely rethink interfaces.

Expect many more types of head-based displays, gesture controls – all of which will ultimately be threatened by direct digital-brain interfaces. The first such devices are helmets for gamers, which use brain waves to control the action.

Many people already have biodigital brains

As I predicted 18 years ago, we have seen rapid advances in the creation of biodigital brains, where brain cells grow into the surface of chips. The first experiments were in 1993, implanting small chips into the brains of mice and rats, which were able to transmit thoughts to each other at the speed of light – such as requests for food or drink.

More recently, rats have sent messages to each other over thousands of miles, from North Carolina to Brazil. Several rats were connected in a 'brain net' so they could collaborate on problem-solving, mind-reading each other.

Doctors have already implanted similar chips inside the heads of more than 600,000 human beings, and are implanting chips into

50,000 more people every year. Most of these are cochlear implants, which connect with the auditory nerve inside the inner ear to restore severe hearing loss.

Send an email (or possibly an image) by thinking alone

Other experiments have given blind people primitive sight – with chips implanted into the visual cortex of the brain, or connected to the optic nerve inside their eyes. I have met a paralysed man who controls his arm, hand and fingers by thinking alone, not by chips in his brain, but by chips in his upper arm that sense nerve activation.

Scientists at Harvard Medical School have enabled people to send simple messages to each other by thought alone, using a helmet to detect brain waves, and another head-mounted device to create sensations in brain tissue.

On current trends, biodigital brains will be a relatively normal part of life for over 25 million people by 2050, mainly to restore hearing or sight, as well as to overcome brain or spinal cord injuries, or, more rarely (for those who are wealthy and curious enough), to try to extend mental horizons, memory, intelligence, thinking speed and powers of concentration. One challenge to overcome is that chips planted directly into brain tissue can increase the risk of epilepsy by irritating the brain.

Digital insights will become common but strange

How will such digital insights feel? Imagine walking down the street and just sensing, by instinct in a way very hard to describe, that the shop you need is on the right, or having a 'gut feeling' that your heart rate has increased to around 80 beats a minute, or 'just knowing' that the person walking by is a relative of someone you know very well.

Most people feel very uncomfortable about chips being implanted into their brains, or the brains of their children. What about health risks or being hacked? Here is yet another example of how the future is not just about innovation, but also about emotion. You can have the smartest invention in the world, but if it fails to connect with passion, sales will be low.

Worries about electromagnetic radiation

Expect growing concerns about lifetime effects of exposure to electromagnetic radiation from overhead power lines, smartphones and other devices. Some studies have suggested that tumours are slightly more common on the side of the head that a person usually uses for mobile phone calls. Expect further evidence that mobile phone radiation affects the brain, as well as other cells. Expect legal action too, even though risks to an individual from normal use seem to be extremely low, and will become lower still as phone calls become less popular, replaced by texts, apps, browsing and so on.

Ongoing boom of recorded video moments

I predicted years ago that personal video would be really important, but I was wrong about the speed of uptake of *live* video.

People love uploading *recorded* video – carefully checked, edited, selected – to match their personal image. YouTube users are uploading more than 300 hours of video every minute, and 1.3 billion different people use YouTube each month, watching an average of 6 hours each, of which 55% is already watched on mobile. Around 5 billion videos are watched every day. At present, 80% of traffic is outside the US, but YouTube reaches more American 18- to 25-year-olds than any cable TV network.

Why people still hate live video at work

Live video links will continue to be unpopular in most workplaces, compared to video calls between close family. The reason is data leakage. Did you brush your hair before the call? Do you look like you have a hangover? For a homeworker – did you remember to shave? Can they see the washing up in the sink? For family calls, such data leakage is enchanting and delightful – a feeling of being there.

Mandarin will dominate future of the web

Mandarin is the most common web language spoken by 800 million online users, and China is the world's largest e-commerce market, with 40% of global share. Chinese people will spend

$1.8 trillion online by 2022. Alibaba is the largest online retailer in China, with revenues growing by around 50% a year, over $40bn in 2018 (compared to $180bn for Amazon), with 600 million registered accounts and 100 million e-commerce shoppers every day, representing 60% of all China's e-commerce.

Expect new Asian competitors to become significant global players, with extremely attractive, simple, clever innovations – things that capture the imagination of hundreds of millions of people within days or weeks, making existing dominant players look like dinosaurs. Expect many of the most innovative new web companies to be bought by larger familiar brands.

Google will try hard to manage your entire life

Google will continue to set the pace for innovation across many new sectors over the next two decades, ranging from driverless cars, to next-generation biotech, and smart homes linked to voice recognition. To achieve this, Google will acquire a very wide range of much smaller companies. Take the $550m purchase of Deep Mind for example, which teaches computers to think like humans. Or the purchase, for $3.2bn, of Nest Labs, a leader in smart home technology.

By 2018, Google Android had 85% of the mobile market for operating systems, compared to only 14% for Apple. Google will come under major scrutiny in Europe – over possible abuse of monopoly, given its more than 90% share of search queries compared to 68% in America – and in nations like Russia, which will impose more web censorship. Google will continue to feel a cool wind, along with other large American IT companies, following revelations of deep co-operation with American spy agencies, as well as further losses of personal data.

More web-based billionaires with a touch of genius

Expect many new web billionaires with a typical time frame, from startup to buyout or stock market flotation, of 4 to 5 years. In most cases, at least half the value will be in their loyal user-base, which enables the buyer of the company to reach a new community.

Some of the most successful will be in very well-defined areas, as we have seen with taxi-ordering apps like Uber or holiday sites like Airbnb. The secret of success will usually be a really smart, elegant and 'cool' site or user interface. YouTube was not the first video streaming site – but it was by far the easiest to use.

The future of entertainment

The music industry will face meltdown and chaos

Music is still a $74bn-a-year industry, and spends $15bn a year on new recordings, but big Labels have been in crisis, threatened by streaming services that already generate $8bn a year in revenues. American music revenues collapsed from $14.6bn in 1999 to $6.3bn in 2009, but are now recovering after slashing costs. Over 50% of their revenues in some nations already comes from digital streaming, which grew 45% in 2017 in the UK, with overall revenues growing by 10.6%.

But as streaming has swept the world, the quality of the listening experience has collapsed, with far lower resolution of musical data compared to music CDs using 1980s tech. Speakers and headphones in most people's homes are capable of far better reproduction than the poor signals they are now being fed most of the time. Expect a major upgrade of online sound by 2025, as we have already seen in video streaming and satellite TV. At the same time, expect further growth of retro vinyl and cassette sales, driven mainly by millennials.

Young listeners expect all music to be free – or nearly so. The music market will continue to be flooded by highly talented home-based musicians, artist-entrepreneurs churning out millions of hours of free entertainment, building their own online brands, in the hope of being 'signed' by a big Label. Many unsigned artists will earn a basic income from Spotify and other streaming platforms.

In the past, big Labels used to invest in lots of small bands, hoping one or two would really take off, but in future they will sign very few, after early success online. Labels will continue to dominate global album sales well into 2025, but 85% of their revenues will come from a handful of ultra-successful bands. Most up-and-coming artists will be forced to bypass Labels altogether, and sell direct, working with promoters and event organisers.

Expect over 150 million people to be paying for unlimited streaming via services like Spotify by 2022 (Spotify alone already has 87 million paying subscribers, over 6 million in the UK) – but most musicians will earn less than $0.002 per play. Expect streaming services to become more like traditional radio stations, playing curated lists influenced by the media campaigns of big music Labels.

Radio music will survive and live gigs will boom

Radio will continue to enjoy huge audiences because it is convenient as background entertainment at home or in the car. Another reason is the feeling of companionship, with tens of thousands of others listening to the same radio show.

Some 60% of music industry revenues are now from live performances, up from 33% in 2000. Live music will be a $30bn industry by 2023, growing 3% a year. Expect more blockbuster tours, each playing to more than 5 million people around the world, typically grossing over $600m. Most successful artists will generate the bulk of their income from live events, sponsorships, commercials, film scores, celebrity appearances, and so on. More top artists will give away their music, aiming to use it as a way to grow income from these other sources.

But clubbing will face a tough future in nations like the UK, because so many younger people now prefer sitting at home and being on social media to going out to get drunk, take drugs, or party all night.

Future of the film industry and gaming

Compared to the drastic transformation in the music industry, the film industry will change slowly, with even more sequels, more mega-budget films, and astonishingly realistic imaging of imaginary creatures, worlds and events. The industry will struggle to generate enough quality output to satisfy ultra-high resolution home-based cinema, just as TV and cable companies will struggle. Ultra-HD will continue to pose challenges for actresses and actors, directors, make-up departments and lighting teams, with every minor blemish exposed in detail by hyper-real screens.

Most film-making will continue to be directed first at the US market – responsible for 31% of around $40bn global film revenues. America generates 29% of global and media sales, followed by China. The global market will be worth $2.5 trillion by 2024.

Boom for live cinema

Piracy will remain a constant and annoying issue, but will not prevent rapid growth in cinema audiences across the world, attracted not only by breathtaking visual immersion but also by excitement in sharing the experience. DVD and Blu-ray sales will collapse across the world, wiped by streaming, even though, as with music, most sources of online or broadcast video will struggle to match even Blue-ray for quality until beyond 2025.

Films in 3D will continue to impress and disappoint, depending on audience and genre. Ten years ago, I expected 3D TVs to be successful, but the last manufacturer ceased to make them in 2018 – yet another example of how easy it is to be innovative, yet fail to engage with passion.

On-demand watching is already dominating how millennials consume TV, but big live TV shows and sporting events will continue to command huge viewing figures (people like to participate in a communal experience – we used to call it watching TV).

Augmented reality and total immersion gaming

The computer games market is worth $140bn, and will grow 11% a year for the next decade. Very successful new games will win over $12bn of total sales each by 2025. The fastest growth will be on smartphones.

Half of the entire £7.3bn entertainment market in the UK is now gaming, larger than video and music combined, and 66% of the US population plays them. Growth will be driven by breathtaking creativity, astonishing graphics, and game streaming (where people learn by watching favourite experts play). Watch out for new game genres targeting mainly women in China, where 50% of players are female, for example highly realistic and interactive virtual boyfriends.

The film industry will continue to merge with gaming, with interactive HD animations and sequences by 'real' actors. Headsets will be more widely used, with higher-resolution screens and smoother response to head movement, and with gimmicky features to allow gaming by thought control (detecting brain waves). However, headsets will be rejected by most gamers for day-to-day use for the next decade, because of eye strain, weight, poor resolution, lack of comfort, cost, being uncool, and short battery life. That will not stop expensive experiments, as we saw with the $2bn spent by Facebook on Oculus. Expect worries about the hours of 3D gaming on the brains of young children.

Augmented reality glasses will be used in a wide range of specialist applications ranging from those aimed at surgeons (to enable them to see extra data), and tourists (to wear when visiting museums or galleries or monuments), to the military.

Future of infotech

You will see more changes in the next 15 years than there have been since the start of personal computing in 1975, with rapid development of Artificial Intelligence linked to Big Data, robotics and rapidly growing security threats.

China will dominate Artificial Intelligence research. Expect the US and EU to be overtaken by Chinese IT systems within 15 to 20 years, maybe far sooner. Microsoft and Apple both face the same challenge over the next decade: how to find radical innovations to drive growth when both are burdened by a range of well-optimised but ageing products, and when the market for computers continues to be wiped out by sales of larger mobile devices.

Microsoft will be addicted to revenues from Windows and Office, well beyond 2025, and will struggle as a global mobile company. Most new investment and revenue growth over the next

20 years will be in cloud-based services, plus Artificial Intelligence, smart homes, automation and robotics, and various collaborative experiments in financial services.

Apple will need to reinvent itself

Apple urgently needs at least two more breakthrough products in the next 5 years, each equivalent to the first iPhone and iPad, that is, totally different to anything seen before. The trouble is that products like smartphones are now highly optimised, and room for radical innovation is very limited.

Apple will continue to be threatened by giants like Samsung Electronics, and by many Chinese companies, who are copying or improving on Apple genius. Apple will invest heavily in a rapidly growing range of wearable tech, going far beyond the i-Watch with medtech sensors. Apple will also make much better entertainment hubs, with web, mobile, and home integration, as part of deep investment in home automation.

Expect big investment to integrate all channel activities into a joined-up experience. So the iPhone knows you are watching a TV quiz show, and the iPad knows you are also on the phone to a call centre while searching for better online offers. Every other manufacturer will follow.

Quantum computing means a million times faster

As I predicted, we are already seeing huge investments by government secret services and military into quantum computing (QC), mainly to crack strong encryption, especially by America and China. QC will also be used for complex tasks like long-range weather forecasting and simulations of nuclear weapons. In addition, QC will transform personal computing, because we will all be able to access QC power in the Cloud, as we will see later.

Quantum computers use qubits, not bits. Each qubit can have many different forms, based on varying properties of atoms, ions, photons or electrons. Imagine writing a book in Morse code using just dots and dashes, and then writing the same book using an alphabet or Chinese characters. That is why a single event in a quantum computer has a million times more processing power than in a normal computer. So a secret military code that takes two years to crack will be decoded in minutes or seconds.

For ordinary computers, Moore's Law will continue for the next 25 to 30 years, that is, computing or storage capacity will halve in price for the same capacity every 18–36 months, extending gradually, because there will be limits to size and speed of on/off memory stores – whether magnetic, or on chips.

The next great digital revolution

We need to take a close look at four areas that will really matter to our future: the *Internet of Things*, *Big Data*, *cloud computing* and *Artificial Intelligence*. Each has been around for a while, but it is the *combination* of all four in new ways that will create the next revolution. These four factors will merge to create immense and lasting opportunities for good, but also for evil on a gigantic scale when abused by governments or criminals.

The truth about the Internet of Things

The Internet of Things is about the tracking, monitoring and management of billions of different things. Automation and robotics rely on it. At least 60 billion different items will be communicating with each other online by 2025, rising to 130 billion by 2030 – hard-wired into the web, or using radio-frequency identification devices (RFIDs). These are tiny chips, the size of a grain of sand, plus a small aerial, which is used to power the device and receive or transmit as needed – so-called near-field communication.

More than 19 billion new RFIDs are already entering the environment every year, attached to clothes in shops, food packaging, airline baggage, supply chain components, farm animals and pets, and tickets and passports. Most have one-time use and end up in rubbish. Airbus has tagged 1.5 million different components used in its latest planes. RFIDs are already a \$12bn-a-year market. It all adds up to greater efficiency, fewer production line faults, automated supply chains, fewer stolen goods and reduced human error. It means that a clothing retailer can provide live data on mobile apps showing which store has what dress sizes and colours in stock – and, as the customer walks in, where to find the garments, to within one metre.

RFIDs have limits: it is hard to read them in general groceries because water, foil and steel can interfere with radio signals, and transmission distance is usually only a metre or two. More reliable is a permanent web connection, using a fully powered wireless device such as a watch or a light.

Expect all new fridges to be able to sense a lot of what is inside them, or changes in outside weather, so that they might, for example, make extra ice on a very hot day. Expect all new gas boilers to send alerts if they break down – to service engineers as well as owners. Expect your alarm to wake you earlier if it is snowing. Some of this will turn out to be almost useless information – for example, who really wants a fridge that automatically reorders the same food?

Human bodies merge with the Internet of Things

Human beings are already part of the Internet of Things, despite health risks. Some people have injected themselves under their skin, with the same RFID devices as vets use in animals. In 2002 VeriChip gained a US licence to implant RFIDs into humans but then it was revealed that hundreds of animals with RFID implants had developed cancer, and the company collapsed.

People have injected RFIDs under their skin as keys to gain access to secure facilities. The Baja Beach Club, a nightclub in Rotterdam, has used VeriChip implants to identify VIPs and to enable them to pay for drinks.

Four thousand people in Sweden have been 'chipped' in this way, which means that they no longer need paper travel tickets or plastic travel cards to take a train journey.

In the meantime, larger GPS tagging devices will be widely used by governments to tag criminals and political activists under house arrest, as well as by worried parents to track children. Expect rapid growth of all kinds of secret tracking, mainly by collecting data from smartphones using hidden features in apps. Expect abuse by oppressive regimes to control hundreds of thousands of dissenters, as well as by family members to spy on each other.

Expect wearable devices inside your body: monitoring or controlling your health, sensing blood sugar, heart rate or other things, connected at all times to health services.

Expect many new hacking threats. What happens, for example, if a terrorist or hostile government hacks into 10 million driverless cars while they are on the road? Or takes control of 35,000 pacemakers?

Big Data – why it really matters

Around 90% of all the data we have ever created has been generated in the last two years – 2.5 million trillion bytes a day, much of it from the Internet of Things. Data collected each year by US companies alone is enough to fill the Library of Congress 20 times over.

Marketing directors and insurance underwriters need this data, but most companies will really struggle to get a return on their investment, losing data to criminals will be a constant nightmare, as well as the risk of breaking ever-stricter privacy laws.

On the world's busiest websites, up to 2,000 companies are watching everything you do. Even if that data is anonymised, it is usually very easy to work out who you are, with the right tools. Every web page you visit may be collecting your screen size, operating system, location, web browser type and many other things that form a unique digital footprint, which can be cross-referenced against other data they have from forms you fill in. The information is being used to target online ads that already account for 25% of the $500bn global marketing spend. Expect waves of new regulation to make such data collection far more difficult in future.

As we saw when Snowden leaked secret US documents in 2013, every large intelligence agency is also using Big Data to track people, detect patterns, prevent or solve crimes, and for political surveillance.

Big Data will save money and lives – but over-reliance will be lethal

Here are some examples of the value of Big Data:

◆ Your bank sees an unusual pattern of purchases from strange locations – and creates a Fraud Alert.

◆ Amazon predicts which products to stock in warehouses close to your home, before you order them, based on your shopping habits, age, income, and how long your screen cursor lingers over a button.

◆ Tesco led consumer marketing using Big Data, with its loyalty card in the UK. From the data it collects, it tailors eye-catching offers for a specific customer.

◆ Los Angeles police use past crime data to predict areas where new crimes are most likely – sending in extra officers. Result: 26% fall in local burglaries.

◆ The Pentagon looks for hidden patterns in aerial footage from drones, links between regular events on the ground, and local explosions or attacks.

◆ The World Health Organization and Google monitor the spread of viral epidemics such as Ebola by looking for new patterns in Google search requests in different cities.

◆ Weather agencies look for patterns going back over decades, to improve long-range forecasts.

◆ Employers look for patterns in what people do at work in order to detect fraud in banks.

A personal guide on your journey of life

In a mobile world, the most important thing to know about any customer is where they are located right now and where they were before. That tells you a huge amount about how they are likely to be feeling, especially combined with other data. Tesco created a special offer for young women within 400 metres of a store, and 40,000 walked in. It takes seconds to set up such offers, targeting small groups with personal discounts.

Who is watching you right now?

I have sat looking at a client's web page and watched individual letters and numbers appearing in a web form, in real time, as they were being entered by a customer living in another city. The customer was totally unaware that they were being closely monitored, second by second, even though they consented to 'cookies'.

Imagine someone is trying to buy a very expensive holiday. You see that she has entered her passport number three times incorrectly, her mouse is hovering, you sense her frustration, and fear she is about to give up. Do you phone the mobile number she entered earlier and say: 'Hello, is that Mary Jones? I see you are having trouble with entering your passport number on our web page. Would you like me to take it from you over the phone?' Or do you wait an hour or two and pretend to be making a random sales call from the company? Answer: don't interrupt. Use the data to learn how to improve your web form, and phone tomorrow.

Little Data matters far more than Big Data

Big Data is about spotting a pattern, but *Little Data* is all about spotting a person. Most large companies need to take very small elements of their Big Data, and focus on little things to make a practical difference to customers – or they will get buried in analysis. Billions of dollars will be wasted over the next decade by companies on useless Big Data systems that produce nothing except frustration.

Let us imagine a wealthy telco customer. He likes sailing, and is about to buy a yacht. Here is the *Little Data* picture and how it develops towards the sale:

◆ web page searches on his smartphone for yachts and marinas – over months

◆ visits to marinas, many of them

◆ purchases of yachting magazines

◆ several holidays over 18 months, payments to yacht charter companies

◆ web searches for yacht finance, yacht insurance, yacht ownership

◆ smartphone sees the person arriving at national Boat Show, the largest selling event in the calendar for yacht manufacturers.

Many months before the boat show, the phone company or bank will be sending apparently fairly random messages from time to time about boats, or displaying them in Facebook ads, on YouTube video clips, next to web pages, and so on. We are seeing the same thing in supermarket checkouts, where face recognition is used to match cash purchases to the individual, triggering customised offers at the point of sale.

All humanity will be found in the Cloud

More than 90% of all web users globally are already using cloud-based email, or sites such as Facebook, LinkedIn, YouTube, Twitter or Instagram, where the information is held in networks of computers linked together in different parts of the world, rather than on your own computer or smartphone. Cloud computing will become the main way to prevent data loss, backing up automatically the contents of every computer or mobile.

Most software will be rented by the day, week, month or year, running in the Cloud, rather than on your own machine. The savings can be colossal, not only in development, but also in keeping software updated.

Salesforce.com is a prime example of a cloud company – able to set up and run call centres almost instantly and manage customer relationships. Salesforce has capabilities that very few global corporations could possibly afford to develop on their own, with 30,000 employees and a budget of over $8.3bn a year.

Corporations are rapidly shifting most of their systems into the Cloud – in many cases by setting up private clouds. At the same time, boardroom debates about cyber risks will intensify, especially in banking and financial services after yet more large-scale attacks.

Artificial Intelligence – controlling the whole world?

Artificial Intelligence (AI) is gradually taking over and dominating our world, and will become more powerful than the president of a large nation. That said, hype has often run far ahead of reality.

There has been much talk of a Technical Singularity – a computer with neural networks greater than human intelligence that could dominate the future destiny of humankind, producing runaway technological growth, and ushering in a post-human era. Science fiction, or a wider reality that is already almost upon us?

It is true that we have built huge super-brains that learn for themselves, gain knowledge, and are able to make more accurate decisions than any human expert. Three decades ago the great debate was about whether a computer could ever beat the world's best chess players – but today they do it every day, and the same for complex computer strategy games like *StarCraft II*. Back then the great debate was whether computers would ever understand human speech without hours of adapting to each person's voice – but today we take voice recognition for granted.

Robot doctors, who never trained at medical school, are now more accurate at diagnosing many medical emergencies than most doctors or nurses. AI is better at detecting payments fraud, predicting crime or the weather, forecasting which oil rigs will blow up next, and so on. AI is already able to predict, with 90% accuracy, a wide range of gene defects, just from the shapes of people's faces – a variant of face recognition.

AI is already starting to control web access for over 1 billion people in China according to their personal social responsibility scores, which are also set by machines. Scores can be based on social media postings, web search requests, criminal record, debt history, the scores for members of someone's family or friends, and so on.

The reality is that billions of small decisions are already influenced by AI – for example selecting the route you drive, the suggestions made to you on Amazon about other products you may like, newsfeeds adjusted automatically depending on your reading habits. In the UK, one police force is investigating only half the number of assaults and public order offences than it did in the past, based on AI predictions about how likely a conviction will be.

A major threat is that AI will be harnessed by criminals and rogue states to automate tasks such as hacking passwords, or writing totally customised, highly convincing phishing emails. AI has been widely used to create fake videos of famous people saying bad things or even having sex. It is being harnessed by governments to provide 100% tracking of citizens, combining facial recognition with hundreds of other inputs and to write propaganda.

AI has the potential to manipulate markets and develop weapons that human beings don't even understand, becoming smarter every day by further self-learning. See p. 335 for AI in 2100.

Cyber-crime – one of the world's greatest threats

When you combine all the power and all the weaknesses of the Internet of Things, Big Data, cloud computing and Artificial Intelligence, together with 6 billion smartphones, computers and other smart devices, the result is a gigantic range of criminal targets, and a potential future global emergency. As I warned years ago, every large company in the world is now experiencing frequent, severe cyberattacks, on their own systems or in the Cloud, whether they know about it or not.

As we will see, over 4 billion people have already been personally affected by theft of their private details – and this is just the beginning of the security nightmare, which will drive huge investment in new security measures by all large corporations and by governments.

Never in human history has it been possible for one person, sitting in a bedroom at home in a distant land, to create such havoc and chaos, or seize such power, using a few lines of computer code to hold entire nations or governments to ransom. Such hackers are often teenagers. There is no way back from such a future, except by dismantling our whole digital universe.

Losses are likely to be more than $5 trillion a year by 2025, especially if we include wider-scale attacks, linked to hostile governments, which are associated with 70% of major attacks. In companies with over 50,000 records, the average cost of a single data breach is $6.3m. We are not just talking about attacks on traditional targets such as bank websites, but also commercial aggression like the blackmail of Sony, after the company released a controversial film about North Korea.

There is nothing new about web abuse. *At least 80% of 247 billion emails sent every day are spam*, many of them so-called phishing attacks, pretending to be from a bank, encouraging people to enter passwords.

McAfee is already detecting over 600 million new and different computer viruses, malware or Trojan horses every year – several per second. Pharma, chemicals, mining, electronics and agricultural companies are seeing increases of 600% a year in malware attacks. Energy, oil and gas attacks are growing by 400%. Attempts to steal data from retailers are doubling every 12 months.

Three billion people's personal details stolen in a single theft

If you have a number of online accounts, chances are that your personal details are already being sold to fraudsters – passwords, name, address, bank details, credit card numbers and date of birth. The scale of these hacks is shocking and scandalous, since in many cases the companies concerned have been sloppy about basic security measures.

Hackers recently stole information from 3 billion Yahoo customers in a single attack – a fact that Yahoo took two years to reveal. It can take up to eight years in some cases for large companies to realise they have been hacked. In 2019, a file was published online by criminals revealing 3 billion different names and passwords, stolen from 25 billion different records.

Other recent cases include Adult Friend Finder (412 million); LinkedIn (164 million); Adobe (164 million); eBay (142 million); Equifax (143 million – including social security numbers); Marriott Hotels (500 million – including passport numbers); and Sony (100 million). The list is endless, grows every day and includes

Facebook, Uber, DropBox, Tumblr as well as many of the world's largest airlines, retailers and banks. JP Morgan Chase lost 76 million names, addresses, telephone numbers and email addresses – affecting two-thirds of households across America. Bank of New York Mellon saw details hacked on 12.5 million accounts; CitiGoup on 3.9 million; and Bank of America on 1.2 million.

Some 43% of people use identical passwords across the web, so a single theft means that criminals often get access to many other private accounts owned by the same person. The other problem is that so many people use terrible passwords – 1% of the entire world uses 123456, for example.

We have to conclude that web security is completely broken, and it will take at least two decades to fix.

Payments fraud on an unimaginable scale

The Heartbleed bug is yet another example of a viral attack that caused huge damage as it swept globally, invading the websites of many multinationals, retailers, banks and email companies. Expect many more highly sophisticated attacks, aimed at forcing people or companies to pay ransom money, or forfeit their entire digital existence and lose all their old data.

Online fraudsters are now earning more than $66bn a year – $19bn in the United States alone – but most cases are not reported: 99.6% in the UK never result in any prosecution, so what is the point? This kind of crime is the most profitable and safe in the world, and this will continue to be the case for at least the next 15 years.

At least 8% of all online merchant revenues are fraudulent in America, rising to a staggering 43% in fake transactions in peak months. Over 17 million US citizens are victims of identity theft each year, approaching 7% of the entire adult population. In a single year, the number of people whose bank accounts were taken over by criminals grew 66%.

Expect many new steps to stop fraud, for example, forcing people to use stronger passwords, forcing regular password changes, and using fingerprint access. Customers will also be urged to set up two-step authentication, with confirmation of passwords using codes sent to mobile devices. As a result, expect huge growth in attacks on telco companies and mobile devices, as criminals seek to hack SMS, or emails, and intercept these codes. Attacks on two-step verification have grown more than a hundred times in 12 months.

Why bank hackers will often escape prosecution – even when caught

I have met bankers who don't prosecute or even sack staff who hack into their own bank systems. Terrified of bad publicity, they pay them off, give them a wonderful reference, and let them go and work for a competitor – where exactly the same thing is likely to happen again. There is no legal requirement in most countries for any bank to report when they have been hacked and lost data, which means that most attacks will never be known, and the true scale is far larger than most people think.

Large corporations will be forced to encrypt stored data

All IT and smartphone companies will step up personal security with end-to-end encryption during data transmission, and encryption of all data 'at rest' stored on servers. It is really shocking that most banks still do not encrypt data on their servers, so once a hacker gains entry, which they do in every large bank several times a year, they usually have no trouble at all reading files. Best practice will mean universal encryption, which makes a large attack significantly more difficult for hackers.

Cyber-war – a new kind of Cold War

As I say, expect many significant large-scale cyberattacks against entire nations and groups of enterprises over the next two decades, often directed by criminal gangs rather than government staff, but paid for by secret agents of other countries. The largest of these attacks are likely to form part of next-generation conflicts / disputes between nations, paralysing entire government agencies for days or weeks, causing major disruption to banking and telecommunications, and damaging utilities such as power stations or parts of the national grid.

It is already happening: for example, a blast furnace in a steel mill was hit by hackers in Germany recently, causing parts of the plant to fail. Most successful attacks on major installations will be kept secret, in the national interest. A common trick will be to hijack thousands of computers and order them to attack a corporate website, with multiple visits. The site crashes – until a ransom is paid (Denial of Service). It costs less than $10 to order such an attack using websites accessed in seconds on normal search engines.

Cyberattacks on people, companies and nations

Cyberattacks are easy to carry out on physical web infrastructure too. Why bother to attack a government website when you can knock out the whole web communication system for a week or more between an entire nation and the rest of the world? Depending on the nation, this is very easy to do at low cost, and will be absolutely impossible to prevent. It's much cheaper and more low tech than launching cruise missiles. Any nation in the world could do this because of a fundamental vulnerability of the entire web, despite the fact that it was designed to be impregnable.

The weakness is a physical one: most bandwidth in the world is carried on a few, very vulnerable, fibre-optic cables, which often span oceans. But cutting underwater cables is very easy, in waters less than 30 to 40 metres depth – they are even marked on every marine chart to warn fishermen to be careful, and are usually just lying on the sea bed.

All you have to do to wreck a vital cable is drag a ship's anchor along the sea bed on a long chain. And it is very hard to detect which ship did it, especially in relatively busy shipping areas. Even worse, it is also really hard to locate exactly where the actual break has taken place.

It has already happened. Recent underwater cable damage reduced web access right across India by 70%, and in Egypt by 60%, while many other nations were also badly affected in the Middle

East. In another episode, divers were arrested off the coast of Egypt in the very act of sabotage.

You don't even have to have a ship, or a tiny submarine, as the same maps also show precisely where each cable comes ashore over rocks or mud or sand, so anyone who wants to create havoc can drive along the coast to various points, and cut each cable in seconds with a $50 angle grinder or electric saw.

For all these reasons, NATO includes major cyberattacks as one of the events that could trigger military or other action by the Alliance. However, it will be almost impossible to prove who is really behind such attacks, and therefore impossible to retaliate effectively. Meanwhile, the US Navy is being hit on a routine basis by *over 100,000 separate online attacks every hour*, according to Hewlett Packard. But from where, and by whom, and for what purpose?

Sometimes debris is left by accident, which gives clues about origin – for example naming a piece of code, deeply encrypted inside a complex virus, after a popular TV comedian in a particular country. But subtle clue-dropping will also be used as a deliberate decoy by secret services or gangs to cast blame on an innocent nation.

Viruses designed to seize control of an entire country

Energetic Bear is a cyber-espionage weapon that infected vital parts of Europe's energy infrastructure during the Ukraine–Russia–EU crisis. It targeted a wide range of industrial control systems, national grids, power stations, wind turbines, and biomass fuel plants. It was designed to monitor energy use in real time and to disable systems on command – but on whose command?

Future energy viruses will target smart grids and smart homes – imagine the impact, for example, of a hacker from a hostile state or group turning on 15 million air conditioners simultaneously, causing instant power cuts, or hijacking and crashing 5 million cars on the road. These things are easy for small groups of clever IT teams to achieve. The digital weapons have already been built in many cases, as we know from leaks of information by worried security service agents.

A few weeks after the discovery of Energetic Bear, Russian telco and health companies, utilities and government agencies discovered that they too had been hit by one of the most deadly and sophisticated clusters of viruses ever created, called Regin. The cluster was designed with multiple apps to steal passwords, extract information on a huge range of systems, and take total control of many different types of industrial equipment.

'Digital bombs' inside large organisations

Targets were also hit in Saudi Arabia, Mexico, Ireland, India, Iran, Belgium, Australia and Pakistan. In many cases, it turned out that the viruses had been hidden away for up to six years without detection, despite every check. The viruses were constantly listening online for a single command to detonate tens of thousands of digital 'bombs' across every part of the nation. The Chinese, meanwhile, are building a quantum computing link between Beijing and Shanghai, which they hope will lock out foreign surveillance. Russia has created an internet within its own nation, which allows vital online traffic to continue while shutting the entire country off from global connections, to protect the nation in a crisis.

In 2007, Estonian banks, government agencies, parliament, broadcasters and newspapers were hit by three weeks of cyber-attacks that completely paralysed their web capabilities. These followed a disagreement with Russia, though responsibility was never proven.

So we will see huge investment in cyber-resilience, by governments, banks, stock exchanges and utility companies in particular, in the wealthiest nations, but smaller nations will remain very vulnerable. At least a quarter of all attacks will be espionage – directed at stealing state secrets or corporate research that has yet to be patent protected.

Hackers will be recruited by spies and gangs

Expect growing numbers of full-time professional hackers, operating as independent consultants to criminal gangs and secret services, offering services in combination with others to plan major attacks. In many cases, these hacking geniuses will never realise who their end client really is. They may think they are working for MI6 in the UK, for example, when they are actually working for a Bulgarian gang, which is assisting Russian Federal Security Services, or for the CIA or Mossad.

Many attacks will be multidimensional. So a large-scale identity theft takes place a couple of hours before a vital payment channel is hacked, to create new PINs. Minutes later, 200 people with cloned cash cards start withdrawing cash from ATMs in over 50 cities.

Hackers will be turned against other hackers

Expect a radical rethink about what to do with convicted hackers: people with proven genius in cracking open systems, who may well be the best people in the world to test your own security, and help improve it. Do we really want to see young lives wasted in prison? Some companies are offering over $1m for every major new bug which is found. The HackerOne community is just one example of a major new industry that will grow rapidly over the next three decades: their community of 200,000 hackers has already earned over $31m in rewards in just over three years, identifying 72,000 vulnerabilities between them in more than 1,000 corporate systems.

The best hackers will be offered secret rewards by governments, to attack and destroy the criminal web. One aim will be to identify activity by many millions of users of Tor web browsers (these are like normal web browsers, but prevent ANYONE monitoring your web activity) and other 'secret' tools: people who want to keep their activities and payments 100% untraceable.

Over 400 dark websites were closed in 2014 alone, including sites that sell illegal drugs, facilitate illegal arms deals, advertise professional assassins to kill spouses or politicians, and service every kind of depravity. However, many dark web users in future will simply be trying to evade 'oppressive' state snooping – particularly in countries like Russia or China where web controls have become severe. Use of Tor in Russia leapt from 60,000 to over 200,000 people in just a couple of months following the seizure of Crimea.

Cryptocurrencies like Bitcoin will be a major boost for web criminals

Of course, there is no point in holding a government or company or nation to ransom unless you are sure you can get paid without being arrested. But Bitcoin and other cryptocurrencies have proven the best criminal payment system ever invented. Cryptopayments are completely secure and anonymous, which is why 70% of such payments in 2018 were to buy illegal drugs, buy illegal weapons, pay ransoms or pay for assassinations.

Future of surveillance, spies and state snooping

BIG BROTHER IS WATCHING YOU – George Orwell's *1984* offers a chilling picture of how technology could be used by a dictator to control millions. But the tools available today have advanced far beyond what Orwell saw. Most governments of larger nations are using a wide range of digital tools to secretly monitor people on a very large scale. Tomorrow's tools will take this to an entirely new level, including instantaneous, accurate face recognition from fixed video cameras in public places, through to recognition by mobile cameras worn by police or undercover agents. China will lead the way in face recognition algorithms, which will then be used globally.

Security agencies have never had so many different and easy ways to invade privacy, spy on every citizen and blackmail people into cooperating. Expect rapid scaling up of government budgets in most developed nations for surveillance using public or commercial data, images from video surveillance, and legally, semi-legally or illegally, intercepted data. Cyber-espionage will become a crowded world with the constant risk that experts are working for more than one master.

You should expect intelligence agencies in most developed countries to have complete remote access to any computer, phone etc., they wish, with the ability to listen using built-in microphones even when devices are 'not in use', to watch using built-in cameras, and to monitor every screen, every keystroke. The implications of all this for the future of freedom and democracy are very profound and deeply disturbing. These are the dream tools for any dictatorship that aims to identify, isolate and wipe out dissenters.

Secret back doors into every device

As we know from recent leaks by whistle-blowers, all computer and mobile phone operating systems have become targets for the CIA, MI5, the Chinese and Russian governments and so on, with the aim of being able to control devices or entire systems belonging to private individuals or companies or other governments, read files, intercept passwords, and turn on built-in cameras and microphones remotely. That is why Chinese companies like Huawei will continue to come under close scrutiny over major contracts to supply other countries – with worries that such IT systems may have been compromised by their host nation.

Expect further revelations to show that secret 'back doors' were successfully coded long ago into most versions of Windows, Mac, Android, and so on, including back doors into encryption and security companies like Symantec, without any knowledge of the companies concerned. As a result, we can also expect growing numbers of worried consumers, living under oppressive regimes, to turn off all their devices whenever they wish to be 'alone'.

But that will not be enough to escape. Safer to wrap a phone in silver foil, or put it in a bucket of water, or leave it at a different location altogether. For example, even when iPhones are turned off, they continue to log all your geo-tracking data as usual. And even when the battery dies, iPhone apps can go on measuring the number of steps you have taken, and use other clues, to help plot your movements from your last known position. But these are just official Apple system design features. What about secret services code?

Companies like Google have been criticised for handing over security keys to government agencies to make spying easier. Many IT and phone companies are hitting back by developing systems that are so secure that they cannot decode customer data even when ordered to by secret service agents, in large part to help restore trust by customers. Apple and Google have already begun this process, creating security worries that newer smartphones could be used by terrorist groups to evade surveillance. However, some media interviews about these 'security worries' are no doubt a smokescreen by intelligence services, who do not want criminals or terrorists or other security agencies to realise that security services are right inside all these new systems as well.

The trouble is that such ultra-secure innovations are easily banned by governments – and will be. For example, a nation can announce that no cloud provider or mobile phone manufacturer can sell IT services or handsets in that nation without back-door keys so that police or secret services can instantly access all private data, whenever they feel the need. Australia took this path in 2019. The days of private, encrypted data are already numbered, because many governments will argue that guaranteeing your own privacy means dangerous criminals can also hide from sight.

Many future 'techies' will continue to innovate as a matter of principle, as a silent protest against state interference, exploiting little gaps in government surveillance, inventing clever ways to beat the system, and offering them to groups of friends – but governments will relentlessly hunt them down. And with huge improvements in face recognition, expect many people to develop ways to try to deceive the all-present cameras, ranging from 3D printed face masks to hoods, make-up and other techniques.

So how will terror cells and criminals communicate in future? Or people who are just obsessed with their own privacy? Expect many new generations of techniques and online tools (many developed and launched covertly by security agencies themselves, masquerading as entrepreneurs wishing to help people stay private).

Every meeting and conversation recorded

On top of all this, individual do-it-yourself spying has never been easier – and will become even more so – via wireless devices hidden in standard power adapters, or pens, or ornaments, or concealed micro-cameras, each able to transmit over 1,000 metres to a base station which then transmits instantly online, or using apps installed secretly onto anyone else's phone, which can take just a few seconds, or using a drone equipped with a video camera.

All business leaders should assume that every meeting may be recorded, or is being transmitted live to a wider audience – using just a voice memo on a smartphone concealed in a jacket pocket, or just an open voice call, set to hands-free, on a phone slipped into a pocket.

Doctors, nurses and home carers are already discovering that their careless habits may end up immortalised in YouTube videos. The same applies in every other kind of workplace. And then there is secret tracking of family, friends, competitors or enemies – made so much easier by automatic trace facilities built into every mobile device, and the wide availability of spying apps.

Future of publishing, paper and news

We have looked at spying, but what about public media and government scrutiny by news agencies or book authors?

Printed books will have a future for a long time. Yes, it is also true that e-book sales have grown over the last decade, together with devices or apps to read them, but sales of children's physical books are increasing, and sales of e-books fell 10% in 2017, the third year of falling sales, while the sales of audio books soared – so what is going on?

In the longer term, expect e-book sales to grow, bouncing back somewhat from the fall in sales since 2016, and a gradual decline in sales of paper books and magazines, except in niche areas such as glossy travel books or 'experience books' for children. But the physicality of books will become more important: touch, look, feel and smell.

Specialist magazines will be more resilient – indeed, throughout the last few years, magazine titles in many countries have boomed in number, for ever more niche groups of readers. Magazines will continue to benefit from convenience, and from a superior look and feel to reading matter on a mobile device.

Paper will still mean a faster read

Stupid predictions have been made for years about the 'paperless office', when the truth is that more paper is printed each day per manager than ever before in most corporations: 92% of executives print something each day, 45% print ten pages or more and 15% print more than 50. As I predicted years ago, paper will be with us for a long time yet.

All electronic media will continue to face a challenge from print, because of the higher reading speed associated with it due to larger page size, format and resolution. Reading speed is less of a consideration when enjoying a novel on an e-reader, but it really makes a difference at work.

As every busy executive knows, the fastest way to read and mark up a set of lengthy board papers, or a long contract, is to print it out. Most people read printed pages at up to ten times their on-screen speed, using unconscious techniques such as page scanning, and are less likely to miss important sections than if they scroll through endless electronic pages of text. Their recall is usually better with paper, especially if they have a 'photographic' memory, and they are better able to reproduce important thoughts at the relevant part of the board meeting, because of their notes in the margin. And they usually find what they are looking for more quickly than by using the 'find' function in an e-version of the text.

Speed-reading will help newspapers

Set the speed-reading challenge to any group of friends and see for yourself. Most senior leaders can only read around 500 words a minute on screen, but can easily make overall sense of an entire 40,000-word publication in less than five to ten minutes. So any corporation running a strict paperless office is wasting a huge amount of time and money.

You may think that all this will change with higher resolution, larger screens, but this will not be the case for a long time. We already have large 'retina' screens, operating at the maximum resolution the eye can process, but they are hardly mobile. We will need to wait for electronic paper: flat, foldable membranes with the same contrast, resolution and convenience as large sheets of paper. Expect prototypes by 2020, but large retina-resolution sheets will be unusual and costly until well into the 2030s.

Future of news agencies, newspapers and reporting

It has often been said that 'News is what someone else does not want you to print. All the rest is advertising.' But the fastest spreading online content is heart-warming videos, funny lists, and eye-catching headlines on sites such as BuzzFeed or ViralNova. These appeal to positive, affirming emotions, and are promoted by friends.

Newspapers in crisis – but growth in emerging nations

Newspapers will rapidly decline in almost all developed nations over the next five to ten years, while readership will grow in news-loving nations such as India, driven by expansion of the middle classes.

In 5 years, newspaper readership fell in America by 47%, but will grow by at least 15% in India in the next five years. One in five of the entire world's daily newspapers is published in India – more than 100 million separate titles, with 45% of all advertising spend.

In developed nations, traditional newspapers will struggle to convert readers into profitable online subscribers, losing over 60% of their previous income in many cases. Expect closures, mergers, consolidations and serious downgrading of content, as staff are laid off, offices closed, and regional and specialist reporting stopped. The number of newspaper journalists in America has fallen by 45% since 2004.

At the same time, some free newspapers will do rather better, whether dailies given out in metro stations with minimal editorial teams, or local weekly papers in areas with robust local advertising, particularly from estate agents.

Future of news media

More Americans now watch news online than on cable TV. Around 61% of 18- to 29-year-olds mainly watch streamed content online. Over 5,000 new full-time jobs have been created by around 500 digital news firms, including jobs for experienced journalists who have left newspapers like the *New York Times* and *Washington Post*. Digital newspapers will develop a new working model – for example, there is no cost limit on length of an article, nor any need to make it all fit neatly in pages of a printed newspaper.

Growth in digital news will not halt the declining audience of news companies. For example, Facebook users who click on news links only spend 90 seconds a month on news sites, on average.

As I predicted, news broadcasting is now a social activity – half of all social media users already share news, and comment on news posts, while 7% of American adults have posted news videos they made themselves to a social network or news site.

Research shows that sad news stories are least likely to go viral. Positive stories get the most share-time. Expect these trends to profoundly shape our communities, and impact all news companies. The fact is that entertainment has always been a bigger business than news.

Who cares about depressing news online?

The challenge for fee-paying online news sites will continue to be strong competition from hundreds of well-respected, free sources such as the BBC, the *Guardian* and the *Huffington Post*, and sites such as Google. In addition, we can expect to see more 'community' news sites, similar to the *Huffington Post*, again all free access. Curators of content will multiply: people who gather various types of related web content, sometimes adding editorial of their own, despite stricter copyright rules.

In 20 years' time, high-quality, in-depth investigative journalism for print media will have almost died out in developed nations. Aspiring journalists will be working instead for TV news, with linked (free access) web pages. But even large TV news companies will struggle in future with the cost of maintaining their own reporters across the world. The three largest news channels in America – CNN, Fox and MSNBC – lost 11% of the prime-time audience in a single year.

Expect rapid growth of freelance reporters and camera teams, without formal backing of news companies, or their protection, working alone or in packs, taking huge personal risks in the competition to get stories and sensational images. The result will be more frequent deaths among journalists in war zones, together with growing worries about loss of professionalism and possible bias.

News fatigue will cut audiences further

In the past, most news tended to be sad or bad. Slayings, beatings, rapes, job losses, natural disasters, air crashes, bomb blasts, wars, business scandals, and so on. Editors cram all the worst and most sensational events onto the front page, or the first 60 seconds of TV headlines. The more gruesome the images, or the more sensational the event, the more it will be broadcast.

Audiences are experiencing 'news fatigue', fed an ever more sensational diet of stories, built mainly around availability of images. This matters most for TV news, where it is almost impossible to report a story without video. Any citizen with a smartphone can be a news source, but quality is declining.

TV news distorts reality, even more than printed news or web pages. You could be forgiven for thinking at times that the entire world is affected every week by terrorist bombs, or by terrible murders, or by natural disasters. Whereas the truth is that on most days of the week, there is not enough real national news to fill bulletins.

Audiences will also be increasingly bored by current affairs debates and political interviews. As we will see in Chapter 5, differences between politicians are usually exaggerated in media debate. Most people in developed nations don't trust politicians anyway, so why bother to listen to what they say?

Democracy will be weakened as a result of all these different factors, with less media scrutiny, and greater susceptibility to being hijacked by relatively ill-informed, viral social media campaigns (see Chapter 5, 'Radical') – which will, of course, set the scene for a further extension of the same malaise.

Fake news will become an even greater global obsession

For the last 20 years or longer in the UK, journalists have scored among the lowest in society for trust, equalled only by politicians. Compared to doctors or church leaders, trusted by 70%, journalists have often scored a mere 10%. This has been corrosive for democracy and government accountability. In my experience, such mistrust is unjustified. Almost all journalists I have worked with have been obsessed with accuracy, meticulous in detail, careful in checking quotes, and deeply knowledgeable.

It was easy, when President Trump was elected, for him to play on commonly held mistrust, whipping up suspicion, even open hostility. And that of course is a really smart thing for any politician to do, if he or she fears public criticism in future. President Trump also perfected the art of going direct to the people, using his Twitter account just like dictators in the last century used state-owned TV and radio stations, to broadcast a constant stream of comments and favourable stories.

But it is only a small step from ridicule of journalists to verbal attacks, and from verbal attacks to physical attacks or even murders. No surprise then that in the last few years we have seen many high-profile investigative journalists murdered in many different nations from Slovakia to Ukraine, Malta, Russia, Saudi Arabia and China.

In many nations with autocratic leadership, the more respected a journalist is, the shorter their average life expectancy will be. The purpose of such killings will go far beyond silencing the writer or broadcaster: the primary aim will be to intimidate and silence an entire community of other media critics, and such aims will often be very successful.

But in the end, all politicians and business leaders need independent media validation to win the greatest respect, amplify their messages, and transform whole societies, so there will continue to be an uneasy alliance. The rest is mere propaganda.

And at the same time, autocratic leaders will continue to step up surveillance and control of all online influencers, however informal they are, who they will tend to see as other potential threats.

★

In this chapter I have shown how the speed of change is accelerating. I've described the risk of Wild Cards, how emerging economies will grow, and the benefit as well as risks of digital. And also the paradox that some things are changing surprisingly slowly. We need to look next at how our world is *physically* moving, with a billion migrating to cities, huge demographic changes, rapid improvements in life expectancy, and what it all means for your future.

Chapter 2

URBAN

THE SECOND FACE OF THE FUTURE IS URBAN – radical changes in megacities, migrations, demographics, health and life expectancy. Show me the demographics of any town, city, nation or region, and I will tell you its future. It all depends on how many people live in the area, how old they are, how well educated and so on. For example, more than half the world will be living in Asia by 2025, and India will be the largest nation on earth, full of young people.

One billion children will become consumers in the next 15 years, the biggest jump in human history. Today in Africa 350 million children see glimpses of your lifestyle and compare this to their own poverty, surviving on less than $3 a day. Most of them will spend their entire adult lives chasing dreams of your wealth.

85% of the world's population is already living in today's emerging markets, mostly in cities, driving over 90% of the entire planet's economic growth. In the global population of those aged under 30, 90% are in these same nations. This single fact will dominate our world for the next 100 years. The so-called developed world is rapidly becoming irrelevant, less powerful or influential, and will represent less than 8% of the world population by 2060.

Expect massive shake-ups and takeovers, with many boardroom upheavals, as old companies are hit by new Asian mega-giants, invading their markets, and buying competitors. Many takeovers will happen at high speed, as old companies run out of cash and ideas, to the dismay of governments, workers and shareholders.

Population will peak at 11 billion

More than 9 billion people will be living on earth by 2040, around 1.6 billion more than in 2020, despite the fact that the number of children born per couple globally has already fallen to only 2.4 (replacement level is around 2.2). Across sub-Saharan Africa, the number of children per couple is still 4.9. Expect 11 billion people on earth before 2090.

This will be a very crowded world, with massive pressures on land use, which will create internal and international tensions. Land pressures will be even greater because climate change will dislocate many of the world's poorest and most vulnerable, with flooding, rising seas and extended deserts, all of which is likely to be blamed by many on carbon emissions over decades by developed nations.

Many nations have young populations, with 50% of them under 25 years old. Even if there is not a single baby born in these communities over the next 20 years, this age bulge guarantees a boom in the number of parents – barring global plague or catastrophic world war.

A huge challenge will be to feed, clothe, shelter, and provide power and water to 11 billion people without destroying the planet, especially as all these people will expect middle-class lifestyles. If leaders fail to deliver, especially in nations like India or China, expect radical unrest.

Population growth cannot be slowed suddenly without producing other crises, with huge populations of elderly people that will dwarf problems in Europe or Japan today. Some 20% of Japan is older than 65, and its 124 million population is likely to be only 88 million by 2065. Globally, expect 1 billion people over 60 by 2025. Expect 1 million people over 90 in Italy alone by 2026 – enough to alter every election.

One billion people on the move due to vast wealth contrasts

More than 1 billion people will migrate to cities over the next three decades, in search of a better life. Around 300 million people will move from rural areas to cities in China alone over the next 25 years, 300 million in India, and a further 475 million across Africa. Half the world's GDP growth over the next 20 years will come from around 450 cities in emerging markets, mostly places you may never have heard of.

These cities will create the world's greatest new markets, with hundreds of millions of new city retailers – many of whom will be street traders. Most of the world's largest corporations will be based in emerging markets by 2035, compared to just 5% in 2000.

When a third of the entire human race lacks basic necessities, such as running water, basic sanitation, and adequate food, it is hardly surprising that a billion people will want these things. More than half our world is living on less than $3 a day, and 22,000 children die each day from poverty. A billion people have no safe water to drink. Nearly 1 billion people cannot read or write. Every day around 840 million are hungry. A billion people have no access to electric power. Almost one in three of those in the least developed countries die before the age of 40.

Large-scale migration is an unstoppable force, as we have seen many times during wars or civil conflicts, and on the Mediterranean. When 200,000 people all decide to move, many willing to risk death, no army or navy on earth can stop them without a police state, gigantic walls or massive costs patrolling seas. And there are easy ways around barriers. For example, someone can buy a flight and a holiday to Disneyland in Miami, enter on a tourist visa, and disappear. Or do the same on a student visa.

1% of humanity will own 65% of the wealth

The wealthiest 1% in our world own 50% of the world's wealth, and 20% already own 75%. Their income is 60 times that of the poorest 20%, and the gap is increasing rapidly. In 30 years' time, on current trends, 1% of the population will own 65%. This is a worrying and completely unsustainable situation. If you own this book, you are probably one of the 1%.

History shows that when such inequalities exist, resentment and anger usually grows, and violent revolution can follow. In our social media age, new revolutionary movements will erupt from nothing in minutes, hours or days, just as we saw on the streets of Paris in late 2018.

History shows that the only way to reduce the risk of large-scale, bloody convulsions is for governments to deal with public resentments, tax wealth on a much larger scale, and pay for better public services. Or for the super-wealthy to give much of their wealth away.

For all these reasons expect more effective taxation, especially of the super-wealthy and of global corporations, and the funding of better public services. More wealth may need to move from wealthy to poor nations, invested in better education, health care and infrastructure. As in Saudi Arabia and in China, many governments will take very public action to prosecute corrupt leaders, to reduce public resentment.

The richest 80 people on earth own as much wealth as the poorest 3.4 billion people, and such people and their families are likely to be targeted if there is large-scale civil unrest where they live. Next in line could be 1,600 billionaires and their families, who own $6.4 trillion more than the combined income of the poorest 120 countries. Many very privileged people seized by mobs in some emerging markets are likely to end up in prison, accused of all kinds of things, while others will not be so fortunate.

In America the contrasts are also growing rapidly; 1% now owns 40% of the wealth. The three wealthiest Americans own more than 160 million other US citizens (50%). The same kind of shift has taken place in most other developed nations.

Contrasts are even greater in the poorer nations, especially in cities. In Mumbai, for example, in the shadow of the most expensive real estate in the world, you will find slum dwellers in shacks of plastic and plywood, and street pavements crowded with sleeping workers at night.

If just 0.1% of low-income migrants become politically motivated and well organised the result will be new, revolutionary, protest movements that will dwarf anything our world has ever seen, probably starting in the poorest nations, overthrowing governments and powerful leaders, seizing the assets of the wealthy, and crossing borders at astonishing speed, changing history for a hundred years. We saw a tiny foretaste of this in the so-called Arab Spring in 2010, partly triggered by the rapid rise in food prices hitting the poor.

Living in cities

More than half the world already lives in cities, of which a large number are megacities of more than 10 million people. By 2025, many nations will boast of smaller, so-called Smart Cities, where digital tech has been used widely to radically improve efficiency of transport, energy and utilities, as well as improving workplaces, homes and leisure.

A decade or more ago, many forecasters came out with wild, idiotic statements about declining cities. They claimed that many millions of wealthier people would move to rural areas, working virtually, driven away by noise, pollution, house prices and fear of violent crime.

It was obvious to me then that this was nonsense. People love busy communities, the buzz, opportunities, bars, cafés, clubs, restaurants, cinemas and theatres. And crime rates in many cities have fallen significantly – with some exceptions such as London, with the growth of teenage gangs. Cities are good for the environment: they pack people into small areas, and protect countryside from sprawl and destruction. Cities are efficient, with smaller distances from work to home, school to home, shops to home, home to hospital, and have the advantage of major economies of scale.

A billion live in city slums

In most emerging market cities, a taxi can drive you in minutes from a smart hotel to slums, where makeshift homes rise precariously to four storeys. Take a walk down dark and narrow pot-holed streets. You will see children and animals play in open sewers, stagnant streams, piles of stinking rubbish, tangles of electric cables strung from houses, and evidence of disease and deprivation.

Yet if you have the privilege to be invited as a guest into such homes you will usually find immaculately kept rooms, smartphones, well-educated, ambitious young people, and maybe parents with professional qualifications.

Come back in a decade and most of those slums will be middle-class districts, with concrete homes, running water and sewage. But another million new people may have arrived, building new shacks, and so city growth continues.

Some slum dwellers become millionaires

In former slum districts, urbanisation is creating real estate millionaires – people who built informal dwellings on land some time ago, and somehow gained land rights – and such places are now surrounded by high-rise blocks of smart new apartments.

More than 2 billion people will find themselves empowered by new wealth over the next 25 years, with more choices, better access to health care, e-commerce, banking, and so on. At least 1 billion will be first-generation middle class – first to go to university; first to own a car; first to own property.

Many megacities will plateau at 20 to 25 million people, as infrastructure limitations start making life unpleasant. So for every million low-wage migrants that arrive, another million middle-class workers will leave for smaller cities. And eventually rural to city migration will end. This is already the case in Brazil, where cities like Rio de Janeiro are no longer seeing waves of new migration into densely packed favelas.

Mega-infrastructure

As a result of all this, we will see more investment in infrastructure from 2020 to 2050 than in all of human history – in schools, hospitals, power stations, national grids, water supplies, sewage treatment, roads, railways and airports. Linked to this, we will see booms and busts in real estate, construction and commodities.

Much of this infrastructure will last far longer than people imagine. The impact of each city on nature will be clearly visible for 30,000 years into the future, even if that city is abandoned. Ports have been, and will be, used by travellers or traders for thousands of years. Many Roman roads built 2,000 years ago are still busy routes today. Many Stone Age earthworks are also clearly visible in rural areas, though abandoned 5,000 years ago.

Commodity instability

Rapid urbanisation will create instability and chaos at times in commodity markets such as steel, copper or aluminium. Expect large price spikes and falls as speculators trade on uncertainty. Steel prices will be affected by real estate booms and busts in China, and by global overcapacity, with 1.6 trillion tons a year produced. China uses twice as much steel as India, America and the EU combined.

Mining companies will be forced to mine deeper for lower-quality ores, and will need to take a 40- to 50-year view, to recoup investment. As commodity prices rise, waste (slag) heaps will be re-mined to extract additional material. China will snap up mining rights, mining companies and mining technologies.

Countries with the greatest mining wealth will spend more on armies and internal security. They will be more likely to have ultra-wealthy leaders, see huge finance siphoned out of the nation, to have a corrupt judiciary and to experience civil wars. They will also be more likely to have lower growth economies, because exchange rates rise as soon as commodities start to be exported. And as soon as that happens, every other exported good and service becomes less competitive.

The future of Africa will be driven by cities

Africa will continue to be the world's fastest growing continent in industrial output, barring a regional disaster such as a new, very widespread pandemic. Despite a bloody history of tribal conflict, sub-Saharan Africa has been almost entirely at peace for over a decade, with no substantial cross-border conflicts, and the resolution of many civil wars.

I have worked closely with people in many countries across Africa over the last 40 years. While traditional ways of life are still found in almost all rural areas, the speed of growth of many major cities is remarkable and relentless.

Take Kampala in Uganda, which I first visited in 1988. People were dying of AIDS all around us, and a third of sexually active adults were infected with HIV. The country was also recovering from civil war. Kampala is now a vibrant, noisy, thriving, cosmopolitan high-rise city, full of hotels, new offices, and surrounded by new factories. Yet, just 25 miles out of the city, along dirt tracks through the bush, most people live in mud-brick dwellings with thatched roofs, as subsistence farmers, with no running water and with unreliable power.

Expect huge investment into Africa

Businesses like Primark, H&M and General Electric are moving into Africa. National economies are being stimulated by the rapid adoption of smartphones, which has accelerated mobile payments and business. Tens of thousands of Chinese nationals are staying in Africa when Chinese-sponsored contracts end, investing in local businesses. The number of scientific papers published by Africans has trebled in a decade to 55,400 a year.

I recently visited an income-generating project linked to our own AIDS foundation, in rural Uganda, eight hours drive on a terrible road from Kampala. We passed a giant motorway being built by the Chinese, using local labour, which will transform the incomes of those in mud huts, and help the Chinese to win influence for a generation, gaining access to oil, minerals and food. Decades ago, this part of the world was dominated by British aid, but today the only growing global empire is Chinese. I saw the same in Colombo, Sri Lanka, where China is building an entire city in the sea, on the edge of a strategic port, in a nation where wages are half that in India.

We are likely to see economic growth of 5 to 8% a year in many African nations over most of the next 20 years, despite regional challenges and corrupt governments. Manufacturing and service industries will grow fastest within 50 miles of sea ports, as Asian costs rise.

Nigeria – rapid migration to coastal towns and cities

Nigeria is Africa's largest nation, and largest economy, even though average earnings per person are only a third of those in South Africa. Nigeria will soon have a population of 300 million people, up from 185 million. Expect 440 million in Nigeria by 2050, the third-largest nation on earth by then.

For the next four decades, most wealth will be in Christian-dominated southern cities, because of oil, and access to ports. Most instability will be in the poorest parts of the Muslim-dominated north, where the terrorist group Boko Haram has roots. Nigeria could see another prolonged civil conflict, as it did in the Biafra war from 1967–1970 in which a million died, but next time the result could be partition. In the meantime, cities like Jos will remain on the front line.

South Africa will struggle to keep pace

South Africa is the second-largest economy in Africa, but has seen very slow growth compared to that of the region overall. South Africa's greatest miracle has been peaceful transition from apartheid, widely credited to Nelson Mandela, and to the influence of prominent black Christian leaders.

South Africa's greatest challenges will continue to be very high unemployment in young, black communities, and white dominance of big business leadership, with huge disparities of wealth and opportunity; city violence; gated white communities; and revolutionary undercurrents.

Sending money home

One consequence of urban migration is hundreds of millions of workers from poor nations sending money home. Most remittances in Africa are from young adults in cities to parents and other relatives in rural areas. Such income will be a growing proportion of future income in rural communities.

Global remittances are already worth over $650bn a year and contribute up to half of some nations' GDP. Take, for example, Tajikistan at 47% of GDP, Liberia at 31%, Kyrgyzstan at 29%,

Lesotho at 27%, and Nepal at 22%. Whole industries are booming to move such cash across borders, which will shift rapidly from Western Union, and human beings carrying bundles of cash, to mobile payments.

Birth rate decline will add to city migration in Asia

Travel around India today and you see children everywhere, on streets, hanging onto buses, crammed into schools – yet China's children are hard to find. The impact of China's one-child policy, even though partially abolished, will be felt for the next 70 years. Migrants from rural areas will continue to make up the gap caused by an ageing workforce in coastal cities, but eventually this source will also decline.

South Korea and Japan need more babies

The same is happening in South Korea. Just 40 years ago, the average couple had six children. By 2018, that had fallen to 1.1. Across the world, once income per household reaches $12,000 a year, numbers of children per couple drop dramatically. But we need 2.3 children per couple to maintain population without migration.

If the fertility rate stays low in South Korea, without greater immigration, by 2050 South Korea's population will have fallen from 50 million to 40 million, of which 38% will be retired.

In Japan, unless something changes, over 1,000 rural towns and villages will have no women of child-bearing age by 2050. The population will fall by a third, from 127 million, over 50 years, and there will be only 43 million Japanese by 2110.

Japanese society has not welcomed migration, and less than 2% of the population was born overseas. Expect this to change, and for child-rearing to become more fashionable, with all kinds of government incentives as raising a family is promoted as a national duty.

Population decline has been a national security issue for nations like Russia, which saw a fall of 10 million in a short period, although birth rates are recovering. France has been offering generous tax and benefit subsidies.

Here is a paradox: a billion people in poor nations will look to move for a better life, many of them very well educated, while many of the wealthy nations to which they want to move face a collapse in population. So the real issue is cultural.

Migrations to cities across Europe and Central Asia

From Central Asia to Western Europe, people are on the move: Kazakhstani workers to Russia, Ukrainians to Poland, Poles to the UK, and Britons to America. There are already so many Central Asian workers in Moscow that over 20% of the city's inhabitants are Muslim.

We will see similar migrations from Africa to Europe, with growing pressures on Spain and Italy, who will at times be over-whelmed by highly motivated, younger migrants who enter illegally. More than 600,000 Africans are waiting at any time in North Africa, and 650 boats full of migrants have been rescued at sea since 2014 to be 'processed' in Italy. Over 100,000 more people a year are entering Italy illegally without detection from North Africa, often at great risk in tiny boats, while migrants from Turkey to Greece have grown 150% in a single year, partly as a result of civil wars in the Middle East.

North Korea is sitting on a migration time bomb. At some point, the pressures on the regime will become overwhelming. In the meantime, there are still risks of more military provocations from North Korea, despite recent discussions with other nations. The end of the current very strictly controlled regime may be a peaceful adjustment or result in bloody chaos, but expect the Chinese to be deeply involved in any longer-term transition.

Wherever they go, new migrants tend to settle in their own cultural communities (almost ghettos). Many will retain their customs and ways of life, alienated from their adoptive nations, adding to local tensions. Birth rates of lower-income immigrant communities will usually be much higher than in wealthy host nations. These imported baby booms will help re-balance ageing populations.

Europe was dying – but expect a baby boom

In Germany, on current trends, you need eight great-grandparents to produce a single great-grandchild. That is the simple consequence of couples having an average of just over one child. The situation is similar in Italy, Portugal, Spain, Greece and in parts of the UK.

However, birth rates in some Western EU nations are likely to rise rapidly, partly as a result of migration, as in the UK. More than 1.7 million people a year enter the EU, and a further 1.7 million migrate within the EU – mainly from newly joined EU nations where wages are very low. Most migrants are young, single adults who are likely to settle down and raise families. Another reason why birth rates may rise is that a generation of women delayed motherhood by 10 to 15 years, and biological clocks are ticking.

10 million more people want to head for Britain

For the past decade, more than 500,000 people have moved to the UK every year, and just over 300,000 have left (many of them British born). Of those arrivals, 40% have been from the rest of the EU, with the majority from all over the world. If past trends were to continue, over 10 million people more would move to Britain in the next 20 years, and 2 million babies would be born to those 10 million arrivals, offsetting low national birth rates. White children would be a minority in schools in England by 2037. The number of ethnic minority children in primary and secondary schools has soared by over 60% in a decade.

Immigration will continue to be a hot political issue for the next three decades, made even more sensitive by Brexit tensions. Brexit can only reduce some of the migration from other EU nations – just a small proportion of those that settle in the UK each year.

We will see many attempts (and failures) to control numbers, of which a vote for Brexit was only one, with growing popularity of extreme right-wing groups, and attacks on minorities. However, the UK will remain a very attractive global destination, and employers will continue to make a very compelling case for worker visas, especially in times of low unemployment. In every nation, population size is strongly linked to size of the economy, so the UK economy will also grow.

At the same time, expect serious decline in the numbers of people living in rural areas and smaller towns or cities in countries like Poland, the Czech Republic, Bulgaria, Albania, Slovakia and what was East Germany as over 15 million younger workers leave for better opportunities during the next decade, many of whom are well educated. Most will only work in other nations for a while, and then return to the largest cities in their home countries.

Germany is likely to develop a more polarised attitude to immigration – especially following admission of a million Syrian and other migrants in a single decision – with street protests a common occurrence. At the same time, the challenges arising from an ageing labour force will deepen, which will threaten economic growth.

Future of real estate linked to cities

Despite all the real estate booms and busts that we will see in major cities around the world over the next three decades, more than $100 trillion dollars will be added in real terms to the total value of global real estate, from $228 trillion in 2017, simply because cities are expanding, economies are growing, and numbers of middle-class property owners are rising.

Globalised travellers remain near airport hubs

All globalised executives will continue to need to be close to a large international airport, however virtual their teams. This 'hub effect' will also be true for high-speed train networks.

Those who are fed up with city life can afford the luxury of bucking the trend, going 'back to nature', getting out of cities for a greener life, greater security and lower costs. However, the wealthiest will just live in both, with two, three, ten or twenty homes. An increasing number of super-wealthy will have private helicopters and planes that link their offices, homes, hotels and holidays direct.

Future of UK property linked to largest cities

UK property prices will be linked to the future of London, Manchester, Edinburgh, Glasgow and other major cities. As I predicted many years ago, and more recently, real estate has, for many reasons, remained a good long-term investment, despite the 2008–9 crash and Brexit-related worries.

◆ Rapidly growing population due to net immigration – unlikely to fall as dramatically as many think post-Brexit as net migration from *non-EU* nations has been running at over 250,000 a year compared to only 74,000 from the EU in 2018

◆ Acute shortage of land for new housing in a tiny island, and severe planning controls

◆ Outsourced jobs in other nations coming back to the UK (e.g. call centres) as it becomes more competitive due to low wage inflation and exchange rates

◆ Recovery of banking since 2009, despite Brexit

◆ Strong growth in services and creative industries

◆ UK seen as safer haven for investors than other regions where there is conflict

◆ Family breakup means smaller households, more homes

◆ Ageing population, and better care to help stay at home

◆ Equity release by parents to help children buy property

◆ Bank of England policies to keep interest rates low, until certain of recovery, even if the result is a new real estate boom

◆ Low rates of return from government bonds, bank deposits and company shares so real estate more attractive

◆ Many people don't trust pension saving and prefer property

◆ Traditional mindset/psychology of property ownership as an investment

◆ No capital gains tax on your own home – yet

◆ Tax benefits for personal pension funds that own property.

Future of London

The population of London has grown by more than 1 million in a decade and, despite Brexit, will grow by a further million in the next 20 years, while the number of houses will hardly increase. In the medium term, London will continue to experience a top-end boost from international buyers who are worried about the future of their own nations, and whether they might need to make a rapid transfer of assets or even of their families.

London will continue to be firmly placed near the top of the world order in popularity as a 'good' place to live. Private schools and private health care are world class, and the streets are so safe that police don't routinely carry guns. London is likely to remain France's sixth-biggest city by French population for the next 15 years.

Restaurants and wine bars have multiplied, together with cinemas, hotels and nightclubs. London has become one vast work and leisure complex offering the very best of world-class time-out for busy executives, round the clock. Some of this will be dampened by Brexit until the UK economy adjusts to exploit new markets.

London will continue to be a major global centre of financial services, despite efforts by the EU to end its regional near-monopoly. Expect a fierce fight from London to remain the main player for global foreign exchange. The City will struggle to retain the world's largest collection of foreign banking offices. There will be growing competition from New York and Shanghai, together with Singapore, Hong Kong, Tokyo and Mumbai – but the pull of Paris and Frankfurt will be less than many predict. London's banks and other financial services will remain dominant employers, even though the total number of workers is unlikely to match that of the period before the 2008 economic crisis until beyond 2025.

London will also continue to be a huge magnet for creative, imaginative people – for free-thinkers, digital marketers, computer games designers, film-makers, artists, entrepreneurs, FinTech startups (mobile payments, for example), management consultants and advisors. Expect London's tech workforce to grow by at least 5% a year for the next decade, fuelled by a flood of new venture capital, much of it from other nations.

Property in America, Eastern Europe, China and Russia

As I predicted, America's real estate market had recovered by 2016 across almost the entire country, following the crash of 2008–2010, and the US GDP has grown well.

Some East European countries suffered falls of over 40% in house prices in the 2008–2011 crisis, and in some nations such as Ukraine it will be some time still before these levels are seen again. In contrast, China's evolving real estate market will continue to wobble from booms to busts across different regions, as the nation rapidly urbanises, in a poorly balanced process driven by migrations, real estate developers, over-ambitious property owners, varying availability of credit, and government policies.

Across the former Soviet Union, it will take more than 50 years to replace Stalin's world of concrete, identical, low-grade apartment blocks, and rehouse the 175 million people who still live in them.

Future of health

We have seen how the future of every nation is linked to demographics, migrations and cities. But these things are also linked to health.

The fact is that 65% of all health spending in developed nations is on those over the age of 65, most of whom have several chronic conditions, almost all related to the ageing process. Therefore, it could be said that every pharma company and every hospital exists primarily to serve the needs of older people, in those parts of the world.

The greatest health challenges in the next two decades are almost all related to ageing, as many emerging nations also become older in average age.

Shift from sickness to enhancing performance

The whole emphasis of health care is already shifting from treatment to prevention, wellness and improving performance. Many drugs used today to treat illness will be used tomorrow to enhance performance. For 15 years we have seen this in sexual health and memory loss. Drugs like Viagra and Cialis were first prescribed for men with varying degrees of impotence, but both are now widely used to enhance 'normal' performance, with growing 'underground' sales online.

The same happened with Ritalin and other drugs to enhance brain function, either in hyperactive younger people, or in older people with memory loss. Some 20% of all US and UK students are now using such drugs to help pass exams.

The commonest complaint of older people is lack of energy. The greatest blockbuster drugs of all time will rejuvenate old bodies and brains by targeting systems in every cell, increasing efficiency of mitochondria, for example, which generate electrical power.

Mitochondria have their own genes; they divide and can be swapped between animals and humans. Old mitochondria have been revived in mice and rats, with treatments such as alpha-lipoic acid in combination with other drugs. The old mice run around faster, and solve mazes more rapidly. Imagine the impact of such a therapy on human health: on memory, healing, heart output, as well as sexual or athletic performance.

Future of cosmetics, skin care and face lifts

We are seeing a similar trend in cosmetics. The global cosmetics market will be worth around $420bn by 2022, growing by 4% a year – with greatest growth among older consumers and those in the emerging middle class.

Hundreds of millions of women over the age of 30 will seek to look younger. Some will pay more than $1,000 every year for their latest 'miracle' skin treatments, creams, lotions and other therapies. We will see reliable research over the next decade that demonstrates clearly that certain formulations really do stop wrinkles, restore the skin colloid that gives the skin its natural thickness, help restore elasticity, and make people look up to a decade younger.

The damaged ozone layer still covers 8.8 million square miles and will continue to fuel tourist concerns about skin cancers.

Sunlight will be blamed for many disorders, including cataracts and non-Hodgkin's lymphoma (a type of cancer). Skin cosmetics will increasingly emphasise ultraviolet ray protection.

Some sun screens are so strong that it is now impossible to develop a 'normal' tan, and growing numbers of cancer-obsessed middle-class parents will be horrified to discover that their children have rickets because of lack of sunlight. Over 50% of UK adults are short of vitamin D, including many children, mostly in winter and spring, and rickets is more common than it has been for 50 years.

Sun-tanned skin will be less fashionable in Europe, as in India, with paleness a sign of sophistication. Increasing numbers will view beach holidays in hot countries with suspicion.

And plastic surgery will continue to offer remarkable remoulding of faces, ears, necks, breasts, buttocks and thighs – all increasingly common as a death-defying generation attempts to stop the ageing process.

Nutrition and feeding your gut bacteria

There are more bacteria inside you than there are human cells, and those in your gut weigh 2 kilograms. Expect huge research into how to feed them better in order to stay well. As part of this trend, global sales of probiotics – yoghurt-type foods containing live 'healthy' bacteria – will grow to $60bn by 2024 (see p. 281).

We will see routine treatments to alter mouth and gut bacteria (your microbiome), including transfer of faecal material from healthy people. Gut bacteria affect risks of many things, from depression to immune dysfunction, stomach ulcers, obesity, autism and, possibly (in the case of gum disease), Alzheimer's.

Greatest health challenges in the next 40 years

Brain degeneration of all types – Alzheimer's disease is now the commonest cause of death for men and women in the UK, but research has so far been very disappointing. Over 130 million people globally will be affected by dementia by 2050, up from 48 million in 2019. Fear of Alzheimer's will spread globally to become the number-one health concern for hundreds of millions. Alzheimer's is a particularly distressing condition. It often takes over a decade from major memory loss to death. Progression can mean that someone cannot recognise family, is distressed and confused, and doubly incontinent – maybe for years. It robs people of personality and insight, often turning them into gross caricatures of their former selves. Expect really huge research efforts to be ramped up over the next 15 years. A key will be to find an early marker to detect whether drugs are really working, without having to wait two decades for trials to complete. This research will also teach us about the physiology of the brain – how we think; how memory is stored; how decisions are made; what is conscious thought.

Cancers – most types / cases are already curable with early diagnosis and the best treatment. Expect many new therapies that teach the immune system to attack cancers, and gene screening to select anti-cancer drugs based on the precise character of each tumour. Most people with cancer over the next 30 years will be treated by combinations of different therapies. Death from cancer will become very unusual in most developed nations by 2065.

Obesity-related conditions including diabetes – 30% of humanity is overweight, which costs around 2.8% of global GDP (in health care and lost work days), and causes 5% of all deaths. Half of the world will be obese by 2030, as more people become wealthier. One in three babies born in New York in 2020 will develop adult-style diabetes as children because they are so fat. Obesity is costing the US economy over $100bn a year in ill health and lost productivity – with over 300,000 deaths a year – while 20% of all health costs in all developed nations are linked to obesity. Just one example is nonalcoholic steatohepatitis (NASH), a form of fatty liver disease, which now affects 12% of American adults, costing $5bn a year. Expect new therapies for obesity, such as ones based on the hormone thyroxine, which are designed to speed up metabolism without affecting the heart. Expect huge growth in regulations, ranging from a ban on chocolate advertising to children, to sugar content in convenience foods, or drinks, and major initiatives to encourage fitness.

Heart disease and strokes – we will see further astonishing reductions in deaths worldwide from heart disease and stroke due to screening of adults for blood pressure and cholesterol levels, and because fewer people smoke tobacco. Blood pressure tablets and statins to lower blood cholesterol will be used by over 350 million older people in 2025. We will see more widespread insertion of small tubes (stents) to unblock cardiac arteries – 127,000 people in America are treated with these each year, whereby a flexible tube is inserted through a tiny hole in the groin, and then guided using a thin wire, through blood vessels right up to the heart. Strokes will also be less common, with better recovery, as clot-busting drugs are used more widely.

Chronic wounds – around 100 million older people around the world will be affected by chronic wounds by 2025, particularly in their lower legs, caused by poor circulation. Expect huge investment in new dressings and therapies to accelerate healing, including the use of telomerase enzyme to reactivate old and tired fibroblasts in wound margins. (When cells have divided too many times, the ends of strands of genetic code inside them become shortened so the cells cannot divide any more. Telomerase is an enzyme that lengthens those ends or 'telomeres' back to a more 'youthful' state so they can divide again.)

Bacterial infection and sepsis, including TB – drug-resistant bacteria are a nightmare for surgeons and patients, and make 2 million people ill each year in America, costing $20bn in health care and killing 23,000. If irresponsible prescription practices continue, we could see more than 8 million deaths globally each year by 2045, 150 million deaths over 30 years, wiping out $50 trillion of economic activity. The last major breakthrough in new antibiotics was in the 1960s. Pharma companies do not make big money from antibiotics, because they are taken only for days, and several global pharma companies have recently closed down their antibiotic teams. Expect new government and industry partnerships. Expect much stricter controls on over-prescribing and bans on use in animal feeds by farmers. The TB pandemic has also been made worse by drug resistance, often linked to HIV infection.

Parasitic infections including malaria – malaria will continue to be one of the world's worst medical problems for the next 20 years, with 100 million cases a year, killing 660,000, especially young children. As I predicted, we are now beginning to see major breakthroughs in vaccines for malaria – expect growing numbers of vaccination programmes in every hard-hit nation by 2030.

Infertility – we will see an 'epidemic' of infertile, older aspiring parents. This is because more women wait until age 35 or older to try to conceive, and fertility falls rapidly with age. Sexual diseases are also rising globally and sperm counts have halved (see p. 94 for reasons).

Care of older people – over 100 million older people in the EU will need care, at home or in an institution, in the next 20 years. Despite popular perception, most older people die peacefully after a short final illness. Others will need heavy-duty care for many years. Expect huge growth in home carers, and more e-monitoring of health. Robots will not form any significant part of this solution, even by 2050. Low-cost migrant labour will fill many new, relatively low-skilled care jobs in the EU over the next 25 years.

Viral pandemics – major risk to every nation

Every year we see new virus variants, and as populations grow and travel more, mutations develop and spread even faster. Mutation is particularly likely when viruses from animals infect humans, or when people are treated with antivirals.

Humankind is very vulnerable to viral attack because we have very few, and relatively feeble, antiviral therapies. There is not a single antiviral today that is as effective as penicillin when first discovered. Antiviral research is 50 years behind antibiotics. Our only really effective weapon is vaccination. Hepatitis C virus is just one threat, carried by 3% of the entire world, including 4 million in America and 215,000 in the UK. Hepatitis B and C kill over a million a year.

AIDS will be a global menace for decades

AIDS has killed over 40 million people with a further 35 million infected, mainly in Africa, and continues to be a major global health threat with 1.8 million new infections a year. HIV mutated as it jumped from animals to humans decades ago, and is a warning of other mutants to come, against which we will have no immunity, vaccines or treatments. While infection rates have fallen as a result of effective projects, AIDS will still be a major health issue in 2040.

I have been deeply involved with AIDS work since 1988, when the international AIDS agency ACET started in our family home. This was as a result of my NHS work with people dying of cancer in London, during which I discovered people with AIDS who were dying in great physical and emotional distress. Today ACET has prevention and care projects in 15 nations, mainly in the poorest parts of the world.

Back in 1987, I said that developing a vaccine against HIV would be very difficult, because the virus keeps changing its outer surface, and escapes every vaccine trick we know. I predicted back then that it would be at least 15 years before a vaccine would be developed, and today there is still no likelihood of an effective, widely available vaccine by 2035.

Treatments have improved dramatically, as their availability has too, and AIDS is now a chronic illness in many nations where antivirals are widely available. We are also able to prevent most babies born to mothers with HIV from becoming infected themselves, using antiviral medication. But there is still no cure, and treatments can be toxic and are taken for life. We are discovering rare genes that provide partial or complete HIV protection, and which will lead us to gene-linked therapies.

But even if a cure is discovered tomorrow, it will take over 12 years for clinical trials to prove safety, and at least 25 years more to bring HIV under control. TB, for example, became curable in 1944, yet we still have the world's largest pandemic today.

The good news is that prevention works, with falling or stable infection rates in many nations like Uganda where up to 30% of all sexually active men and women were infected at one time, now having fallen to around 7–8%. However, complacency will be a constant challenge in many nations among different parts of the community, especially as treatment and life expectancy continues to improve.

Mutant flu will continue to be a hazard

Another mutant virus on the scale of HIV was the Spanish flu epidemic of 1918–19, which spread across the world in months, on foot, horses, donkeys, trains and ships, eventually killing over 30 million people, out of a world population of 2 billion. If a similar highly infectious and lethal pandemic begins tomorrow, it is likely to spread on international flights in days and weeks, not months, with no time for vaccine development or global distribution, and could kill 100 million people within a year. That is why the World Health Organization keeps warning governments about these threats.

From swine flu to Ebola

The genetic code of the Spanish flu virus is almost identical to that of swine flu. Therefore, it was worrying when swine flu reappeared in Mexico in 2009. It spread globally in weeks and caused 14,000 deaths, despite mass mobilisation of health resources, bans on travel, and almost instant lock-down of parts of Mexico.

SARS also appeared without warning in 2003. Over 8,600 people were infected with the virus within a few weeks, despite huge containment efforts, and 860 died. And 1% of carriers were so infectious that even touching a light switch 24 hours after they had done so could have been enough to kill you. SARS was only stopped by aggressive contact tracing and quarantine, in China, Canada and other nations. The outcome would have been very different if a single 'super-spreader' had travelled across Africa in a crowded plane, seeding clusters of infection in remote rural areas.

The 2014–15 Ebola outbreak killed and orphaned many thousands, paralysed West African economies, stopped farming, closed markets, and caused widespread hunger and deaths from other treatable diseases, with constant threats of more outbreaks from infected animals in the bush.

Mutant viruses will be a major future threat, and we will see far greater investment into antiviral therapies, rapid vaccine development and epidemic monitoring as a result.

The ultimate nanotech robot

Over 30 years ago I predicted in *The Truth about AIDS* that doctors would one day use viruses as a therapy. Such an idea sounded very strange back then, but I was until recently chair of a biotech company that is looking to do just that in order to destroy cancer.

Viruses are naturally occurring nanotech robots. They are not living, need no food, use no energy – they are just biological machines. Viruses have legs with sensors to detect what kind of cell they are touching. Once the legs latch onto the cells they are programmed to infect, the body of the virus fuses with the cell membrane, injecting a payload of genetic code.

Within minutes, the genes are read by the cell, and new proteins are being built. Every virus contains instructions to hijack each infected cell and turn it into a virus factory. The cell soon starts to fill with new virus particles until it explodes and dies, and the cycle of infection continues.

Scientists have redesigned different types of human viruses to target, infect and destroy cancer cells without damaging healthy tissue. At the same time, many of these viruses provoke an immune response against the cancer. Viruses can also be used to deliver extra genes, instructing cells to behave in certain ways as part of therapy.

Viruses will be used as weapons of war

These same techniques can be easily used to design viruses as weapons of war, perhaps with receptors that have an affinity to a particular race, for example. But while bio-weapons undoubtedly exist in different nations, most will be very poorly targeted, with extremely high risks for those who deploy them.

And we also need to recognise that old viruses will *inevitably* be used as 'low-tech' weapons at some point – for example, to deliberately cause a huge outbreak of foot and mouth disease across farms of an enemy nation. Very easy to do – just one person driving a van for a day, dropping bits of infected meat near pigs on a few farms. And how could anyone prove which country was responsible? The cost of a single outbreak in the UK was more than $13bn. In terms of cost of action and impact on a nation, such a viral attack promises a tremendously attractive payback for a small terrorist group, or for an individual with strange motivations.

Medical technology will change all our lives

Almost all the greatest medical advances will be from medical technology, pharma or biotech, or a combination of these. Medical technology alone will transform health care over the next 20 years. Here are just a few examples:

- **Endoscopy** – rapid growth of tiny telescopes, keyhole surgery, shorter hospital stays. $75bn a year market by 2022.

- **3D imaging** – ability to watch living tissue in astonishing resolutions, 'travel' inside blood vessels, see inside the heart, detect cancer cells during operations.

- **Ultra-resolution microscopy** – able to observe things going on inside an individual cell in real time, watch a photon of light excite a retinal cell, a drug molecule attach to a receptor.

- **Digitised patient records** – instant availability in the Cloud of all tests, scan images and other medical records.

- **AI-aided diagnosis** – let robots treat the sick, using Big Data to predict what will happen. Computer-assisted diagnosis will be universal in some countries for some types of conditions by 2025, with doctors forced to use it not by law but by insurance companies.

- **Telemonitoring, telemedicine and home diagnostics** – huge growth in virtual medicine and home monitoring devices, where doctors and specialist nurses make decisions in a faraway location. However, we will *not* see many surgeons controlling robots thousands of miles away, because speed of light is too slow, with delays from surgeon, to robot, to image, to surgeon, as well as risks when things go badly wrong.

◆ **Deep brain stimulation** – electrical stimulation using implanted electrodes or external devices to reduce depression, drug dependency, improve memory or symptoms of Parkinson's disease.

◆ **Growth of do-it-yourself health care** – web-based diagnostics and mobile apps with a wide range of biosensors, so that many patients know more than their doctors about their own condition. Breath sensors, attached to a smartphone, to diagnose cancer, sophisticated heart monitoring and prediction of heart attacks using a wrist-worn device, and so on.

◆ **Social media and sharing health experience** – scoring carers, rating doctors and hospitals.

◆ **Replacement of reading glasses** by a tiny implant into the cornea, made of hydrogel, to change the curvature of the eye.

◆ **Low cost gene readers** – see p. 91.

Future of dentistry

Dentistry will also change rapidly over the next three decades, mainly as a result of medical technology. More people will be able to afford cosmetic dentistry, and the governments of emerging nations will provide more access to free dental care.

Treatment will be transformed by huge advances in diagnostics, instant 3D imaging, local 3D manufacturing and printing, plus advances in new tooth-filling materials and 'invisible' braces to correct poorly aligned teeth, with near perfect results. Many dental clinics will offer completely integrated cosmetics. The key question will be whether you want to *restore* how you looked before, or whether you want to *change* how you used to look – in which case Botox, dermal fillers, bone reshaping and other things will combine routinely with major dental work.

Next-generation tooth cleaning will improve daily repairs of microscopic defects. However, the greatest transformation globally will be due to the wider consumption of fluoride in emerging nations.

Future of pharma

Traditional pharma will face a major crisis – how to ensure good returns on risky investments, in a highly regulated industry, and one which many people in future will criticise for being greedy or even corrupt. If you want to know the future of medicines, take a look at the list of drugs in clinical trials on pharma websites. The global pipeline is short, unexciting, and stuffed full of 'more of the same'. I qualified as a physician over 35 years ago, and, sadly, many drugs used today are ones that we used back then.

Big Pharma finds real innovation difficult, slow and expensive. The largest five companies have a combined research and development budget of $32bn, while the 50 largest have a combined budget of around $100bn, which is larger than the GDP of the world's poorest 35 nations. Despite all this, Big Pharma will generate less than 40% of the world's new drugs over the next 25 years.

Most breakthroughs will take place in over 20,000 smaller biotech companies, most of which do not yet exist, often partnered with universities then bought by larger pharma. Biotech products already account for 21% of the $750bn a year of pharma sales, and are likely to grow by around 7% a year over the next decade, compared to only 4% for small-molecule drugs.

$1.3 billion for a new drug to market

Over the next two decades, the cost of bringing a new drug to market will rise by over 4% a year. It already costs $1.3bn to bring a drug to market in a 15-year process from discovery to early development. Around 80 to 90% of experimental drugs do not make it, and all pharma will remain high-risk. In five years, more than $240bn has been spent on drugs that failed in final clinical trials.

Since patent life is likely in most cases to remain 25 years, of which 15 are lost in development, pharma companies will have to make a good return in less than a decade of sales.

But pharma companies will see lower sales than in the past for many new drugs, as gene profiling is used more widely to select the right treatment for each person (pharmacogenomics).

The price of the world's latest drugs will fall dramatically over the next 15 years, as almost all patents expire on drugs sold today. We are talking about billions of dollars of lost revenue over a decade (and corresponding savings to governments).

A drug therapy that costs $100 today will typically cost less than $5 as a 'generic' by 2030. Of course, doctors will be offered a new range of expensive therapies by then. But most will be incremental changes made to extend patent life.

To make matters worse for pharma, if a drug shows huge benefits for a disease like malaria in the poorest nations, the company will be under huge pressure to give it away 'at cost' for ethical reasons. Some large pharma companies could also lose up to 35% of revenues almost overnight if forced to withdraw one or more well-accepted 'blockbuster' drugs because of unexpected risks.

Orphan diseases will get special treatment

Yet in spite of the above, our world needs a profitable pharma industry, able to take risks to develop new therapies. So we will see more concessions by regulators, to balance patient safety with the need to accelerate development, particularly for people who are expected to die soon.

Governments will expand lists of 'orphan diseases', where numbers of sufferers are too few to generate much interest. These will attract subsidies, tax incentives, fast-track approval, better pricing and longer patents.

Expect new models for drug development where knowledge and patents are owned by the public, with work funded by the taxpayer, while production and distribution are carried out by pharma – as in AIDS research. Expect big changes also in medical publishing. More public bodies that fund research will insist that published results are freely available to all. It is shocking in our digital age that most published research is kept secret from most of the scientists in emerging markets who need it – and who cannot afford journal subscriptions. Expect new patterns of collaboration: co-opetition, crowd-sourcing, open innovation, crowd-funding. Super-wealthy patrons will also fund many biotech innovations, as social enterprises.

Many new pharma blockbusters

We will see gigantic sales and profits from key breakthroughs. Just imagine sales from a new drug proven to delay onset of Alzheimer's by three years. Even if governments and insurers refused to fund, many people would take out loans on their homes to get it. Other examples will include breakthroughs in rheumatoid arthritis, asthma and diabetes, and drugs that make people 'feel' much younger.

Many of the most innovative products will be molecules which are too large to absorb through the gut wall when swallowed. Examples will include antibodies, targeting cancers and other tissues, as well as chemical messengers or cytokines.

We will see new ways to get large molecules into the blood, for example injecting under the skin using an air blast instead of needles; liposomes (microscopic protein bags containing medication that passes through the gut wall); and viruses that deliver genes to target cells. Expect great advances in training your own immune system to destroy unhealthy cells or foreign organisms – immunotherapy.

Future of biotech – altering the basis of life itself

We have entered the Age of the Gene, as I predicted in *The Genetic Revolution* (1993). Humankind now has the power to redesign the very basis of life itself, and to create a new super-race of people with enhanced DNA. It is impossible to overstate the long-term significance of this, which is the basis of transhumanism.

We share most of our genes with insects, earthworms, rats, rabbits and horses, and 50% with bananas. We can cut and paste genetic code very easily, without needing to know in advance what the results might be, using techniques like CRISPR in labs as small as a single Portakabin. Human genes have been added to mice, cows, sheep, rabbits, rats and fish, to name just a few.

Huge numbers of designer animals are born every year, each a unique mix of two, three or more different species – transgenic sheep, for example, which are programmed to produce human hormones or other complex molecules in their milk. Scientists have created a goat with genes from a spider, so that web proteins are excreted into milk. These proteins can be extracted to create a kind of textile fibre that is highly elastic and almost as strong as Kevlar.

Expect humanised cows to produce low-fat milk. Another goal will be cows that produce human breast milk. Biotech farming raises new animal welfare issues – for example, in the case of cows that are programmed, or driven by hormone injections, to produce many times their natural daily yield of milk.

And, of course, food scientists can and will also re-engineer fruit, vegetables, cereal crops and rice on a huge scale. There is nothing new about this: genetically modified crops have been around for over 25 years. But the precision with which scientists can now redesign is breathtaking. Just one example is a tomato that grows to three times normal size, containing five times normal levels of the red pigment lycopene.

Ability to read your genetic code (genome)

It took $3bn and 15 years of work to decode a single genome, a cost which has already fallen to around $1,000. By 2025, it is likely that doctors will be able to read an individual's genetic code in less than two hours for less than $500, enabling us to predict our medical future with far greater accuracy – comparing patterns of genomes, medical records and lifestyle data.

Expect gene readers on devices as small as today's USB sticks by 2040, taking 30 minutes to decode each strip of genetic code. Gene screening will be free for many people within 20 years, paid for by pharmacies for loyal customers, or by companies wanting to protect employee health, or by insurance companies and governments

More than 100,000 genomes have already been sequenced by the UK health service. We can already predict gene-related future illness in 10% of babies tested at birth, such as heart disease or hearing loss.

Big Data has already identified genes associated with speech, memory, murder, addiction, excessive risk-taking, shyness, obesity, faithfulness, psychosis and happiness, among other things. And once a gene is located and a test devised, it can be used on IVF embryos before implantation, raising a host of ethical issues. It is one thing to decide not to implant embryos that carry genes that guarantee a very serious, lifelong illness, but quite another to select embryos for some preferred feature.

Researchers have already found that a high proportion of murderers on death row in the US share a common gene or genes, raising profound questions about responsibility or therapy. Having the 'wrong genes' has been cited in mitigation against sentence of execution in America over 50 times since 1994. Men with XYY chromosomes are more likely to commit murder, while the gene affecting production of monoamine-oxidase-A in the brain is called the Warrior Gene, because it is linked to very aggressive behaviour.

Researchers have also discovered that many 'epigenetic' changes take place to our genes during our lives, affected by the kind of lives we lead, activating some and suppressing others, and that these changes can be passed on to our children. So exposure to environmental risks, or major stress, or to other things, may have impact on more than one generation. These findings will increase parental worries.

Improving your own genes – and Hyperlympics sporting events

Once you find a rogue gene in your own genome, which is almost certain to make you very sick, why not correct the defect? This is the basis of gene therapy and, as we have seen, a relatively simple method is to use human viruses. Another method is to use various gene editing techniques. Very precise changes can be made, letter by letter, in genetic code, taking the very best genetic variants from many different people.

And, of course, such changes may well be passed on through sperm and eggs to alter the genetic code of many generations to come. But what if we make a mistake? What if we create dangerous new variants of bacteria or viruses, or carry out edits on humans that have unexpected health consequences for future generations?

Some athletes are already experimenting with injected gene fragments, which have short-term effects and are very hard to detect. Bio-doping will be a major problem in all future Olympic events, and is already raising questions about the validity of new sporting records. If an athlete is winning every event because of specially engineered and 'alien' gene sequences, what then? We already have the Paralympics – so maybe a new competition will be named the Hyperlympics.

Altering the human race

The desire to alter the human race is an old one. Around 60,000 forced sterilisations of women with 'unwanted mental and physical characteristics' were carried out in Sweden from 1935 to 1976, with similar practices in Denmark, Norway, Finland and Switzerland. And 20% of the world's population – in China – is already banned by law from having children if the state decides that their genes are not worth reproducing .

Who owns a species?

Is it right for a company to own an entire new species? Is it right to create a species that is guaranteed to suffer? Both questions were raised by the creation of the Oncomouse, which was designed to develop fatal cancer 90 days after birth, and was created in America to test new cancer treatments, is commercially owned, and is protected by patent.

Patents on human genes

Is it right for companies to own human genes? A man in the US developed cancer and gave cells for research. The genes were used to develop a diagnostic test, which was patented. He was furious. 'I own my own genes,' he said. He challenged the company in the Supreme Court, but lost. As a result, humans do not have the right to own their own genes in America.

New ways to make babies

Every year puberty comes earlier in boys and girls. By the age of seven, 27% of African American girls and 7% of white girls in America have obvious pre-puberty body changes, for example breast enlargement. Female cells produce oestrogen so the larger a girl is, the more oestrogen in her blood. And there are also naturally occurring oestrogens in food, plus contamination of water supplies with oestrogen from contraceptives.

Doctors are having to rewrite medical textbooks. What is normal, and who needs treatment? Doctors will take steps to delay puberty in significant numbers of very young children in developed nations by 2030, at the request of worried parents.

Children molesting each other and having babies

Earlier puberty and exposure of millions of young children to web pornography is a particularly hazardous combination. Teachers, parents, doctors and social workers are already dealing with an explosive rise in the numbers of children sexually abusing other children, including rape. Expect to see much younger children as 'parents', with nine-year-old boys impregnating nine-year-old girls. Expect to see much heart searching, as parents struggle to work out what to do.

A sterile generation?

Environmental oestrogens, such as phthalates from plastics, may also be the reason why sperm counts have halved per millimetre in many nations since 1973. Total sperm counts are down by 60% in many nations if you take into account loss of volume of semen.

In Denmark, 20% of men cannot father children. On current trends, 50 million men will be infertile by 2050. If this continues at the same rate, sperm counts will be seriously low in most men globally in 80 years.

Testosterone levels are also falling dramatically. As a result, cases of undescended testicles and testicular cancer are increasing. It seems highly probable that chemical pollution is responsible, and it is possible that this effect is also being passed on from father to son, by epigenetic changes in sperm.

What it means is that men are becoming *less male* in how their bodies function, and maybe also in how they feel or behave.

We can hardly imagine anything more profound for survival of our species, and for gender distinctiveness. Consider the outcry if we knew that most younger women were ovulating only half as often as 50 years ago, that breast sizes were falling, and that all girls and women were being affected by significant levels of environmental testosterone.

If phthalates are indeed toxic to men, then we have a huge problem because they are found so widely – in gelling agents, lubricants, detergents, medicines, toothpaste, packaging, paint, payment receipts, nail polish, liquid soap and hair spray, as well as in the tubing that processes liquid food and in all plastic containers. Expect further research, and major steps to reduce phthalate exposure within 30 years, if evidence becomes compelling. The challenge is that our world is so totally dependent on plastic, one of the most useful innovations of the last hundred years.

The problems of infertility are also growing rapidly in women. As we have seen, most women in developed nations are waiting longer to have children, and the mean age of mothers at first birth is now 30 in many EU nations. That means many women have been ovulating for over 20 years before they first try to become pregnant. Yet by then, fertility is already in decline, and complications more common.

New combinations of parents

We will also see more men desiring to be women, and women desiring to be men, many of whom may wish to parent their own biological children, even after surgery to permanently reshape their bodies. The number of people requesting gender changes is growing 20% every year in the US.

Within a few years, two women will be able to conceive their own biological child without sperm needed at all, and two people born male will be able to do the same, implanting their embryo into a surrogate mother's womb, or perhaps into a womb transplanted into one of the two of them. And human cloning will one day create the possibility of people giving birth without any genetic contribution from any other human being (see below).

Retired mothers giving birth for the first time

Expect a growing but controversial fashion for women in their late fifties or early sixties to have babies, using donated eggs or their own, held for years in freezers before use. This may even extend to women in their seventies by 2050, given longer life expectancy. The next two decades will see extraordinary advances in child-making technologies, each of which will push the boundaries of social acceptability. Exotic treatments will be very costly. Expect to see a reaction against 'playing God', and a growing desire for 'natural-ness' in conception as well as in home births.

Epidemics of infertility

Expect epidemics of infertility caused by a combination of older women trying to conceive and rapid spread of infections such as chlamydia. Over 48 million couples are unable to conceive from many different causes, despite all efforts, while 44 million abortions take place every year. In many nations, abortion rates will continue to fall over the next two decades, as contraceptive use improves, and as attitudes harden against abortion as an alternative to protection.

Numbers of babies or young children available for adoption in developed nations will also continue to fall. Despite there being 18 million young children in the world with no parents, many of whom struggle on the streets to survive, international adoptions will also decline, banned already in many of the poorest nations.

We will continue to see unease, particularly in many emerging nations, over abortion. Imagine a busy hospital in Delhi or Moscow with two women sitting next to each other, both with problems in early pregnancy. One wants to see the gynaecologist about 'termi-nating the pregnancy' while the other wants to see the paediatri-cian for advice on 'saving my baby'. If a gynaecologist talks about 'terminating a baby', or an obstetrician about 'saving a pregnancy', both will likely be condemned as uncaring – or even unethical in their attitudes.

Era of the precious child

We live in an era where anything that might threaten the health or emotional happiness of a baby or younger child, even for a few moments, is severely frowned upon in many nations. We see this in concerns about safety of children in cars, exposure of children to undesirable influences at school or online, and in even greater outrage over paedophilia than in the past. This era worships the image of a little child, a symbol of innocence and perfection in an increasingly tarnished, polluted and self-centred world.

Child 'cocooning'

'For the sake of the children' will be used as a motto to justify more or less anything, from marital fidelity to getting married in the first place or getting divorced, to cleaning up the environment, or banning cigarette advertising. The same sentiment will drive new waves of online censorship and attempts at control in many nations, aimed at stamping out child or young teen access to pornography. And we are seeing similar anxieties over web/videos/games exposure in general.

Parents will become even more obsessed with the well-being of their child, creating cocoons in which (they hope) each is totally protected from risk. So, for example, fewer children will ride bikes on their own in the park or walk on their own to school. As a reaction, we will also see a new generation of parents who believe children need to be allowed to grow up in the 'real world', less tied to adults for every waking moment.

Paradoxically, desires to protect precious children are almost certainly increasing their risks of a wide range of illnesses including asthma, chronic bowel disease and other immune problems, linked to lack of exposure to normal dirt containing bacteria, viruses and fungi at an early age. Expect all kinds of new behaviour patterns in parents, as a result.

Human cloning will continue to fascinate

Animal cloning has been possible for a long time, and was first conducted in frogs in the 1950s. Mammal cloning is relatively recent. The technique is now well developed using fresh or frozen cells.

1. Remove the nucleus from an egg.
2. Inject the nucleus from any adult cell into the egg.
3. Give a small spark of electricity to simulate fertilisation.
4. Incubate the cell in a warm watery bath full of nutrients.

All the genes in the nucleus are activated by the cytoplasm of the egg, and the cell begins to divide to form a new embryo. If such early embryos are implanted in a womb, they grow into an identical twin of the adult donor. If they are harvested instead, they can be used as sources of stem cells to treat the person who donated the adult cell.

Many claims for human clones but when will we see them?

Many laboratories have carried out early-stage human cloning experiments, and some claim that their embryos failed to implant or miscarried. No cloned babies have yet been shown to the world as babies, but it can only be a matter of time. Cloning of favourite pets is already available in several nations.

Even if such human cloning is successful, 'parents' and doctors are likely to feel rather sensitive about the new person they have brought into the world, and may want to protect such an unusual child from being stigmatised in any way. So there may well be a significant time lag between a clone being born, and the world learning the truth about what has taken place.

Big market for human clones

The idea of cloning will be very popular among some wealthy people: the ultimate in pedigree children. It also means that parents can 'recreate' a dead child, or that a clone can be created to assist in tissue donation for the existing child or adult. However, there will be major safety and psychological risks. Even if the cloned child is healthy, what will the emotional impact be of growing up knowing that you are your mother's or father's twin? Malformations and miscarriages are common in cloned animals. For these reasons, cloning is unlikely to be used widely as a technique to create designer babies for at least the next 35 years.

Designer babies – made to order

Scientists can already design young children to order, using some of the same technology used routinely in IVF to select embryos, and this could be coupled with gene editing and other techniques. Expect furious debate among scientists and philosophers about the ethics of all this, and for some nations to outlaw such procedures. As always, the usual justification will be to prevent illnesses, but others will wish to use the same methods for human enhancement as an expression of parental choice.

Cloning raises interesting long-term possibilities: women would no longer need men to fertilise their eggs, and could produce an entirely female society, for example.

Cloning the dead – or the extinct

Animals have been cloned using frozen cells, so any human can in theory be recovered from the grave as a baby, so long as cells are suitably frozen before death, or up to a week after.

As I predicted some years ago, we are now quite close to recovering extinct animals – by using genes in frozen tissue, for example from mammoths buried in tundra – or to partially recovering them by adding a few clusters of recovered genes to an existing animal. In 2003, Spanish and French scientists brought the bucardo wild goat back from extinction, cloning with frozen cells from the last survivor of the species, which had died. The clone was born successfully but rapidly died of a malformation.

Ultimate miniature factories

A conventional laboratory to make insulin would occupy a vast area and cost several billion, yet that entire factory unit can be compressed into the cytoplasm of a living cell. Once a single bacterium receives the human gene for insulin, it carries on dividing forever, eating food and making insulin in a process similar to brewing beer.

Every complex chemical you can think of will be made by gene technology in brewing vats containing bacteria or animal cells. Medicines, vaccines, precursors of new plastics, new fuels – whatever. More complex substances such as human hormones or cancer drugs will be made in genetically engineered insects or in the milk of mammals such as cows and sheep, or in chicken eggs.

Growing whole organs

Whole organs may be grown one day inside young animals of suitable size. Organs are already being built layer by layer, using Bubble Jet printer cartridges to print a matrix full of nutrient jelly and different types of human cells.

How close is a monkey to a human?

Hybrids are very easy to create. Take geep, for example, a combination of goat and sheep made by rolling together two balls of cells from two different embryos shortly after fertilisation. It will not be long before humonkeys are with us. Perhaps such embryos already exist. The technology is proven.

But how many human genes does an animal have to have to gain human rights? We differ genetically from monkeys by less than 2%. So if you are adding 1% of human gene material to a fertilised monkey egg you had better brace yourself for the results – a mere 0.3% of human gene material could be more than enough to give the monkey speech.

Can monkeys go to heaven?

Theologians, philosophers and lawyers need to consider what their reaction will be when such a hybrid is displayed to the world. Does it have human rights? Can it be eaten? Is it morally responsible before a court of law? Can it be tried for murder? Is it allowed to marry and procreate with 'normal humans' or to mate with other animals? Is it in need of salvation? Does it have a soul?

Many biotech inventions are already blurring the distinction between animals and humans. It could all produce a crisis of faith for those who accept traditional teaching that humans have been created 'in God's image'. So what is that image? Are monkeys 98% of the image of God? Is all life a manifestation of the image of God to some degree or another?

New ways to stay young (forever?)

Future generations will treat ageing as a disease. The life of every reader of this book has increased by an average of 15 minutes in the last hour – the pattern in many nations of the world over the last two decades, in people with reasonable education and wealth.

Take London, for example, where average life expectancy increased by a year between 2004 and 2010, both for those at birth, and for those aged 65. We have seen similar things in Japan and Germany. In many emerging nations, life expectancy is improving even faster. But what about the next 50 to 100 years?

Expect Ageing Immortalists to grow in number: wealthy people obsessed with living forever. These are people who dream of being able to improve their own life expectancy by more than a year, with every year that passes.

Here is the truth about life expectancy, and why there has been collusion by governments and corporations to underplay the situation. Every time you add a year to the expected life of an individual, you add over 3% to their pension deficit. So adding five years to projections can wipe out the entire reserves of many large corporations, or make government liabilities soar.

Slowing down or reversing the ageing process

Scientists have already produced mice that live to the human equivalent of 160 years and earthworms that live to the equivalent of 500 years. The gene activated in long-living worms is the same one often found in people who live until at least 100. Scientists at Harvard Medical School reversed the ageing process in mice by increasing levels of NAD protein. This protein restores communication between DNA in the nucleus of a cell and the DNA in the mitochondria.

As a result, the body tissue of a six-year-old mouse was converted back to that of a two-year-old. It would be the equivalent of some of the tissues in a 60-year-old man or woman becoming as young as those in a 20-year-old.

Some animals do not age at all and others regenerate perfectly

We have identified types of rockfish and some whales that show no signs of normal ageing. Rougheye rockfish live to 200, while other rockfish live only to the age of 20, even though they are identical in every other way. Naked mole rats can live in captivity for over 28 years, nine times longer than similar-sized mice. They show little sign of ageing and never develop cancer. The same is true for whales, where individual life expectancy can vary from 20 to over 200 years in the case of bowheads, depending on their genes. Aldabra giant tortoises live for up to 255 years, and ocean quahog clams can live for over 400 years.

We are also learning from animals that regenerate, such as lobsters, naked mole rats and planarian worms, and learning from animals that regrow entire limbs, such as lizards.

Nine mechanisms of ageing in almost every organism

Almost every group of cells, in every organism, in every corner of our planet, is ageing in similar ways. Insects, worms, frogs, fish, mice, tigers, elephants, monkeys and humans – it makes very little difference. You will find a mix of:

◆ Telomere shortening – preventing cell division
◆ DNA damage – including cancer generation
◆ Gene expression errors – epigenetics
◆ Proteins becoming less functional or accumulating
◆ Cells that don't die when they should – senescent cells
◆ Energy production falls in mitochondria
◆ Inefficient cell communication – insensitive to cytokines/ hormones

◆ Unbalanced metabolism / sensing nutrients

◆ Stem cell exhaustion – less regeneration / renewal.

Each of these nine mechanisms will become a target, in the search for 'negligible senescence'. Touch one mechanism, such as mitochondrial mutations, and you may improve the function of 37 trillion cells in a single human being.

Alteon 711 is an interesting compound that produces a permanent reduction in blood pressure levels in old mice and rats, as well as restoring elasticity of the skin. Sadly, clinical trials found only a small effect on arteries and no effect on human skin, but we can expect many more such trials, targeting a fundamental part of the ageing process. Consider the demand if Alteon 711 *had* worked in humans: a drug that permanently cures high blood pressure *and* produces a face or body lift.

Gene mapping is showing us precisely which genes are the ones to slow down ageing in the long-lived animals discussed above. Genes tell cells to build proteins of a particular shape. So once we have found the right genes, pharma companies will make proteins as therapy, while biotech companies will try to activate the same genes instead.

Blood or plasma from younger people

We are going to see many more centres offering blood or plasma as an anti-ageing therapy, following research showing reverse in mental decline in mice transfused with blood proteins from younger mice. The next stage will be to identify the correct proteins and to make them into a specific treatment. The rejuvenation of old mice, conjoined to young mice in order to share their blood supply, has been well known since the 1950s (parabiosis).

Using stem cells to grow new organs

Another way to keep people young is to repair old organs by injecting them with fresh stem cells. Bone marrow is the favourite source of stem cells, as techniques for bone marrow extraction are so well developed for the treatment of leukaemia.

Such treatments have already begun and will be routine for many conditions by 2025 in developed nations. As I predicted in *The Genetic Revolution* (1995), despite many claims, there is no justification any longer for taking stem cells from embryos or foetuses. We can get adult cells to revert to more primitive types, to repair just about any tissue we want. The source of such cells can be many tissues, including skin (to grow new retina) or blood (to repair brain or heart). When we use a person's own cells, we don't see rejection by their immune system, unless they already have an autoimmune disease.

Stem cells may work by forming new functioning tissue in organs like the heart, but it is more likely that they release cytokines, which stimulate repair by other cells. So we will also see research into the production of cytokines to be injected into damaged organs. We can also expect to see new types of drugs that encourage large-scale migration of stem cells, from locations such as bone marrow, to repair damaged tissues.

Expect other therapies that stimulate different types of brain cells to convert into new, fully functioning neurons to reverse local damage by stroke, Alzheimer's and a host of other conditions.

Repair of brain or spinal cord

Cells from the olfactory bulb, high up inside the nose, will be used to repair the brain and spinal cord. The bulb is the organ that we use to smell, and is packed with brain stem cells. We have already seen successful repair of broken spinal cords in animals, and partial spine repairs in humans, with people regaining some sensation and movement.

All nerves naturally regrow at around 2mm a day, but in the brain or spinal cord this growth is stopped by scarring and debris. It is very likely that at some point in the next three decades people with new spinal cord injuries may recover complete sensation and movement – as long as they are treated early enough, and the spinal cord either side of the wound is undamaged. We are already seeing some early success.

Head transplants – to get a new body

Such a breakthrough in spinal cord repair will open up the longer-term possibility of head transplants, to enable someone to survive who would otherwise die very soon, using the body of someone who has died from severe brain injuries. Short-term head transplants have already been successfully carried out in rats, dogs and monkeys – and also carried out in China, as a technical test, using a human corpse.

The procedure was well developed over two decades ago. Under anaesthetic, the 'old' head is cut off, and the new one stitched on, with careful connections of major arteries and veins as well as the windpipe and gullet. During the process, the transplanted head needs to be cooled to protect the brain from damage during the short interruption in blood supply. In these animal studies, there was no attempt to reconnect the spinal cord or other nerves, nor was there any attempt to prevent the transplanted head from being rejected by the immune system, so the transplanted heads rapidly deteriorated after a few days. However, the experiments continued for long enough for animals to wake up, and in one case a laboratory worker was bitten by a monkey after the operation was completed, which the researchers took as added proof that the mental processes of these reconstructed animals were intact.

Head transplants in animals or humans may seem grotesque, weird and unethical, but if someone is already completely paralysed from the neck down, and dying from something like combined total liver and heart failure, there is no practical reason why their head could not be transplanted today onto the healthy body of someone who is totally brain dead. It is just an extension of organ transplant technology.

And of course, once spinal repair techniques are perfected (and they will be), head transplants could allow an older person to jettison a worn-out body and enjoy becoming a young adult again (from the neck down).

The astonishing truth about future life expectancy

Leaving aside such an exotic and controversial possibility, and only taking into account medical advances in the general ageing process that we considered earlier, we can see how human ageing could look rather different in the longer term.

More than 320,000 people around the world are 100 years old or more. By 2050, that figure could be more than a million in Japan alone, with a further 4 million in America and 280,000 in the UK. But these modest figures assume very little innovation in health care.

Let me take you through a discussion I have had with hundreds of actuaries, whose job it is to predict life expectancy – for banks, insurers, pension funds and government.

My grandmother is a guide to your future

Let us start with my own grandmother. She was born in 1905, retired officially in 1970 at 65, but continued to enjoy working part-time as a physician until she was 82, playing bridge most afternoons and also playing golf twice a week. She died a decade later.

Even if we were to say that each generation can only expect an additional *five years* of life, that would mean that the same grandmother today would retire at 75, then work part-time as a physician until her 92nd birthday, with over a decade of full retirement ahead, before she died at the grand age of 102. Indeed, one of my cousins died a few years ago at the age of 103, with all her mental faculties intact.

The real future of a 40-year-old today

Now let us look at a more recent generation. Let us suppose that a woman called Jane is 40 years old and is now reading this book. If she was from Western Europe, Japan or North America, government figures would give her an average life expectancy forecast of 82, or 42 more years. However, the fact that she is reading this book gives her an extra 5, because it means that she is in an upper socio-economic group: well-educated, middle class. So on average she would still be alive at the age of 87.

But as we have seen, to keep pace with endless small corrections made over the last 20 years, we need to add 2.5 years in every decade. So on that basis alone, without even considering any major advances, it is perfectly logical to add a further decade over the next 45 years. That would give an average life of 97 years for our example.

However, if you look at the rapidly growing pace of medical research, it is reasonable to assume that knowledge and capability in health care will continue to double every 24 months – just genome research alone could do this.

That means we will know ten times as much as today in a decade, 100 times as much by the end of the following decade, 1,000 times as much by the end of the third decade, and so on. Therefore, we are bound to see several major advances in health care over the next 30 years and these must surely add at least five more years to Jane's life during that period, which takes her to an average life expectancy of 103.

The most spectacular medical advances that Jane will witness between now and the age of 103 will of course be in her final two decades, because of this relentless acceleration of health-related science. During that 20-year period there will almost certainly be more medical advances than in the whole of human history before that point, many times over.

It is hard to fully comprehend the scale of health advances over the next 63 years. To help us, look back 63 years for a moment, and consider what life was like in the mid 1950s.

So it is perfectly reasonable to add a further 5 years to Jane's average life expectancy to allow for what new medical advances are likely to offer her by the mid 2080s. That would mean a 'true' life expectancy for Jane of at least 107 years. And because this is only an average, it means some of her generation will still be alive at the age of 120, while a few may see the dawn of the twenty-second century.

Social meltdown or a welcome transition?

We can see now why most actuarial experts believe that commonly quoted figures for life expectancy are completely misleading, and a dangerous basis on which to project the future of societies. This will be one of the world's greatest social adjustments, and will affect every aspect of every nation, the solvency of every pension fund, and the balance sheet of every large corporation.

It will also affect your own average life expectancy, of course, if you are in reasonable health today. Most people are out of step with their own biological clocks. And most have underestimated the costs of funding their retirement.

Some forecasters have made dire warnings about social meltdown, with countries crippled by tens of millions of ancient people, who have no money left, but who need constant care. While there is an element of truth in this, it is also true that, as in the example above, most older people will enjoy very extended working lives, biologically much younger than those at the same age a decade or two ago, and will also enjoy extended retirement.

But all that said, in some nations there has been a recent small *fall* in life expectancy: so what is going on? The trouble is that many different factors are in play at the same time, in different parts of the population. Take, for example, the effects of anti-smoking campaigns on the one hand and the rise in obesity on the other. Both are due to lifestyle choices, and the balance can shift a major trend. But the underlying science points to long-term, step-by-step improvements in treatments, cure rates and new ways to help people survive longer.

Health messages will start to backfire

When it comes to health messages, we will see a kind of double-think: on the one hand, obsession with ageing and with staying healthy forever, and on the other, increasing apathy about personal health.

So, for example, we will find 80-year-olds who decide to enjoy all kinds of risky activities for the first time in their lives – who have no wish whatsoever to live to a very old age in a very frail state, in dire circumstances, and are more than happy to 'go out with a bang'. Expect more headlines like that of the woman who celebrated her 100th birthday in the UK by going skydiving. More eating, drinking and smoking – 'Who cares. Life is for living. When life is short, eat dessert now.'

First Life and Second Life

By 2040, childhood, youth and young adulthood will be defined as up to 30 years old, because of delays in settling down to have children, and longer education or training.

First Life will be defined as 30 to 65 years – what people used to consider their normal working lives. Second Life will be defined as 65 to 100 years – an identical length of adulthood. A period of many surprises, new skills, new jobs, new purposes and patterns of life. Old age will be those over 100.

Growing costs of health care – and rationing

So how will government health budgets cope? Every nation that provides free medical care will be faced by almost unlimited demand, which they will deal with, as they have done in the past, by rationing – mainly by making sick people wait, sometimes a very long time.

Doctors have been rationing for over 100 years. Expect debate about these choices to become more strident, linked to social media. Health will be in competition with education, infrastructure, defence and other government departments.

Every health specialty will also be in competition: cancer with asthma, hip replacements with stroke rehabilitation. Within specialties there will be competition, with questions, for example, such as: more money for breast cancer or prostate cancer?

Future of health care in America

Nearly every developed nation except America provides free health care to all, 'as part of living in a civilised society'. In many nations, universal access to health care has become as widely accepted as access to education, but this will be questioned. Expect gradual introduction of a wide range of small health charges, to stave off bankruptcy of health services and to choke off demand.

America spends more per head on health than any other nation by a wide margin, but 12% of non-retired adults in America still have no health insurance, and face huge worries if sick. Despite popular perceptions, most health-care spending in America is funded by taxes. US health care will need to be more cost-efficient, with stricter controls on insurance claims and authorised treatments, and a clampdown on massive fraud. At present there are many incentives for over-treatment, and over-billing is hard to prevent.

Future of the NHS in the UK

As the UK's largest employer, the NHS faces a deficit of around $4bn a year, when everything is taken into account, and that includes insolvent hospitals. Expect rapid shifts to community care, fewer hospital beds, shorter stays, more community-based clinics, and more privatisation to cut costs. Private health insurance and treatment will grow, as people become more fed up with waiting lists, and more worried about the quality of NHS care.

Expect a crisis in general practice as many family doctors retire over the next decade, with acute shortages of new doctors willing to work under less attractive contracts. The same is happening to hospital nursing, where chronic understaffing and stress will lead to more resignations. As a result, more doctors and nurses will be employed from other nations, some with poor English and cultural understanding. Expect higher salaries, better contracts.

Better outcome measures

Surgeons will be measured by the numbers they treat successfully, complication rates, length of hospital stay and the numbers they kill. Expect a rethink as these crude measures encourage bad practice – for example, surgeons may refuse to operate on those who could be a 'bad risk'.

Medical tourism, medical migration and illegal trade in human organs

One way to reduce health costs for individuals, insurers or government is to move patients abroad for treatment, and we will see a lot more of this.

'Medical tourism' is already a $40bn industry, growing 20% a year, with over 11 million people annually travelling to another country for private treatment, and possibly convalescence in a nice hotel. The market could be worth over $130bn by 2025.

The savings in all types of medical tourism can be huge: private health care in Brazil is only 25% of the cost in America; in India it's 73%; in Mexico 50%; in Thailand 65%; and in Turkey 60%. Within the EU itself there are also major cost differences – for example, dental treatment in Hungary is far cheaper than it is in Paris.

Governments are already signing contracts with private providers in other nations. Thousands of elderly people have moved to Eastern Europe and Asia for long-term care and re-habilitation. According to the German government, over 400,000 older people cannot afford a German retirement home – a cost that is growing by 5% a year, and 7,000 are in retirement homes in Hungary alone.

As part of this, transplant tourism is also growing. Demand will be even greater in future from ageing, wealthy populations. In America alone, 20 people die every day while waiting for a suitable or willing organ donor. Families and patients are often desperate and many are willing to pay large amounts to fly to another nation to get a new organ. The black market rate in America can be over $150,000 for a kidney or liver. Despite the legal ban, at least 2,000 low-income people in India donate one of their own kidneys to medical tourists each year, mostly for a few hundred dollars.

Life expectancy is similar with one or two kidneys, but many other organs cannot be removed without death of the donor imme-diately after, so organ trade can rapidly become a very macabre business.

Growing numbers of men and women are being kidnapped every month as part of the organ trafficking industry, and forced into operating theatres where surgeons are waiting to cut their organs out.

Over 7,000 kidneys are trafficked a year, just some of the 11,000 organs sold on the black market annually. There have been cases where a child has had both eyes removed (cornea transplant) before being abandoned onto the street. Unconfirmed reports suggest that over 12,000 post-execution transplants may be taking place in China a year. Organ trafficking could already be worth $1 billion a year.

We are also seeing the migration of health professionals. Vietnamese doctors and nurses, trained at huge cost by their own nation, are working in Thailand. Filipino nurses are attracted to work in the UK. This is a very worrying and unsustainable situation for 'donor' countries that can ill-afford the escalating costs of losing the majority of those they train to wealthy nations. Expect some kind of training tax in future, or binding contracts with those trained at government expense.

*

So, then, we have seen how a billion people moving to cities will transform our world, how growing contrasts in wealth are a threat to society, how demographics is the key to the future of every nation and market, how life expectancy is radically changing, and how ageing itself could be halted one day. Now we need to look at the most powerful force in the world: the power of tribes and how we all relate together.

Chapter 3

TRIBAL

TRIBALISM IS THE MOST POWERFUL FORCE in the world today, more powerful than the entire military might of America, China, Russia and the EU combined. Tribalism is the basis of family, belonging, culture, language, relationships, brands, communities and nations, but tribalism is also responsible for nationalism, sectarianism, ethnic conflict, genocide, civil wars and for all the darkest moments in human history.

Most people belong to many tribes

Neighbourhoods are tribes, members of sports clubs are tribes, football supporters are tribes. If there were no tribes, human beings would create them in a day. We need tribes to exist, to make sense of our world.

Tribes will create new languages

We see tribalism in our love of national languages. Gaelic in Scotland was more or less a dead language 30 years ago. Now it is spoken in shops, heard on radio, taught in schools, and road signs are in both Gaelic and English. With French radio there is a strict limit on the amount of English language music that can be transmitted on air. The medieval French tongue *langue d'oc* is also experiencing a revival.

Language preserves ancient literature, poetry and songs – and vice versa. Language communicates who we are; even the accent in which we speak our mother tongue reveals our tribe.

That is why it was so provocative when the new president of Ukraine announced in early 2014 that it would be illegal in future for children to be educated in Russian in Russian-speaking parts of the country.

Why people are hungry to join new tribes

As many as 2 billion people around the world have lost their birth tribes, or tribal ties have weakened. The most common reason is that they have moved to towns, cities, or indeed to other nations. Another common reason is that their parents have split up, which can bring pain in their family tribe.

Tribalism is a basic human instinct that every culture celebrates, whether in birthdays, or marriages or festivals. We all need to belong. And into that gap have come new tribe-makers: brand directors, marketing managers, football coaches, social media gurus, club owners, church leaders, mosque preachers, music celebrities, mother and toddler groups, head teachers of schools, university professors or even friendly neighbours. Each creates new groups of followers or supporters.

Tribalism has driven 68 million from their homes

There are 68 million refugees in the world today, most of whom are victims of tribalism. Every day, over 44,500 more people are forced to leave their homes and 40 million are sheltering with friends, family or in camps within their own nations. A million more seek asylum each year, and a further 10 million are stateless – with no passport and no means of getting one. The poorest parts of the world house 86% of refugees: 6 million are internally displaced inside Syria; 4.5 million more in Colombia; 1.4 million in Sudan; and 1.3 million in Iraq.

I have met many refugees and their children in over-crowded, muddy camps, living in temporary huts of earth and corrugated iron. It is a huge decision to leave everything and flee. For every refugee, there are many others who also live in great fear, but choose to remain. Over 350 million people today are either refugees or thinking about becoming so, have been refugees in the last decade, or have relatives who are refugees at the moment – 4.8% of all humanity.

Tribal impact on the future of the EU

Tribalism was the primary driver for the formation of the European Union, and tribalism will continue to dominate and threaten the future of the European Union, as a Tribe of Tribes.

The EU was founded after two world wars, conflicts that devastated both Germany and France. The primary aim was to weld major European powers together in an economic and political framework in order to prevent wars and build prosperity, and in this the EU has been very successful. Those who are most passionate about the European project often have family stories of wartime tragedy and chaos, which drives their fervour to weld EU nations even more tightly together, even if it means sacrificing national freedoms to do so.

However, while peace has endured, the European Union has no common language or shared culture, and national interests are still fiercely defended. The EU has muddled along, avoiding many tough decisions, but it will struggle to respond rapidly in a crisis, so will continue to be vulnerable to internal or global shocks.

Post-Brexit, the European Union will remain a cluster of inter-tribal compromises, dominated by 'pro-business' Germany and 'socialist' France, without the free-market influence of the UK. Brussels will struggle to balance budgets without the UK's significant contribution, which will mean smaller grants to poorer members, and more money from France and Germany, adding to tensions.

The EU will be held back for the next 5 to 10 years by economic malaise in several of its poorest members. The EU is very good at passing new laws for trivial matters, and very bad at tackling fundamental issues. But hundreds of new laws make life more difficult and expensive for factories and retailers, and enforcement varies from country to country.

More strains in Europe from monetary union

I predicted before the 2008 crisis that tribal and economic strains in Europe were likely to become immense, so the vote for Brexit was hardly a surprise. It is difficult to see how the eurozone will survive in its current form without further major pain and unrest during the next major economic crisis. Countries with very different economic problems and business cycles remain locked together by common exchange and interest rates. Expect further steps to more closely integrate Euro economies, with more loss of national powers. The euro is still a young currency historically, born in 1999, and vital economic control mechanisms are still missing.

Greece has been overwhelmed by government debts, greater than 180% of the size of its economy, while its economy shrank 25% during 2008–2014, with 20% out of work, 40% cuts in pensions, and, of course, a fixed exchange rate as part of the eurozone. If there is no agreement to write off much of the debt, Greece is likely to default at some point, and could end up leaving the euro.

Italy is also in trouble: it is ten times the size of the Greek economy, has eight times the debt, and is reluctant to abide by EU economic rules. At the same time, Poland and Hungary are flouting EU principles of democracy and the rule of law.

The wider EU project is in deep trouble with ordinary voters, as I also predicted, with 30% of European MPs belonging to protest parties like UKIP (28% of the vote), France's National Front (25%), Denmark's People's Party (27%), and the far-left Syriza in Greece (36%). Meanwhile, 60% of people across Europe distrust EU politicians, few can name their Euro MPs or the president of the European Commission, and voter turnout is low.

This underlying malaise in the EU has been a key reason for inflexibility in Brexit negotiations, since the EU cannot afford to appear weak.

America will continue to be a dominant EU partner

American business still invests three times more in the EU than in the whole of Asia. And EU investment in America is eight times that in India and China combined – while a third of all global trade is between the EU and America. The future of the EU will be overly dependent on the American economy for the next two decades, even though strong economic growth will only come from trade with emerging markets.

Farming subsidies still account for 40% of the entire EU budget. But as we have seen, the future depends on rapid investment in innovation, next-generation manufacturing, precision engineering, aeronautics, biotech, medtech, nanotech, Big Data, the Internet of Things, mobile financial services, e-commerce, new venture capital, enterprise zones, joint ventures on emerging markets, and so on. If the EU started with a blank sheet today, it would be more *futurewise* to spend 40% of the budget on some of the above.

The European project may yet be saved by some of the 500 million people from emerging nations who would like to live and work in the EU, legally or illegally. Many are highly educated, entrepreneurial, and bring investment with them, while others do unpopular jobs for low wages.

Corruption and control in the European Union

The EU will continue to be a corrupt, monolithic, non-accountable and wasteful institution. For 19 years, auditors refused to sign off the accounts as accurate, and payments as free from material error. In 2013, for example, they reported that €6 billion had been spent 'in error' – up 23% on the year before.

So how on earth do so many 'errors' and fraudulent decisions get made? I was asked to give a lecture on 'Ethics in Leadership' to some of the most senior leaders in the European Commission. At very short notice, I managed to get hold of an e-voting system, which allowed secret responses to my embarrassing questions. Their answers were very disturbing but hardly surprising. An edited version of the lecture is on YouTube.*

Many participants admitted that they had recently been put under pressure to do something that they thought was morally wrong. In many cases, this was something so serious that in their

---

* http://www.globalchange.com/leadership-ethics-and-dealing-with-corruption-eu-commission-lecture.htm

own country it would probably have appeared on the front pages of the newspapers, should it have been revealed. What is more, most felt that they had no choice but to obey. The person asking them was usually their own boss, and they had no one to turn to.

Trapped by fear

One leader came up to me afterwards, in obvious fear, to reveal a severe moral challenge he faced, and in which he felt trapped. It was clear from my discussions that EU Commission pay, perks and other privileges are so generous, and employment prospects so poor if someone leaves, that few can contemplate an exit. But when any executive is afraid to walk out over a matter of principle, he or she is already in danger of losing their soul. I am certain, therefore, that corruption will continue to be a feature of day-to-day life in the European Commission.

Despite all this, size and inertia will almost certainly enable the eurozone to muddle along for some considerable time, perhaps even for a generation or two, even if there are changes in the list of Euro or EU members.

Tribalism will reshape the United Kingdom

I was correct in predicting that the short-term impact of a Brexit vote to leave would be very slight on the UK economy, despite wild economic forecasts of immediate collapse, chaos and crisis. As I expected, the UK economy proved very resilient and stable, with low inflation, low interest rates and very low unemployment. UK exports grew 4.4% in the 12 months to October 2018 following the vote, to a record high of $621bn, with 6% growth in service exports. Foreign investment in the year to October 2018 also hit record levels, with the UK being the top destination in Europe.

Longer-term EU–UK trade

So what of the UK's future relationship with the EU? Here is the long-term view, beyond media hype, confusion and political nonsense.

1. **The UK will continue to be part of Europe for a thousand years – whatever happens**
The UK is part of the European continent. Signed pieces of paper will make absolutely no difference to the realities of geography, demographics and infrastructure such as ports.

2. **Regardless of Brexit outcomes, trade between the UK and the EU will continue to be strong, especially in services**
Since time began, human beings have traded across borders. A 'no-deal' Brexit could produce some short-term supply chain disruptions for faster-moving goods, especially at French ports such as Calais with risk of industrial action, but disruptions will mostly be well planned for and will have little long-term significance, with even less impact on UK services to the EU (80% of UK exports to the EU), apart from some aspects of banking. Even if the UK were to leave the EU without a trade deal in place, deals will rapidly be agreed for some products and services, followed eventually by a far more comprehensive agreement.

3. **Even if a full 'divorce agreement' is signed before December 2019, a full trade agreement may not be signed before 2025**
In the interim, impact on trade will be slight. But longer-term impact on EU budgets will be very painful, with loss of UK contributions, once the UK fully leaves.

4. **However Brexit is resolved, UK voters will be very divided over the EU for the next 20 years**
Opinion is likely to shift as older 'leavers' die and are replaced by a generation who identify mainly as Europeans.

5. **At any point until completion of the entire Brexit process, a new election or referendum could result in abandonment of Brexit**
This possibility will be increasingly likely, the more drawn out and fraught the whole process becomes.

6. **Border between Northern Ireland and Republic of Ireland will be impossible for the EU to close in event of no deal**

A huge challenge for the EU is that whatever is agreed (or not) between the UK and the EU, there is no power on earth with capability *and* desire to stop free trade and movement of people across the 310-mile border between the Republic of Ireland and Northern Ireland, however much the EU would like it to be closed/controlled, assuming the UK separates from the EU.

Even at the height of the Troubles, the combined efforts of the UK and the Republic of Ireland failed. The UK will have no interest, while the Irish government will not split the island of Ireland into two again.

So in the absence of a full EU–UK free trade agreement, Brussels will be faced with a terrible nightmare: how to prevent an open EU–UK border, threatening the whole EU market. What options for Brussels then?

a) An abrupt exit with 'no trade agreement' means logically that an EU barrier would need to be erected immediately between the UK and the rest of the EU. But no such barrier would be created, or enforced. This would soon require Brussels taking formal sanctions against the ROI, for 'failing to defend their border properly'. It would be a drastic step for the economy of Ireland, its membership of the EU, and for stability of the EU as a whole. The crisis would deepen every week, and if the EU is aggressive to the ROI, could lead to the ROI forming a free trade agreement with the UK, after the ROI became excluded from the EU free market, which would be the ultimate sanction.

b) Partial or quite comprehensive EU–UK free trade agreement – which would still need some border supervision, but with most checks done away from the border.

c) Persuade the people of Northern Ireland to separate from the UK and join the Republic of Ireland, or at the

very least to have their own customs union with the
EU, and a customs border with the rest of the UK. Not
realistic.

Since a) will eventually create a second major issue out of Brexit,
requiring hostile actions against another member state, we can be
certain that huge efforts will continue to be made by Brussels to
avoid this, despite all the political posturing. And since c) is impossible for Brussels to deliver, that leaves b) as the most likely, with
a chaotic open border in the interim, and smuggling on a massive
scale – also a challenge for Brussels.

7. Sterling likely to trade lower against the euro than before the Brexit vote if Brexit proceeds

Between the vote to leave and April 2019, the pound fell around
15%, and markets are likely to continue to regard the UK as a lower
value economy if it does leave. This will make UK exports cheaper
to buy. Even if an average 5% levy were to be imposed for a very
long period in future in both directions for all EU–UK trade (which
is unlikely), the impact on the UK will be more than offset by
changes in the value of the pound.

So in the example above, products sold to the UK from France
will be 15% more expensive for the British to buy in pounds, plus
5% import tax, resulting in 20% added penalty. But products sold
to France from the UK will be 15% cheaper, less 5% import tax,
resulting in 10% lower prices. Sterling will recover if markets decide
that the UK economy is doing rather well post-Brexit, balancing
things out if there is a UK boom.

We can see, therefore, that tariffs are likely to have a much
smaller average impact on the price of goods between the EU
and UK than likely changes in exchange rates, which will almost
certainly work in favour of the UK, unless the UK economy booms,
in which case sterling will recover, and EU tariffs will matter less.

8. The UK will NOT see a big spike in inflation as a result of a fall in sterling of up to 20%

From 2017 to 2019 the UK saw a 12–15% fall in sterling against the euro, with negligible impact on inflation, coupled by a big rise in employment to the highest percentage of the population ever recorded. The markets are unlikely to push down the value of sterling by a further 15–20% after Brexit but if they did, the positive impact on UK exports of services and goods would be extraordinary.

9. UK exports to emerging markets will grow rapidly compared to UK exports to the EU – whatever happens

The 'economic future of the UK' could never have been 'in Europe', regardless of Brexit, because the future of the EU itself is not in the EU. As shown throughout this book, the economic future of the EU, America and all other developed economies will be increasingly dominated by selling to emerging markets, because those markets will drive almost all economic growth globally over the next 40 years.

Loss of some financial services into the EU by London-based banks will be more than offset by astonishing growth in global financial services from London, deeply inter-connected as they are with emerging markets.

10. Brexit has potential to create tens of thousands of new ways to make money

Every major change creates huge opportunities for those with vision, agility, talent and resources. During any adjustment period, expect many highly profitable businesses to spring up, filling gaps, exploiting price differences, managing supply chains, solving challenges, and stealing market share from previous suppliers.

Expect UK-based Brexit billionaires to emerge over the next couple of decades – who made their fortune by snapping up bargain companies in the UK and EU that ran out of cash in uncertain times, turning them around, or selling off their assets. And for every company that goes out of business, there will be another waiting to seize those customers.

In summary then, by 2035, Brexit will be history, even if it proceeds. Both the EU and UK will manage the changes, vigorous trade will continue in both goods and services, and disruptions will be overcome.

Likely breakup of the UK into separate sovereign states (except Northern Ireland)

Tribal forces have been pulling apart the UK for some time. The Brexit vote has added momentum to this process. The global trend is firmly set towards greater autonomy and self-government.

Some 85% of the UK lives in England, a nation within a nation that will continue to struggle with identity, except during international sporting events. England has no national language (English is global), no well-recognised tribal dress, and has often been defined in the past by being British – which has irritated many who are Scottish, Welsh or Northern Irish. But this will change.

Expect to see a rebirth of the English tribe: a fresh energy in a new generation who want to be as English as the Scots are Scottish, or the French are French. National state funerals, the last night of the BBC Prom concerts, international football matches and other events will help focus this new sense of tribal identity. This sense of Englishness will be strengthened as a reaction to what is happening in the rest of the UK.

Expect repeated votes on Scottish independence

Expect a further vote on Scottish independence in the next decade, encouraged by the fact that the Scottish people voted to remain in the EU. The result will be influenced by whether Brexit actually completes, and by oil prices, which are likely to oscillate – as we will see in Chapter 5. If oil prices are as low as $50 in the immediate lead up to a poll, more will vote to remain, preferring to be subsidised by England.

If higher than $100, more will vote to leave, riding on a crest of optimism about high revenues, financial independence and freedom to spend. And if a second independence vote is lost, we can expect a third vote, some years on. But acceptance of an independent Scotland into the EU, and the eurozone, will take at least a decade more, assuming the UK left the EU earlier.

Northern Ireland will be changed profoundly by Catholic majority voting

Northern Ireland also faces major changes, driven by demographics. Birth rates among Catholic-identifying families will continue to be significantly higher than among Protestants for the next 15 years or more, and Catholic voters will be a majority by 2024 as a direct result, possibly sooner. It is already the case that 44% of all working-age adults are Catholic compared to 40% Protestant. In schools, 51% of children are Catholic by background compared to a mere 37% Protestant. Hardly surprising then that surveys now show voters to be almost equally divided on the question of whether to remain part of the UK or become part of the Republic of Ireland.

While many from a Catholic background may wish to remain as UK citizens, a larger proportion are likely to prefer, by 2030 if not before, to be part of the Republic of Ireland, particularly if it resolves major trade issues post-Brexit and renewed border tensions between North and South. We are therefore likely to see calls for a referendum on the status of Northern Ireland within the next decade, which could well lead to a completely united island by 2030.

England as a sovereign state will be a vibrant, growing economy

Many have claimed that such a dismantling of the UK, perhaps even losing Wales, would be severely damaging to the economy – but to the economy of what, exactly? England alone generates 85% of the entire UK economy, with 56 million out of 66 million people, and would be the fifth-largest nation in Europe if a separate sovereign state: a vibrant global economy, with one of the highest incomes per capita in the world.

Whatever happens, London/England will continue to be one of very few premier destinations for the best educated and most highly skilled people around the world over the next 30 years, attracting new generations of talent and investment.

Such destruction of the old UK would of course be deeply

wounding to the psyche of the English tribe, following loss of the British Empire and decades of relative decline in power and influence, isolation from the EU, and absence from a global stage increasingly dominated by giants such as India and China. But a far bigger change will be the rise of emerging markets, especially the power of India and China, which will dwarf the impact of being a slightly smaller sovereign state.

Royal reforms

Tribalism will save the monarchy, albeit on a smaller scale, because otherwise there would be so little left of British or English culture. The fundamental problem with the monarchy is that royalty is based on genetic discrimination and family lines. This will seem increasingly bizarre and morally suspect to a people who have fought for equality of opportunity, fairness and lack of discrimination.

The transition from Queen Elizabeth to the reign of King Charles will be made easier by great public affection for her two grandsons and their own families, scaled back costs, and a culture of greater informality. The loss of the UK as a single entity is likely to diminish the Royal Family further, despite the continuation of the Commonwealth.

UK government spending and ambition

Discussions on public spending are not going to get any easier, and whoever is in government in the UK (or its constituent parts) will face pressure to cut costs or raise revenues, or both. And the less attractive government debt becomes to the markets, the more that borrowing costs will rise.

Choices on tax or spending will therefore be very limited. This is what we can expect over the next decade – with minor variations depending on which party is in power, and if Brexit actually completes:

- great pressures on government spending
- strict control of public pay awards
- increase in taxes for middle and high earners

- allowing inflation to drift well above 2% targets at times, diminishing the value to lenders of low-interest government bonds
- low corporation tax, compared to many other nations, and other measures to encourage investment into the UK, and headquartering of multinationals
- continued growth in UK strengths such as fashion, film, music, design, pharma, architecture and consulting
- recovery of banking and financial services – with new revenue streams, related particularly to emerging markets, despite Brexit-related uncertainty / disruption
- further automation of UK manufacturing – with exports encouraged by the fall in value of the pound compared to before the Brexit vote
- attracting a new generation of wealthy and highly talented settlers, who see the UK as a refuge
- encouraging sovereign wealth funds to invest in new infrastructure
- growth in exports to many emerging nations, benefiting from historic trade, cultural and language ties, relatively low UK wage inflation as well as from new trade agreements
- limited military spend – confined mainly to replacing old equipment and systems, maintaining minimum commitments for membership of NATO, relying increasingly on other nations within NATO to step up and shoulder their fair share of military spend.

Future of Germany as the central tribe of Europe

Germany will continue to be the dominant economy and voice in the EU, particularly as the French economy continues to falter. Germany has the largest population of any nation in the EU, as well as a strong economy built on high-tech engineering. Such dominance in the EU was an inevitable consequence of the reunification of East and West after the collapse of communism, but may cause increasing resentment in future. Germany's economic growth is likely to be held back to some extent by a rapidly growing number of older people, and by a shortage of low-cost, skilled labour, unless migrants enlarge its workforce significantly.

Germany's geographical position at the heart of Europe will ensure that it has a vital role in brokering tensions between Russia and the rest of NATO. Germany will be a very important partner in economic development for such neighbours as Poland. It will take at least 20 more years for all the economic differences to melt away between former East and West Germany, and for historic reasons for Germany as a nation to feel fully comfortable in exercising a strong leadership role.

France – tribal protests and radical change

France has been a dominant influence in the EU, straddling nations in the north and south, as one of the world's largest and most socially minded economies. However, France is in the midst of a profound economic and social crisis that will take at least a decade to resolve. The economy has been moribund, while public spending is 58% of GDP – more than any other European nation. Debt is 95% of GDP. So how will change come about?

A central part of French history is revolution by the masses against a powerful elite. In 220 years, France saw 11 radical and sudden regime changes. And today, the tradition of protest continues. For example, over 1.5 million people took to the streets in 2006 in a series of 'Liberty' marches against a new law that would have made it easier to fire workers under 26 who had less than two years of service. In 2010, more than 3 million people took to the streets, in a series of protests over many weeks, against a proposed increase in retirement age from 60 to 62 for many public workers. And in 2018–2019, there were prolonged violent protests against fuel price rises and a host of other policies, in the greatest uprising since the 1960s.

The scale of such 'people movements' will continue, from time to time, to make France volatile, hard to govern, and hard to reform. Voters are likely to go on favouring governments that promise higher social spending than in Germany and the UK, even if that means borrowing more money, breaking EU rules, and imposing punitive taxes on wealth creation or business in general.

So what of the future of France? Voters will continue to look for a leader who will save the nation, in the spirit of Napoleon I or General de Gaulle. They will also tend to look more fondly than the UK on the EU, as France was the nation that gave birth to it, and continues to see itself as a twin-power to Germany within it. However, the National Front won 25% of their EU votes in 2014, on an anti-EU ticket, and anti-EU protests could grow rapidly. In some ways, France is likely to remain fiercely tribal, for example in its hostility towards the use of English in speeches by government officials to international audiences.

A radical transformation is likely to be seen eventually, but until it comes, expect further stagnation, leading to more popular unrest.

Future of Russia's 160 tribes

Western Europe's future stability and well-being will depend on many factors, but among the most important will be peaceful co-existence with Russia, something that is all the more important given recent tensions.

Russia will remain strongly nationalistic, as a mega-tribe of 160 different ethnic tribes, and 140 million citizens spread across 11.5 time zones. Russia is a nation that has been forged by hardship and comradeship in adversity. Siberia makes up more than three-quarters of Russia's land mass, with average temperatures below freezing, while 50% is forest and 11% is tundra, a bleak and treeless, marshy plain.

Russia's future economy will depend on energy prices and exchange rates, both of which collapsed in 2014: Russia is the world's largest producer of oil, second only to America in gas production. Oil and gas account for 70% of export revenues and government spending is hugely dependent on them.

Russian desire for strong leadership and nation

The Russian tradition is of strong, autocratic leadership, and powerful figureheads like President Putin will continue to enjoy popular support, so long as these figures deliver increased living standards, improved security and better public services, or at least so long as living standards do not drop too much as a result of the leadership's actions. President Putin is likely to continue his strong grip on media and political movements, by popular consent.

Just 110 of Russia's many oligarchs control 35% of Russia's wealth, some of it gained rapidly by dubious means, at a time of chaos following the fall of communism. Government agencies have a long-term strategy to place great pressure on oligarchs who are 'living off Russian money' in other nations, as well as in Russia.

If you talk with members of the generation who grew up under the Soviet regime, you will continue to find warm nostalgia, tinged with slight sadness, when they look back to life as it was under Brezhnev. They will continue to point to full employment, regular pensions, stability, public order and respect for Russian traditions. But Russians born after 1980 have no such adult memories, and are already 39 years old today.

Daily life in big Russian cities can be expected to be similar to that of many European nations, with vigorous consumerism, capitalist culture and middle-class wealth. However, we may also see what many Russians would describe as loss of 'soul' or 'dushá' in smaller cities like Samara or Tolyatti, with very high divorce rates, addiction, depression, and lack of purpose or moral strength.

Russian foreign policy and military renewal

Russian leaders are likely to promote, with some success, an enlarged free trade area with border nations such as Georgia and Ukraine (but not China) to rival the EU. They will seek to influence former CIS nations with a combination of diplomacy, economic measures, media messages, military pressure and less obvious actions.

President Putin will continue to fret about what he sees as persistent American efforts to undermine Russia, whether economic, diplomatic, military or covert. He will also worry about similar activities by some European nations. The stronger the EU becomes and the more united NATO is, the more threatened Russia will feel.

Russia lost over 20 million lives in the Second World War, which is 60 times the toll of UK military deaths, and 90 times the toll in France. It is very hard for non-Russians to fully grasp the emotional force of that disaster on the national psyche, and on Russian pride. It explains the 'Never Again' and 'Don't mess with Russia' mantras that are set to influence foreign policy for several decades. The nation is also deeply scarred by the loss of the Soviet empire, as Britain was with regard to its own empire in the 1950s to 1980s, and is fiercely proud of its heritage, culture and military strength.

Deep unease and anxiety over NATO and the EU

Therefore, Russia is likely to remain bitterly opposed to any further extensions of EU or NATO influence or control, close to its borders, and will be easily provoked by fear and mistrust to vigorous actions of many kinds to prevent this. Such steps would be likely to damage Russia's economic growth, and we will see Russian rhetoric that may feel like a throwback to the Cold War. However, such rhetoric will be popular at home, unless people are hit by major, prolonged declines in living standards that they come to blame on the government rather than on sanctions or other actions by foreign powers.

Russia is likely to want to spend more on defence than any other nation except China and America over the next two decades, and to seek strategic alliances with China, to reduce political and trade risks to the West.

Russia is already an unbeatable power in the wider European region in terms of tanks and rockets, artillery and troop numbers, but also in locally stored tactical nuclear weapons. NATO has little local strength in comparison, without resorting to the threat of first nuclear strike, which is almost unthinkable.

Russia will also increase spending on foreign aid, to win friends in regions such as Africa, and will strengthen military ties in the region.

Challenges for Russia

Despite former superpower status, Russia's economy was only the size of Italy at the start of 2014, and had shrunk to the size of Spain by 2019 with the collapse of oil prices and EU sanctions. A sustained regional conflict would rapidly destroy a significant part of Russia's wealth.

Internal security will remain a key issue: the interior ministry bill exceeds by far state spending on health. Other challenges include capital flight by Russians moving wealth to 'safe havens' – $170bn in 2014 alone; low life expectancy in men (64 years – fiftieth in the world), partly related to alcohol; corruption – ranked 127th in the world by Transparency International; lack of strength in manufacturing; Islamic separatists; threat of a 'coloured revolution' inflamed by social media; and a crumbling legacy from tens of thousands of Soviet-era tower blocks.

Despite these things, expect a more vibrant, self-confident, militant and wealthy Russia within 15 years, but still bound tightly to global markets, and constrained by them.

Tribalism will undermine Ukraine

Since Tsarist times, Ukraine has been called the 'bread-basket of Russia'. It was the wealthiest part of the Soviet Union, with coal mines, heavy industry and large-scale grain production. It declined rapidly after the breakup of the Soviet bloc, due to bankruptcy and under corrupt and incompetent governments, to the point where it refused to pay Gazprom for heavily subsidised Russian gas, on which the entire nation's survival depends.

The Crimea will remain under Russia's control following its seizure from Ukraine in 2014. The Crimea contains Russia's most important naval base and was a highly valued part of the Russian nation, until ceded by treaty to Ukraine in 1957 in exchange for cheaper gas, at a time when such an 'administrative' step had limited significance in the context of the wider Soviet empire.

Ukraine is likely to split permanently along tribal 'fault lines'. People in the east of the country are mainly Russian speakers who feel strongly Russian in culture. Their region is dominated by coal mining, which used to generate most of the nation's wealth.

As in many other civil wars, the situation has been complicated by volunteer fighters and mercenaries from many nations (particularly Russia), and by maverick local leaders who are difficult for either side to control.

The nation will only be held together if a huge amount of autonomy is granted to eastern areas, in a peace process supported by Russia. Whether this will be within a federal structure of some kind or with the east effectively absorbed into Russia remains to be seen.

We are likely to see a 'frozen conflict' for many years, similar to those still in place today in South Ossetia, Transnistria, Nagorno-Karabakh and Abkhazia, following their own breakaway votes from post-Soviet republics in 1991–1993.

Impact of tribalism on future conflicts

Across the world there have been hundreds of civil wars since the Second World War, of which 20 are ongoing and most of which have been simmering for two decades or more. But there have been very few traditional wars.

We have probably seen around 30 million conflict-related deaths since 1945, compared with 100 million between 1914 and 1945. So our world as a whole has been relatively peaceful, and continues to be, despite news headlines.

Most current conflicts are in poor nations in Africa, the Middle East and places like Ukraine – which together produce less than 7% of global output. Therefore, the impact on profits of global corporations has been very small over the last two decades. Only 2% of American, British and Japanese foreign investment is in such places, for example. Yet the risks of conflict remain and indeed may be growing.

American supremacy will continue to create tension

More than $1.8 trillion is spent every year on weapons and other defence costs, or 2.5% of global GDP, down from 4% in the last days of the Cold War, equivalent to $250 per person on earth. Combined sales of the largest 100 arms companies is around $320bn a year.

However, 40% of all global military spending is by one nation alone: America, which burns up more in this way than the next 15 highest-spending nations combined. This is a truly spectacular imbalance of fire-power, and is unsustainable. Which is why the US will continue to pressure other NATO members to increase military spending. Next is China with 9.5% of global military spending, followed by Russia at 5.2%, UK at 3.5% and Japan at 3.4%.

America needs to spend just 3% of GDP on arms to achieve such dominance – compared to Russia, which today spends 4% of a much smaller economy, China 2%, India 2%, UK 2%, France 2%, Israel 6%, Saudi Arabia 9% and Oman 12%.

This relentless build-up of ultra-powerful weaponry will continue to feed tension, resentment and fear over the next two decades. America's army, navy and air force will be dominant globally for the next 15 to 20 years, despite rapidly increasing military budgets in Russia and China.

However, the perceived 'moral strength' of America and its reputation as the world's 'police force' is likely to continue to weaken rapidly around the world, following adventures in Afghanistan and Iraq, yet more news reports on abuse or torture of prisoners, held sometimes for years without trial, and because of more routine killings, using drones, of foreign citizens in other nations.

China and Russia will enter a new arms race with America also stepping up

So how long will it take China to catch up with the global military power of America? The answer depends on whether you measure this in the size of armies or the smartness of missiles and other tech. Even if China were to raise military spending from 2% to 5% of GDP, and even if China's GDP were to grow 4% faster each year than America's, it would probably take over two decades for overall capability to catch up with US military might, unless America slashed spending.

Russia will not be able to create such global strength in 40 years, but within five years could easily mass a million troops in Eastern Europe, up from half a million today, backed by huge numbers of lower-tech weapons, and smart tactical nuclear delivery systems. And Russia will continue to boast of new and spectacular military weaponry, such as undetectable hypersonic missiles, and huge new nuclear warheads on submarines, as part of a national strategy to project strength around the world. So, then, both China and Russia will be able to engage in significant military excursions in their own regions, if they choose, even if far-flung conflicts of any size will be difficult to sustain should they act alone. Only America will have the global power to try to stop them, which, on the whole, it will be very reluctant to try to do.

New nuclear threats and the Space Race

Expect to see major nuclear scares over the next 30 years as various countries or groups claim to have got hold of nuclear weapons or material, or to have developed their own, and threaten to use them.

We will see an accelerating nuclear arms race in a growing number of emerging nations, with rapid upgrades of small tactical nuclear weapons by Russia and America, and the tearing up of 30-year-old nuclear weapon treaties. The two nations between them could spend over $2 trillion chasing nuclear weapon supremacy over the next two decades.

America will really struggle to develop an effective anti-ballistic missile defence, following many failed attempts to shoot down intercontinental rockets in tests, despite spending almost $100bn in 12 years. Russia and China will also try to crack this problem. The trouble is that intercontinental missiles travel at 10km per second, and can release large numbers of decoys in flight. And 'ordinary-looking' satellites could also be launched, containing hidden nuclear devices that could be detonated while flying over a country like America or Russia.

No nuclear warhead has been used in anger since 1945. As I say, expect someone to use this threat somewhere and for massive international confusion about how to respond. Do other countries threaten to go to war against a nuclear-weapon-using nation, if a warhead is used by such a country in self-defence, after repeated warnings to an aggressor? How would such a war be waged? Where do you target your first or second strike(s)? How many warheads do you retaliate with, of what size, and how rapidly do you press the fire button? How do you counterstrike against an invisible terrorist group that has no national support base? What happens if a group threatens again, and explodes a second warhead?

Countries in such a crisis may have only hours or at most a couple of days to work out how to respond.

National arms industries

As I predicted, there has been significant consolidation in the arms industry, and there will be more to come. Defence research is only cost-effective when there are large economies of scale. That means selling to other nations whose policies and behaviour may make many uneasy, despite the argument that if one country doesn't sell to them, then another will just step in.

Rethink about high-tech weapons

High-tech weaponry will not be enough to win future wars. Most wars will be fought inside nations rather than between them, and will be low-tech, as we have seen in Syria: guerrilla wars fought wall by wall and house by house; ethnic conflicts or terrorist attacks; mucky wars where tank commanders park their vehicles inside a large children's hospital, where civilians are caught up in bombing attacks; traditional military hardware and chemical weapons, fired in shopping precincts, around public libraries, by ancient stone bridges and in fields of corn, reducing entire cities to rubble.

Landmines and other messy weapons

New weapons replace old, which move down the arms chain, into the hands of the poorest (and often most unstable) nations where they are frequently used for internal repression. Then arms fall into the hands of criminals.

Weapons are also lost or unaccounted for, like the machine gun I stumbled across in woodland near London one day. Landmines are a global menace, designed to be hidden and 'lost' from the moment they are scattered. Tens of thousands of square miles will remain uninhabitable because of the indiscriminate use of anti-personnel devices, which will remain dangerous for at least three more decades.

Over 110 million mines have been laid and lost, affecting at least 70 countries, and 2 million more are planted each year. Each mine costs $700 to detect and recover, in work that kills many experts every year. A million ordinary people have been injured or killed in 25 years, mainly children (who often pick them up as toys), women and old people.

A further 100 million landmines are neatly boxed in military stores across the world, waiting to be used. Landmines will continue to be scattered widely, not only to protect bases and kill armed men, but also to stop farming, travel and trade.

Power of the few will break the mighty

Gigantic military strength is almost useless in delivering many types of strategic objectives – as America has repeatedly discovered.

For 50 years, America has struggled to 'win' a single 'foreign' war, and even more to 'win' a lasting peace, whether in Vietnam, Iraq or Afghanistan. This will reduce America's willingness to embark on yet another major war in the next 10 to 15 years, barring a NATO-triggered response to a major Russian offensive against Europe, or more major terror attacks.

As Stalin once said: 'A single death is a tragedy, but a million deaths are just a statistic.' Surveys show that Americans paid more attention to the beheadings of two US journalists in the Middle East than to any other news report over the previous five years. As a direct result, 75% of Americans said they supported air strikes against Islamic State in Iraq, with 66% supporting air strikes against rebels in Syria. This was a complete reversal – 12 months earlier, only 20% supported missile attacks on the Syrian government after chemical weapons were used.

Such huge emotional reactions to tiny numbers of American deaths are proof of how very vulnerable the nation is to being provoked and goaded into large-scale military reactions. This makes further beheadings of hostages or similar atrocities inevitable. Enemies of the US will ask: 'What will it take to tempt America into another asymmetric conflict that will wear it down further? Another ten journalists beheaded, or would it take twenty, or a larger attack on US soil?' The answer of course is that it will depend on many different factors, but probably far fewer deaths than many might suppose.

Fewer unilateral decisions to embark on major wars

As we have seen, by 2030, global military power will be more equally distributed, with decline of American dominance, and this will also result in eventual restructuring of the UN security council, for example to include India as a permanent member.

Individual nations will be less able or likely to embark on major military action some distance from their borders, without acting jointly with other nations. Major multinational wars (or a Third World War) will become less likely, but expect minor conflicts over resources/borders/sea-bed rights and other similar issues.

Worrying results from war games

Every large nation in the world is playing war games on a regular basis, the Pentagon more than most, exploring outcomes of imaginary conflicts in faraway places.

However, many such war games reveal the same pattern as in the Middle East. Small, highly motivated groups on the ground, with tiny budgets, can easily provoke large military powers into long-term fighting far from home at enormous cost. War games also show rather worrying outcomes from any scenarios that begin with a sudden, major Russian assault.

The greatest weakness of American military strategy is that the public is not usually prepared for more than a handful of American forces to be killed abroad. Servicemen are rarely motivated enough by the 'cause' to engage in widespread suicide missions. Therefore, future military strategies will be based mainly on technical power, firing long-distance weapons, at eye-watering cost, using very few human beings on the ground.

So a young drone operator sits in an American city watching live video, firing smart missiles into targets in a nation he has never visited, on the other side of the world. He thinks the enemy are *terrorists* that could threaten America.

On the other side, perhaps, is a young man with a gun who will soon sacrifice his own life as a local hero, for his own people, and for the 'rightness' of his cause. He thinks that he is a *freedom fighter*.

The trouble is that the history of warfare shows that those who fight with greatest passion for the 'rightness' of their cause tend to win in the long term. So which of the above has the strongest passion?

Terrorist or freedom fighter? This battle over perception will be central to many future conflicts, as it was during the Second World War with the French Resistance, and with the Nicaraguan Contra movement that was covertly funded by America in the 1980s, along with the Afghan mujahideen.

More double and treble agents – with strange results

America's intelligence agency budget has more than doubled in real terms since 2001, to $75bn a year, including the Military Intelligence Budget, while Russia's intelligence spending has also soared. Expect huge growth in double agents, treble agents, quadruple agents – people or networks working for more than one intelligence service, infiltrating activists and militia groups, playing one off against the other with disinformation and subterfuge (such as sending a fake report to a drone operator, hoping that women and children will be killed 'by mistake').

Expect many strange events and news headlines. At times the numbers of spies planted inside some smaller terrorist cells may form a very significant proportion of the number of genuine members, as has already happened from time to time in Northern Ireland. Expect many moral dilemmas, and legal action in future – spies will often have to prove they are *not* spies by carrying out attacks or atrocities themselves. And one day the shocking truth will be revealed ... with many ethical and legal questions.

This strange world is being shaped further by the massive expansion of cyber-monitoring and surveillance, which in future will be added to by many tens of thousands of tiny low-cost drones, to watch us from the skies. (See Chapter 1 for more on cyber-crime and state monitoring.)

Hybrid wars – blurring of war and peace

Our world is being subverted by hybrid conflicts that are hard to track, recognise or measure. Future hybrid conflicts will mainly be about enhancing national interests and economic growth in a hyper-competitive world.

We will see combinations of the following being used as foreign policy strategies by various nations: traditional military; threats and economic bullying; humanitarian aid; paramilitary groups; informal militia (volunteers and mercenaries); concealed, rebadged or disguised armed forces with official deniability; criminal gangs; terrorist acts; killing 'unfriendly' journalists; mass rape of women and children; drone assassinations; insurgency of all kinds; and cyberattacks – sometimes accompanied by large secret teams using social media, fear campaigns, subtle propaganda, and fake media bending the truth.

The gap between war and peace is already blurred. And future conflicts will be very confusing and hard to interpret – with conflicting reports and uncertainty about who the 'enemy' is, or if there really is a conflict at all.

Covert activities will include commercial espionage; buying members of parliament as consultants; buying up key companies; blackmailing influential bankers, business leaders, media owners or government leaders; indirectly funding political campaigns; and secretly funding dissident groups. Blackmail will be a particular risk for high-profile business and political leaders who visit or work in emerging nations, where they will be targeted, compromised and corrupted, with the aim of controlling them when they return home.

Challenges from failed states

Time and again, the might of the most powerful nations will be tempered by the difficulties of ensuring stable regime change. Whether in Zimbabwe, North Korea, Sudan or Syria, it will become even clearer that mending so-called 'broken states' by sending in foreign armies in traditional fighting machines is a near-impossible task.

One of the greatest challenges will be how to find ways to bring stability and security by other mechanisms, which may include friendly support from neighbouring countries, IMF development loans, NGO activity, use of UN peacekeepers, and so on.

The net result of all these trends will be a radical reshaping of military spending by all major military powers over the next two decades. It will always be true that 'real' wars will require 'boots on the ground'. Tens of thousands of troops, artillery, tanks and other hardware will always be persuasive when massed close to borders. But we can also expect developed nations to invest in more drones, smart missiles, rapid response troop vehicles and helicopters, and better intelligence, for longer-distance operations.

Tribal leadership will also change corporations

Tribal leadership will be the most powerful type of leadership in our future world. Every great politician understands how to appeal to an entire tribe, as does every great CEO.

Team leadership is always limited by team size, usually to fewer than twelve. But tribal leadership can take a hundred thousand people in the same direction.

Tribal leadership is about relationships rather than structures, aspirations rather than goals. We see tribal leadership in popular movements around the world. Anything that strengthens your tribe will strengthen tribal leadership. Expect huge investment by corporations in tribe-building, with team days, off-sites, staff conferences, celebrations and client events.

Every company is a tribe of tribes

Every organisation is a tribe and there can be many tribes inside corporations. Tribalism in a company makes us proud to belong. Tribalism can weld teams together in a healthy and competitive way. Corporate tribalism raises key issues: can we impose a dominant national culture on a global business – for example, as a *Swiss* bank?

The fastest way to change an organisation will be to address the tribal culture. Tribalism is the reason why most mergers fail to create value: take care to honour and celebrate each tribe, and your business is more likely to grow. Tribes of friends produce three times more manufacturing output than acquaintances and 50% better decision-making, with greater trust, honesty, open communication and respect.

A significant proportion of new wealth in many emerging nations will be created by small companies with fewer than 20 employees, of which most will be family owned. They will continue, despite legal challenges, to favour employing relatives, friends, and friends of friends. Expect new government initiatives to help smaller businesses, to create jobs.

Brands and tribes

Every brand creates a tribe and the more powerful your tribe, the more powerful your brand will be. Apple is the world's most valuable corporate tribe – worth around $813bn, followed by Microsoft at $736bn, Google at $674bn, then companies like McDonald's, Samsung, Amazon and Toyota. Each superbrand will spend billions over the next 20 years to promote their tribal identity.

Consumers in many nations are already exposed to 30,000 brands. Tribal gatherings are an advertiser's dream. Create a tribe and money follows. More global brands will hide inside local 'tribal' packaging, becoming more 'glocal', especially where the brand is too closely linked to one nation, culture or religion.

All great marketing will appeal to tribes

Customers have moved on and left marketers behind. Their big TV campaigns, press releases, mailshots, events, billboards, cold-calling of customers or Twitter feeds – all of these marketing plans still work to some degree, but they belong to the last century. Even worse, most marketing just alienates customers.

Most young people in developed nations are moving from old-style live TV to time-warp TV, where they skip the ads, preferring to surf online. So we need new ways to reach them. But the cleverest campaigns will all be about creating *new* tribes, while taking great care not to violate privacy in data storage and use.

Selling to youth tribes

Young people today in most developed countries are more likely to wear the same kind of clothes as their parents, listen to similar music, frequent similar bars and clubs, have similar hairstyles, and hold similar political or religious views. The main exception to this will be in children of migrants who adopt the culture of their new nation and reject that of their parents.

The M generation, whose entire adult lives have been lived in the third millennium, is on the whole unused to protesting. This generation is anxious about sustainability and the environment, but tends to focus on responsible lifestyle choices rather than taking to the streets.

Surveys of 13- to 19-year-olds in the UK show them to be the most driven generation for 100 years – excelling in their careers is one of their most important goals. This ambition to succeed is also driving youth tribes from middle-class backgrounds in India, China and many other developed nations.

Selling to older tribes

As we have seen, 1 billion people will be over the age of 65 by 2025. This tribe accounts for 50% of US income and 75% of all financial assets, and the UK is much the same. Expect a wide range of products tailored to the 'grey market', such as cruise ships, golf breaks and health spas. This is a generation that thinks young, with a mental age of 60, physical age of 70 and actual age of 80.

Redesign for older customers

Expect a rethink about packaging, restaurant menus, instructions and marketing materials, which are usually printed too small for older people to read without glasses. More role models in advertising will age by 30 years. Grey power will be more visible on the high street, in clothes shops, sports shops, car showrooms, garden centres, travel agents, theatres, cinemas and restaurants.

Personal pension plans and investment funds will be growth areas, and face-to-face banking will be especially aimed at those who are retired. Equity release from homes will be a common way to boost pensions.

Delayed inheritance for middle-aged workers

More than $10 trillion dollars will pass from one generation to another in the next decade in the US alone. These days, people may be in their sixties or seventies before both parents have died. By 2050, they may be working at the age of 75, and caring for an older parent at the same time. Expect an army of fit and active 75-year-olds to become volunteers for hundreds of charities. These organisations will provide a sense of family, purpose and belonging.

People with no pension

At the other end of the social scale, we will see an elderly under class – people who work part-time until they drop in their late seventies or eighties (or in their nineties, by 2040), unable to survive on miserable state pensions, and out of touch with their children.

A huge problem will be growing numbers of people in 20 years' time who failed to invest adequately in a pension fund. A separate crisis will be experienced by those whose pensions have been hit by low yields or inflation, or because their pension company went bust as life expectancy jumped. Others will run out of cash, after raiding their capital or making very foolish investment decisions, following deregulation of pensions in nations like the UK.

Impact of later retirement

As I predicted, compulsory retirement is already illegal in countries like the UK – seen as a form of ageism. Many older people will cash in a partial pension at any stage from 55 to 75 and will top up with part-time work, or low-paid, full-time jobs for worthy causes.

State pension age for all workers will be set at 70 years by 2025 in many developed nations, for those who are younger than 40 in that year.

However, those with adequate personal pensions will retire, or semi-retire, whenever they like. A key recruitment strategy in ageing nations will be tempting people in their seventies out of retirement. It may be hard to imagine the need to do this today, in nations where up to 40% of young people are still out of work because of economic crisis, but hard times will pass, wages and exchange rates will adjust, and the experience of older workers will be needed.

Shift from marketing to information and revelation

Brands that oversell will be quickly exposed. The best products in future will 'sell' themselves. The more you have to 'market' a product, the more people will assume that the product is not worth having. The most powerful messages in future will be information and revelation in a personal 'conversation' within a trusted relationship regarding personal data. At the same time, expect ever more exotic ways to develop messaging – including neuromarketing, which studies how brains react to brands, slogans, shapes, textures, ideas, memories, hopes and dreams.

Reaching tribes through social media

Most people are quicker to believe the opinion of a stranger on a social media site than a marketing executive, chairman or CEO. And the more colourful and negative the social media review, the more customers are likely to read it, especially in China, where 66% of consumers rely on social media reports before buying.

Hotels or restaurants that consistently have 5* reviews will be less likely to get bookings than ones which score 4* or 4.5*.

Customers want to hear authentic, varied and balanced opinions of real people and mistrust information that looks as though it is automatically generated.

Every one of your future marketing messages, slogans and campaigns is likely to be scored by the online community. This is great news for all smaller companies with excellent products or services but tiny marketing budgets.

Millions of fake identities on social networks

In the meantime, marketing companies have hit back, creating tens of millions of new fake people every few weeks on social networks with fake friends, fake life events, fake activities, fake posts and fake product preferences. Their hope is to influence search results. At any time, over 80 million Facebook profiles are complete fakes.

There are probably over 1,000 social media companies in China alone that exist solely to fool the algorithms of Taobao, one of China's biggest e-commerce platforms. Each online store displays recent sales figures – and larger figures attract more customers. Pretend customers linger on web pages to make pages appear 'hot' on many different websites. We will see many more such attempts to corrupt search results with fraudulent data.

Search results are already being profoundly edited by your previous activity. Imagine someone who is very sceptical about climate change science. Such an individual may think he is searching the whole web for updates on the science, but in future he will only be shown results that confirm his own views. This issue will have a huge impact on public debate and opinion.

Does Facebook have a long-term future?

Facebook use is already falling rapidly in the UK, a nation that led much of the world in online sales and networking, and the company urgently needs a radical new approach and to win back trust. New sites will spring up fast, aimed at younger users, but only one or two will become global. Old social sites will be under huge pressure to allow people to move their digital content and networks. Another major risk to sites such as Facebook is that significant numbers of people will decide to 'get a life' by rejecting a hyper-frenetic virtual existence.

Most people would say that social media strengthens friend-ships, but what about real intimacy and personal attention? Expect a premium for the real, the authentic, breathing the same air, being '100% present', enjoying the total moment. Expect growing numbers of people to turn off their devices as a matter of principle for at least an hour a day.

Tribal fashion, clothing and textiles

The fashion industry has always been about tribes: what kind of person do you want to be? With whom are you identifying? In addition to established influencers, each with several million social network followers who read their posts or watch their videos, expect hundreds more highly influential 16- or 17-year-olds, to develop their own superstar status.

Future of the fashion industry

The fashion and textiles industries are worth over $1.8 trillion, growing 5% a year, and employing 75 million people. At present 50% of global growth in apparel sales is in China, which has overtaken the US as the largest market. But prices globally have been falling in real terms for two decades, and will continue to do so as the scale increases.

In the US, the industry employs 4 million people in 280,000 outlets for clothes and shoes. I met an American cotton manufac-turer recently who makes 1,400 pairs of socks *every minute*.

Fashion is worth over $40bn a year to the UK economy, employing over 800,000 people – more than telcos, car manufac-turing and publishing combined.

How catwalks and fashion launches will change

Fashion parades will continue to push towards every extreme, with models parading semi-nude, completely veiled, clean, muddy, soaked, icy, body-painted – anything to get attention. But none of this will create third millennial fashion.

Expect a backlash against the traditional catwalks in New York, London, Paris and Milan, typically with four weeks of shows, thousands of events, tens of thousands of outfits. Some fashion leaders will explore ways to completely reinvent how they launch their collections, for a web-mobile world, where attention spans are only seconds.

Traditional styles will endure at work

Executive workplace clothing for men is likely to remain unchanged for the next 30 years, as a globally accepted but visually boring uniform, dating back to over 100 years ago.

Identikit suits for men will remain the 'safe' norm, as will sober dress styles for women, adapted for life in countries like Saudi Arabia, Brazil, Malaysia or India.

Exotic and unconventional styles will continue to be frowned on, as conveying an image of eccentric and risky decision-making. Exceptions will of course be in fashion, design and other creative industries such as App development and many startups.

Expect leisure fashion cycles for women to be as short as 12 weeks for some design houses by 2025, requiring shorter supply chains and faster design to production, in an ever more frenetic attempt to increase sales. Some of this retail hyperactivity will implode with big losses, to be replaced by slower seasonal stock changes.

New fabrics and textures

Expect revolutions in fabric proportion, especially in new ranges of synthetic fibres. These will create exciting opportunities for designers: clothes that change colour, new textures, textiles with nanotech treatments that self-clean or air-clean or remain sterile through many washings. Expect intelligent clothes with displays and sensors that change with temperature in colour or texture, or made of material which changes colour with temperature, or with accessories 'wired' with functionality, such as belts, hats, glasses, watches or trainers – for example, providing readouts of distance. But most clothes will look quite conventional for the next 30 years.

Future of cotton and polyester

Cotton is a really important industry for many emerging markets, and supports over 300 million jobs. We grow 25 million tons of cotton every year on 2.5% of the world's arable land, mainly on smallholdings of around 2 hectares, and global trade is worth $12bn a year. Largest exporters are America and Africa, while China holds stock equal to six months' global output.

The cotton industry will continue to grow in line with global population, but will decline as a proportion of fibre types. This will be the case even in tropical nations where cotton has a key advantage over polyester in absorbing moisture. Cotton is being displaced by polyester by 7% a year in the US.

Expect huge improvements in water use, pollution reduction, productivity per acre, pesticide reduction, and promotion of certified, ethical, sustainable cotton. In contrast, synthetic fibres are simple, plastic-type products, made from oil. Expect a public relations battle over whether polyester or cotton is the most sustainable and responsible fabric, with growing worries about billions of plastic microfibres entering oceans after a single wash of polyester garments.

Future of sport – tribes at play

Just like fashion, sport will continue to be dominated by tribalism: support for individuals, local teams or national champions, celebration of extraordinary physical skill, cheered on by tribal admirers. And then there is the huge social status from 'owning a tribe' such as a football team.

In some ways sport will change very slowly. For example, expect very few significant alterations in the rules for most sports, and few new sports. Sport will continue to be a focus for entire nations, with huge media pull for important live events, some drawing audiences of more than 1 billion. Revenues from broadcasting and related advertising will continue to dominate the sporting calendar, while most leading sports celebrities will earn far more from corporate sponsorship deals than from winning competitions.

However, we will see more news about fixed results, linked to betting syndicates in countries far away from the event. Multiple scandals will bring entire sports into disrepute – with football and tennis in the frontline after years of problems in cricket. Just about every kind of major sporting event will be implicated. Some ruling bodies may turn out to be implicated or corrupt themselves.

Expect huge bets on, for example, whether there will be three free kicks before half-time, or whether a particular player will be injured or will score a goal, and similar things in cycling, Formula 1, and so on. And as we have seen, there will be many questions in future about the credibility of athletics world records in the light of biotech doping.

Future of family and relationships

So, then, we have seen the importance of tribalism for the future of the EU, for nations, companies, brands, marketing, fashion and sport. But the family is *the* primary unit of tribalism. How will family tribes change in future?

Despite nonsense predictions by many social scientists, family life has continued relatively unchanged in most parts of the world. Couples develop relationships, usually get married, want to have children, and often live in extended family situations, especially in emerging markets or immigrant communities.

Family breakdown

Developed nations – and a growing number of emerging economies – are experiencing a cluster of inter-connected trends: family break-downs; more absent fathers; emotional upset and behavioural problems in children; poor school performance. Teachers, social workers, probation officers and judges in family courts see these trends every day.

In the UK, most couples over the last ten years have decided to have children without getting married. Yet most studies show that the happiest couples, and the ones most likely to stay together, are those who are married, particularly if they have had few other relationships before their wedding day.

The popularity of marriage will vary with income. Wealthy, middle-class couples in some nations are far more like to marry before they have children and are less likely to divorce. Many of the poorest and least educated are rejecting marriage altogether.

Absent dads

The UK has one of the highest percentages of absent dads in the world: fathers who have little or no contact with their children, following breakup of the relationship. That means absent male role models, less money to support the children, and higher costs for housing. Family breakup is often a fast-track to poverty.

Family breakup is also strongly associated with higher risks of mental illness in children (and later on in adulthood), addiction, risk-taking, teenage pregnancy, suicide and relationship breakup as adults. So we are likely to see a generational impact, beyond 2050, from events in families over the last decade alone.

The impact on such children is often made worse by the fact that in many cases both parents are struggling to survive financially, both working full-time, possibly with more than one job each. So parenting is often outsourced to childminders, friends or relatives.

The pendulum always swings somewhere new

Over the next three decades, we are likely to see a partial swing away from previous patterns of 'sexual liberation'. In some countries we are already seeing a significant *rise* in the age of first sexual experiences.

For example, in America, the number of 15- to 19-year-olds who have had sex before 15 fell from 19% to 11% in women, and from 21% to 14% in men, in just 13 years from 1995 to 2008. In nations like Uganda, these trends have been driven by the fear of AIDS – most Ugandans have attended at least 20 AIDS funerals in the past decade or so, usually of relatives. But more globally, we are seeing a rethink in many communities about what sex is really about.

Rise of responsible and conservative teenagers

A new generation is emerging that is the most socially conservative for a decade in countries like the UK. Not only has there been a sharp drop in teenage pregnancies to the lowest rate in 40 years, but more young people are rejecting alcohol, drugs and sex at an early age.

One in six admitted to taking drugs in 2014, half the level of 2003, but numbers have risen since. Only 10% are drinking alcohol each week compared to 25% a decade before. The numbers who have ever tried alcohol also dropped from 61% to 44% between 2003 to 2016. Smoking has also fallen, from 41% to 24% – with numbers of regular smokers down to only 3% compared to 9%. These are huge changes, borne out by repeated studies, and also by the experience of retailers/suppliers on the high street.

This generation is likely to question what kind of life they want for their *own* children. Some will want to give their children more parental time than they had themselves when they were young, even if that means working fewer hours, and having a lower standard of living. Such future parents will also be less likely to place their own young children in full-time professional childcare.

Older people as anchors and free childminders

Many grandparents will find themselves helping out with grandchildren, and will become much-loved role models in many areas of life; many happy long-term relationships will be formed, and of course grandparents will save the family money that would otherwise be spent on childcare. As we have seen, for economic and family reasons, more households will have three generations living under the same roof. Some grandparents will provide welcome stability at times of family strain, but others will place impossible stress on the marriages of their children.

We are also likely to see more informal fostering or adoption in wealthier nations of retired people as substitute grandparents, or aunties or uncles, by parents with children at home, where generations of blood relatives are separated by distance or family tensions.

A growing number of children share the same mother but have different fathers, with these father-figures coming and going over the years. Such children will often experience complex rivalries with step-brothers or sisters, and complex relationships with grandparents.

Web censorship and child protection

Many parents of young children that I talk to are very anxious indeed about how to protect their children online. They have sleepless nights worrying about what access to allow, what is fair, and if their children will be teased or bullied if parents don't allow various things. And they know that whatever the family rules are, their children may be getting unrestricted access anyway, to every kind of very disturbing 'adult' material, through friends at school.

Parents are horrified to learn from repeated surveys that most eight- to ten-year-old boys and girls have watched very explicit sex videos; that 30% of teenagers have received sexual images or videos on smartphones; and that most 14-year-olds feel it is part of normal life to be bullied into sending photos of their genitalia to classmates (sexting).

In the UK, 20% of all 11- to 13-year-old girls are already secretly padding their bras before they go to school, because they feel embarrassed to be flat-chested at such an old age. Just another small aspect of the wider issue of teenage angst, self-doubt and social pressure that are the result of a hyper-sexual culture.

Sexual grooming is another major threat, and the time between first online contact by a sexual predator and an illegal offence can be as short as 30 minutes, especially if the abuser impersonates someone their victim knows, and persuades them to send sexual images of themselves. Online-related sex offences against children increased 700% in the UK from 2014 to 2018.

Parents of teenagers are anxious in every nation

I have seen this same parental anxiety in every part of the world, through the work of the AIDS charity ACET that I started years ago. Our educators have seen over 5 million high school students, teaching classes in high schools on relationships and sexual health, in 20 nations, ranging from Russia to Kazakhstan, Thailand, India,

Uganda and Ireland. We usually find that it is the parents who are most keen for our lessons to take place.

Governments of nations like China, Russia, Malaysia and Thailand – which tend to have a more autocratic approach to what they think is good for people to watch or read about – have already taken the lead in global efforts to clean up the web. Remember that 85% of the world's people will be living in these parts of the world by 2025.

These regions are on the whole far more traditional than Europe or America when it comes to such matters, and watch with growing incomprehension what they regard as the 'moral decay' of many developed nations.

Expect more government-imposed filters and other initiatives, aiming to regulate access to 'corrupting' websites, to be active in over 70 nations by 2030, covering over 75% of the world's population, up from 40% today. Even though 400 million people already use private networks to get round such censorship, these networks will become illegal or require a special licence in many countries.

Growing outrage over abuse of children and younger women

Another sign of change in developed nations such as the UK and America is the massive outcry recently over celebrities who abused their status in the 1970s and 1980s to sexually abuse teenagers and younger adults, mainly girls and young women.

In the 1970s and 1980s, many British women accepted that it was normal (but nasty) if a work colleague pinched their bottom in a lift, or tried to put a hand up a skirt in the office. Today, such acts may mean a prison sentence if repeated – even if they took place decades ago, and even if the woman didn't complain about it at the time, or at any point during the following 35 to 40 years.

So while many societies have become hyper-sexualised, as seen in advertising, music videos, fashion, magazines and TV, it is also true that many societies in developed nations are becoming more sensitive and intolerant, especially about the sexual abuse of children and young women. This is a continuation of a trend I first described in 1995 in *The Rising Price of Love*.

Marketing executives, designers and film-makers will all need to tread very carefully as they seek to navigate these profound changes, sensing what is no longer appropriate, and will now risk offending the public, or perhaps even legal action. For example, one of the most iconic adverts of the 1990s was a poster campaign for Wonderbra with the slogan: 'Hello Boys!' The posters were so eye-catching that they were blamed for some car accidents by male drivers. Whether such a campaign would be so widely acceptable today is very doubtful.

The MeToo movement that began in 2017 was inevitable at some stage. The pendulum swing towards sexual respect and constraint has hardly begun, and will continue at many levels in many communities for at least another 30 years. Expect all kinds of actions still commonly accepted in 2025 to be attacked as highly inappropriate or criminal by 2060, in different parts of the world, as all of society's norms continue to evolve, especially regarding relationships, in a throwback to some aspects of an era 150 years earlier. Yet within parts of those same communities we will see profound differences in how attitudes evolve, and in which direction – depending particularly on religious belief and upbringing.

The result of all this will be growing anxiety among many men in particular about how to speak or act in mixed company, especially with men or women from a different ethnicity or background than their own. Will it cause offence to praise a woman's appearance, to open a door for her or to buy her flowers? Will taking a woman's hand in a nightclub be misinterpreted as an unwanted advance? Will placing an arm around someone's waist while dancing risk arrest for assault? If an adult has sex with someone slightly intoxicated with alcohol or drugs, what defence will there be that the other willingly gave consent? Expect a boom in personal guides, websites, agony columns, life coaches and so on, helping people navigate such relational complexities.

Growing number of commercial sex workers and slaves

Prostitution will continue to be a growth industry in many nations where up to 10% of men have paid for sex, and where the cash they are offering is distorting the usual career paths of huge numbers of younger women. And the angst described above is likely to feed this trend further. There is often less ambiguity and uncertainty in a commercial sex arrangement.

In the UK alone, one in ten female students (200,000 across the country) now say that they are working as prostitutes, escorts, lap dancers, filmed performers, or as companions to 'sugar daddies', in order to help finance their education and personal spending money – double the number just four years ago. Consider the social impact for a moment: this is far deeper than a few extra hours a week using Facebook, or playing computer games instead of going out clubbing.

In almost every case, the true source of this extra money is hidden as a 'shameful' secret from their parents, relatives and closest friends. The sex industry will continue to be a major employer of young, female students, and one in five have considered this option.

Globally, at least 40 million women are earning money for sex, while a further 40–60 million are in less formal arrangements, providing sexual companionship in exchange for food just to survive.

Sadly, around 12 million women and 2 million children are being held against their wills as 'slaves' – trafficked, tricked, trapped, blackmailed, assaulted and abused in terrible ways every day. Slavery is now one of the fastest-growing criminal activities in the world, affecting every nation and every large city whether New York, Paris, London, Lagos, Singapore or Rio de Janeiro. Expect many new regulations and deregulations as governments struggle to respond to this terrible situation, in the face of insatiable demand from men who rent such women for cash, with no questions asked. Expect many debates about how best to rescue sex slaves. Some politicians will argue that rescuing sex slaves and providing them all with homes, social support and other jobs will only encourage more women to take risky offers from gangs, hoping that they too will be rescued if something really bad happens.

Rethink on age of consent

In Spain the legal age of consent is 13, compared to 21 in Bahrain, 18 in Turkey and India, 17 in Ireland, 16 in the UK, 14 in China and 12 in Angola. In some nations, all sex outside marriage is illegal, as in Kuwait where the minimum age for marriage is 15 for girls and 17 for boys.

Expect a major debate on the issue in nations where the age of consent is higher for same-sex relationships, as in Finland, Greece, Austria and Malta. Expect harmonisation downwards in some European countries. We will also see a relaxation of laws in some of the 79 nations in the world where homosexual acts are illegal.

However, any future debates about the age of consent in general will be dominated by one argument: if we do lower the legal age further, it will mean that more adults escape justice, because they will not have broken any law by grooming and seducing (even) younger girls or boys.

The romantic dream will remain strong

The romantic ideal is very powerful, has not changed in over 200 years and will endure for the next 200. One reason is the powerful genetic instinct of human beings to form intense bonding relationships.

Almost all young people hope one day to find an amazing person who fulfils them in every way, with whom every day is treasured. If the romantic ideal remains unchanged and powerful, and if breakup is more often the reality, then it tells us that our future world will be full of disappointed people. And also full of people whose self-esteem has taken a knock as a result of an unhappy or broken relationship.

All this will guarantee that in many nations the market continues to grow for relationship advice, marriage counsellors, agony columns, confidence-building activities, dating agencies, romantic city breaks, Valentine's day gifts, bedroom fashion wear, sexual therapists, and a very wide range of other products and services to help couples keep their romance alive.

Online dating will continue to grow in many nations by 5%

a year or more; it is already a $3bn industry, serving mainly 25- to 34-year-olds. One in five US couples in 2017 reported that they had met online, and 50% of UK singles have never asked anyone out for a date face-to-face, while 46% have never dumped someone in person.

In some communities, over 50% of all couples will start their relationships online by 2030. Expect more research suggesting that relationships that start online last longer on average than those that do not. This may be for many reasons, including better sharing about interests and so on in the early stages, rather than going straight into a very physical relationship.

And marriage or remarriage is likely to become more popular again in some nations where decline has been greatest, even if the event takes place only when a baby is expected or shortly afterwards.

Expect many older people, including those in their eighties and nineties, to enter with great energy and passion into new relationships, particularly after major bereavements, which in the past might have led to permanent loneliness and isolation.

Sex industry adds to worries about performance

Recent research cited by *Forbes* magazine and the BBC showed that 4% of websites and 13% of web searches are pornography-related, based on global search teams and an analysis of the world's million most popular sites. These figures are lower than often quoted in older studies – more women are online these days and e-commerce means that the web is used for more things.

Even the most popular video porn sites have only a tiny fraction of the traffic of sites like YouTube. The busiest of such sites globally is used by 2.5% of all online users, with around 32 million visitors a month. Revenues from selling porn have fallen sharply over the past decade, because of wide availability of free online content.

Free, instant access, 24 hours a day, on any mobile device, to watch people having sex, in an infinite variety of ways, has proven an overwhelming temptation for many male teenagers and younger men. And we have no idea what the long-term impact will be on a generation of children growing up who have become used to viewing such material from before puberty and throughout adolescence.

Research suggests that 2% of men are now fully addicted to online porn, to the point where it disrupts and damages their daily lives. A further 30% experience various degrees of dependency, which can damage their relationships. That means that one in three men are affected in some way. Hardly surprising, then, that online porn addiction is one of the commonest complaints cited by women against their husbands in American divorce papers.

Professional help for sexual performance

There can be little doubt that widespread access to porn has changed expectations in teenagers and children, as well as among some men (and women) about what sex is about, as well as altered perceptions about their own relationships and capabilities, often in completely unrealistic and damaging ways, especially in the case of younger people.

One thing is certain: many more men are seeking professional advice because they are anxious about their own sexual perform-ance. At the same time, more women are also seeking ways to achieve greater satisfaction, or to give pleasure to their partners.

Most men over 50 have some degree of mild erectile dysfunc-tion from time to time, a potential market of up to 300 million men by 2025. And 5% of 40-year-old men and 20% of 65-year-old men have serious long-term problems with impotence.

Sales of drugs like Viagra and Cialis are already worth more than $4.3bn a year. Expect a wider range of such drugs in future, with faster action, longer effects, at lower cost – many of which are likely to be available from pharmacists without prescription in some nations within 10 to 15 years.

Busy professionals are becoming too tired for sex

Despite the obsession of many societies with sex, and the constant barrage of media suggesting ways to find greater sexual enjoyment, the reality is that for busy young professionals in relationships, their love life may often be non-existent, which can greatly increase the temptation to look elsewhere.

This is a major paradox – and a stark reality far from media impressions. One of the common causes of lack of intimacy in younger people is chronic tiredness and stress, made worse by obsession with social media. Couples are often affected by long working hours, young children, broken nights or night shifts, financial worries, and crowded housing with lack of privacy, as well as by constant online distractions.

A growing number of male and female executives will be faced with a choice between the aggressive pursuit of an exciting career *or* a fulfilling long-term relationship, with well-balanced children and (hopefully) a happy love life.

Arranged marriages will decline

Over a billion people live in communities where marriage partners are chosen by family, and where marriage is still regarded as a noble and exclusive institution, with dire consequences for unfaithfulness, or for pre-marital sex, especially in the case of women.

Expect more frequent culture clashes in traditional families now living in a developed nation, where children are rejecting arranged marriages, or where there are few suitable matches for parents to select from in the host nation in which they have settled.

Gay marriage and diverse expressions of family

Expect gay marriage to become very widely accepted as a normal expression of long-term commitment between two men or two women, across almost all the EU, most of North America and a growing number of other nations. The same will apply to attitudes towards transgender identity and relationships. It is easy for residents of such nations to think that the rest of the world is just backward, and will soon fall into line with modern thinking, yet laws for gay marriage will continue to be viewed with deep hostility in many of the 72 nations where *all* homosexual activity is still criminal, let alone marriage.

We are likely to see increasing polarisation over this issue between developed and emerging economies, with greatest opposition to gay marriage in strongly Islamic or Christian nations like Malaysia or Nigeria. Nations like Russia and Belarus will also tend to be fairly traditional in outlook for the next decade or two.

The word 'family' is already being redefined in many developed nations by those who believe that alternative models are equally good for individuals and society as a whole. Families with two dads or two mums – using surrogates or sperm donors to create their children. Families with children from one, two, three or four different relationships, or children made by combining genes from three parents.

However, more studies are likely to confirm the findings of a large body of research that already exists, suggesting that, on average, the lowest-risk environment for the emotional well-being of a child is in a happy home in which it is cared for by its own biological mother and father, in a stable and loving relationship.

Extended families will cluster together

Despite many predictions about the atomisation of society, most people in developed nations such as France, Spain or the UK are still living within an hour or two's drive of parents, and not far from where they were born.

What is more, a greater number of young adults are at home until around age 30, or spend long periods during their twenties with one or both parents. A major reason is economics, with rising house prices, more time in education, and higher unemployment. The same has been happening with grandparents, who are more likely to be living under the same roof as one of their children than they were a decade ago, often helping with grandchildren. This is particularly the case if their own child is a single parent.

Products for the 'precious child'

I have already described the 'era of the precious child' (see p. 97).

Part of this growing obsession with children is due to families having fewer of them. The entire hopes and dreams of two parents are often focused on the development of a single child.

We will see rapid growth of products, services, techniques and educational tools to 'hot-house' child development. Ways to encourage your child's genius to shine. How to create a musical prodigy by the age of five. How to help your child to be trilingual by the age of three.

Entire industries will spring up to service the hopes and worries of pregnant mothers. Ways to encourage child development before birth. Hyper-nutrition to boost brain development in the womb. Exposing the unborn child to ambient music or other stimulation. How to give your child a perfect birthing experience.

Environmental factors matter far more than most people realise. For example, we know that the genes your child inherits are permanently affected by your own nutritional status when conceiving, and by environmental factors in the lives of your own parents, and grandparents. So what happens when your unborn child is still in the womb could possibly affect the well-being of your great-grandchildren in subtle ways. Such insights will just add to the pressures felt by mothers-to-be.

Growing concern about transgender children

Many developed nations have seen a huge increase in the number of younger children who are confused about their gender identity, for a longer or shorter period, for many different reasons that can be hard to unravel. It will be a generation before we understand all the reasons for this sudden phenomenon, which may include strong social influences, extensive media coverage, influential role models, more 'open-minded' parenting, as well as hormonal blocks or stimulants from pollutants (see p. 94).

More older children will be referred to gender reassignment clinics, while surgical removal of genitalia and other treatments will become more common in teenagers, despite the fact that in many cases such feelings are temporary, yet surgery is permanent.

These trends are likely to become more widespread, together with anxiety and debate among parents, teachers, guardians, youth leaders, religious leaders, social workers, nurses, counsellors, doctors and politicians about how best to respond. Expect ongoing debates in many nations about whether gender is a biological fact, recognised under law, determined by presence or absence of a Y chromosome, or whether it is a personal choice.

Many schools and other organisations announced a new policy that any child, teenager, or adult who wished to identify as the opposite sex should have full rights to use the toilets or changing facilities assigned to the opposite sex, and to be treated in every way as someone of the opposite sex. But while such policies may satisfy those who seek to make life easier for people with gender identity issues, they will also create a new cluster of important safeguarding issues for other children and adults.

So for example, a heterosexual man with strong voyeuristic desires will only have to announce his gender change choice, to get a passport to spend as much time as he likes in female changing rooms at the local swimming pool, enjoying the view of semi-naked women. A heterosexual, or confused, older teenage boy announces he wishes to be a girl, is accepted into the Girl Guides, and ends up sharing a small tent with a teenage girl on a camp expedition, where he abuses her and ends up raping her during the night.

Consider that almost all sexual crimes are committed by men, which is why most societies create huge numbers of protected spaces for women and children, including separate public toilets and changing rooms. If just 1% of men in prison decided to self-identify as women, the number of 'female' sex offenders in prison would double, creating a major crisis over safety of women in prisons from abuse by predatory men, convicted of sex crimes against women, but now transferred to women's prisons, with huge associated costs to the prison service.

Other safeguarding issues for children include the longer term impact of starting potentially irreversible treatments at a young age when a person's sense of gender identity may not have stabilised for life. These matters are very sensitive and complicated, involving the balance of rights and the need for care, and we can expect a more common-sense approach to emerge, which aims to support and accept those who are feeling emotionally vulnerable, while also minimising risk to the well-being of the rest of the community.

Taken to extremes, the end results will be unhelpful as well as impractical. For example, a sex education teacher decides that they can no longer talk about menstruation in 'girls' or 'women', but instead has to refer to 'people with wombs' in case a girl who is menstruating has decided to be a boy.

Care for children at school will become far more complex

Of course, many combinations of issues affect the emotional health and well-being of young children, and schools, with the involvement of teachers, governors, parents, lawyers and government supervisors, will increasingly struggle to navigate the most appropriate responses. It will not always be possible to isolate the issue of being transgender from other issues – all of which may connect to each other in the classroom or the playground in even more complex ways.

For example, there is a soaring percentage of children in UK schools who are very difficult to integrate into a normal classroom environment because of a wide range of very disruptive, antisocial or violent behaviours. Statistics show that many such children are experiencing great unhappiness at home, caused by any number of things, including absent, sick or fighting parents, issues with stepparents, domestic issues with drugs or alcohol, conflicts with other children in 'blended' households, and so on. But as we have seen, many of these traumatic home situations are likely to become even more common.

We can expect very difficult situations to arise more often in future. Take for example the case of an emotionally disturbed and disruptive ten-year-old boy, who has to be taken out of the classroom many times a day. Suppose that such a child announces one morning to a teacher that they are transgender. The teacher may be very uncertain at first whether this is genuine, or whether the announcement should be seen as part of a wider, daily pattern of attention-seeking behaviour.

One thing is clear: gender identity issues will continue to generate great public debate and sensational media stories for at least the next twenty years, some of which will relate to rules for sporting events normally restricted to either men or women.

Changes in drug and alcohol use

We have already seen how a younger generation in many nations is spending less on alcohol or drugs than a decade ago. People are usually introduced to these things by others in the same tribal group, and consumption is often a social activity.

Alcohol will be a growing problem

Alcohol dependency is one of the world's major and most urgent challenges.

Globally, alcohol kills 3.3 million people every year, which is 50% more than AIDS, and alcohol kills three times as many teenagers than illegal drugs. Alcohol dependency is responsible for 7.6% of all male deaths and 4% of all female deaths. Half the world's population does not drink alcohol at all, but those that do consume on average 17 litres of pure alcohol each year. European figures are higher than the global average.

In America, 6% of the population, or 16 million people, drink more than their bodies can cope with long term, and *10% of all health problems are related in some way to alcohol consumption.* Around 40% of all crimes across America are committed while under the influence of alcohol. In the UK, 9 million people are 'problem drinkers'. The cost of alcohol misuse to the UK economy is over £21bn a year, and every government is picking up the health bill for overindulgence on a vast scale, while the impact on workplace productivity and family well-being is also immense.

So we can expect a wide range of measures in many nations, including education about health risks, stricter controls on sales to young people, and higher taxes on alcohol (the single most effective measure in reducing consumption). Many nations will take the view that alcohol dependency should, after tobacco addiction, be next on the list to tackle as a widespread social evil.

Expect more investment in specialist centres and support teams to help people break a serious drinking habit, and more research into medications that take away the craving to drink, or interfere with pleasure pathways inside the brain.

Tobacco sales switch to the poorest nations

Tobacco will continue to be a huge global industry, as companies switch marketing from developed to emerging economies. The number of smokers globally is slightly up since 2001, despite huge falls in developed nations. Smoking still kills 419,000 Americans a year and costs $100bn in health care as well as productivity losses. However, the proportion of people who smoke in the US has fallen from 43% to 18% – after 50 years of health campaigns, social pressures, taxes, restrictions on marketing, and a ban on smoking in public.

The government of China is also likely to become increasingly hostile to smoking over the next three decades. China lights up 1.6 trillion cigarettes a year (25% of the population smoke, more than 300 million adults), making it the world's largest producer and consumer.

Most Chinese smokers are male and smoking kills over 400,000 men a year, a figure expected to rise to 2 million by 2025. On the other hand, the Chinese tobacco industry is one of the largest sources of state revenues, with total sales of more than $100bn.

Vaping or the use of e-cigarettes will continue to boom globally at 25% a year for the next decade or more. Numbers of vapers increased from 7 to 43 million in the five years to 2016, in a $17 billion market, almost entirely confined still to Japan, the UK and America (the last of which has more vapers than the whole of the rest of the world). The appeal is harm reduction, helping people cut down nicotine intake, and less public annoyance, but the longer-term health impact is unknown.

Traditional tobacco smoking is the usual door-opener to cannabis smoking. Therefore, it is no surprise that cannabis use is falling in countries where smoking is out of fashion. Research clearly shows that cannabis use is not physically addictive, and less dangerous to life than tobacco or heavy alcohol use. However, cannabis alters important brain pathways, and heavy use often affects personal motivation, aspiration and achievement, especially in children and young people, and even more so if stronger types of cannabis are taken. Risks of psychosis are five times greater in people who smoke cannabis products containing high levels of THC every day. In the UK, a six-year study suggested that one in four people with hallucinations, delusions, paranoid ideas or schizophrenia were mentally ill because of smoking extra-strong varieties of cannabis, which are becoming more common.

How the drugs economy will evolve

The global trade in illegal drugs is worth around $500bn a year – now included in official GDP figures of EU nations. That includes 450 tons of heroin, mainly from Afghanistan, which (after seizures by police) supplies 17 million addicts. A further 17 million people are addicted to cocaine or crack, of whom 40% live in America and 25% in Europe.

The global drugs economy will continue to be highly profitable, funding wider criminality and terrorism. Trade in illegal drugs will continue to destabilise several nations.

Failure of drugs control

America has spent over $1 trillion since the 1970s on targeting drug cartels in Latin America. In 2006, Mexico declared a 'war' against drug gangs. In the space of eight years, 100,000 Mexicans died and 27,000 disappeared. A similar 20-year crackdown in Colombia cost 15,000 lives. Yet there is no evidence that these efforts cut consumption in America. The number of heroin addicts doubled to 680,000 in six years, and the price of heroin halved in real terms between the 1980s and 2014.

Uruguay and Bolivia have now liberalised laws relating to illegal drugs, and other Latin American nations are likely to review their own laws over the next two decades. Canada voted to legalise recreational marijuana in 2018, creating huge new businesses.

In the US, 62% of voters now support the legalisation of marijuana, up from 53% in 2015, and several states have already taken that step. The logic is that as prohibition failed for alcohol in the 1930s, drug policies are also set to fail, and merely encourage criminality. Step-by-step decriminalisation across America will be watched closely. Expect small steps in the same direction in many other developed nations, while death penalties remain in some emerging economies for drug trafficking. At the same time, the Netherlands is now moving to tighten up drug laws, having had the most liberal attitudes in Europe to drug use for a generation.

Over the next five years, many more nations that retain a cannabis ban will start permitting retail sales of products containing CBD, derived from cannabis but with very low psychological effects, to people with health problems, such as severe uncontrolled epilepsy in children, cancer pain or arthritis.

Falling drug use in many tribes

The numbers of people taking heroin, cocaine, crack and cannabis have fallen over the last decade in many nations, despite wide availability of cheap heroin from Afghanistan. In the UK, for example, cannabis use fell from 11% of the population to 7.2% from 2001 to 2017, while LSD use has also become less popular. The use of any kind of illegal drug by 16- 59-year-olds fell from 10.1% to 8.5% over ten years to 2017. Heroin and crack use fell from 332,000 to 298,000 in the six years to 2011, although crack use has increased recently. As we have seen, alcohol consumption has also fallen significantly – especially binge drinking in young people.

Expect huge growth in consumption of 'designer drugs', however, created by chemists, of which ecstasy is one of the best known. Each experimenter can make several types of new drug a year, none previously seen in government laboratories nor classified under 'old' drugs laws. Most of those who take these designer drugs do so on an occasional basis, but there are many unknown risks. Governments will struggle to respond to this trend.

Future of crime – tribal patterns

Crime rates have fallen in almost every developed country, in a consistent way, over the past 40 years. In many parts of the UK, for example, rates of reported crime have halved for various types of criminal activity, with the exception of knife and gun crime in London that is linked to gangs. In the past, crime tended to rise or fall as unemployment rose and fell, but the link appears to be broken now. So what has happened and what will criminality look like in a future which is steadily becoming more feminised?

Why recorded crime is falling in many nations

Societies in general are becoming more caring and sensitive. This is based on a wide range of historical trends going back hundreds of years, well described by Steven Pinker in *The Better Angels of our Nature*. Here are some examples:

◆ Attitudes to women have become more respectful as part of the feminisation of men and culture in general; human rights are widely supported; fathers are expected to be involved in caring for their children; most urban dwellers are very squeamish when watching the slaughter of a chicken; cruelty against animals makes many people very angry.

◆ Cruel and degrading punishments such as beheadings, burning people to death, public torture and slow deaths for political enemies are almost unknown today in developed nations.

◆ Falling rates of drug addiction means less crime. A single heroin or crack addict may need hundreds of dollars a day to buy drugs, and may commit several crimes a day to survive. In some communities, a small group of addicts can be responsible for most thefts.

◆ Better security. Car theft used to be very common, but is now almost impossible. Cash machines are better protected. Burglar alarms are more reliable, and more likely to be connected to police stations. Locks on windows and doors are more likely to be robust.

◆ Crime is moving online. E-commerce and online banking have created more than 1 billion people to target with scams, frauds and other activities. Every business has become a target for online theft. The risks of being caught are low, and prosecutions are very difficult across borders. These crimes are often not reported properly in official statistics.

Expect further progression towards less violent and aggressive societies over the next 200 years – punctuated by shocking lapses into atrocities and anarchy, mostly in wars, civil conflicts or terror attacks.

Expect better ways to close down online scams at the speed of light. Expect recent falls in traditional types of crime to stabilise. Expect more wealth to be stolen online than in all other kinds of small-scale criminal activity, by 2020.

Despite falls in crime in many nations, we will see very rapid growth of private security services for people with wealth, because of the unsustainable and growing gap between rich and poor. Private security in America already represents three times the amount spent on the police. Countries like Russia and South Africa have ten times as many private security guards as public police officers.

★

So, then, we have seen how tribalism is the most powerful positive and negative force on earth: the basis of teams, brands, customer groups, nations and families. The balance to the tribal Face of the Future is the Universal one, which includes globalisation, manufacturing, retail, travel and banking. The two faces pull in opposite directions. So what will be the drivers of a more Universal future?

Chapter 4

UNIVERSAL

THE FOURTH FACE OF THE FUTURE, universalism, is the exact opposite of tribalism. Universalism means English and McDonald's everywhere. Tribalism and universalism feed each other, each the reaction to its opposite.

Globalisation is an unstoppable force, despite recent nationalistic speeches and new trade barriers: the result of the free movement of capital, technology, goods, services and information across national boundaries, and the need for gigantic scale in many industries such as automotive and airlines, mobile operating systems, retail or web servers. Globalisation will continue to cut costs, increase competition and lower profit margins in many countries – and will destroy local culture.

Future of regional trading blocs

Expect more of the world to be aligned within regional trading blocs, allowing tariff-free movement of goods and services. The number of regional trade agreements increased from 100 to over 250 in the last decade alone, even though America became more negative about them. Expect strengthening of NAFTA, ASEAN, a Russian-based bloc, and a Southern African trade area, in addition to the EU. And expect growing frustration as many countries realise that they are losing control of their own economies, as a result.

With the expansion of regional trading blocs, interest rate or tax differences between nations become less sustainable, and capital flows unstoppable. Governments will be forced to go much further in harmonising laws, taxes and benefits. Countries out of line with what the global investment community thinks is reasonable will rapidly lose foreign direct investment (FDI).

Costs will converge and power will be centralised

In a globalised world, market forces mean that commodity prices tend to converge in different parts of the world, and this will also be the case with labour costs, despite resistance in developed nations like America and calls for trade barriers. So China's wages will rise, and Europe's will fall, relatively, over the next 20 to 40 years. Expect organised labour movements to campaign increasingly against free trade and in favour of trade barriers.

Global investors, such as pension funds and sovereign wealth funds, will become increasingly involved in big corporate decisions, effectively hiring and firing the most senior executives and exercising a veto on strategy. Trading by institutions is already 90% of the volume and value of transactions on Wall Street. Institutions already own the vast majority of US stock.

Future of mega-corporations

Our world needs more economies of scale to achieve greater efficiencies. Expect to see many more mergers – and also de-mergers as corporations make mistakes, or refocus on key areas.

Scale will reduce choice. It may seem surprising, but even a market of 10 billion people will be too small to support more than two large airline manufacturers. The same will be true of mobile phone operating systems and their communities of App developers; our world may be able to support two, but not three. Android and iPhone will endure beyond 2025, but as I predicted, every other operating system has been more or less completely wiped out. Expect similar consolidation in telcos, defence, banking, car manufacturing, pharma, the film industry, energy companies, and so on.

Illegal cartels and semi-monopolies will grow in numbers and strength – typically raising prices by around 20%. Past examples include: airlines fixing the costs of $20bn in air freight – which led to fines and compensation of more than $4bn; car-part manufacturers fixing a huge range of component prices; rail and subway contract price fixing in Brazil; Libor interest rate fixing in Europe and America; and the huge semi-monopolies of Apple, Google and Amazon.

Global citizens

We will see more hyper-mobile globalised individuals with no national loyalty or identity and no commitment to any geographical area, yet with friends in every city. These industrialised techno-gypsies consider themselves global citizens. They will be hard to tax and hard to count in census surveys, as well as hard to police.

Future of global manufacturing

All successful manufacturers will become far more efficient, and prices of most goods will fall in real terms over the next three decades. They will achieve this with greater automation, larger factories, better design, thinner and stronger materials such as carbon fibre and composites, more recycling, improved energy efficiency, shorter supply chains, lower stock levels, and by moving factories to regions where labour costs are lower or to where demand is growing fastest.

Future of trade, logistics and supply chains

Moving a container 150km by lorry from Birmingham to Southampton costs the same as moving the same container 10,000km by sea from Southampton to Beijing. It is cheaper to transport melons from Istanbul to Naples than to drive melons from a village up in the Italian mountains to the same market.

This overwhelmingly huge difference in freight costs will be one of the single greatest drivers of future global trade, despite increased energy costs. It is the primary reason why global trade has grown at twice the rate of global production over the last 30 years.

Look out for trade growth in Latin America and Africa – both of which have huge manufacturing potential close to the sea. Areas with major container ports will on average grow up to 40% faster over the next three decades than cities, regions or nations that are landlocked.

Expect over $28 trillion a year of global trade by 2030, up from more than $18 trillion in 2019. Global trade will continue to grow around 25 to 35% faster on average than the entire global economy. For two decades, the use of shipping containers grew twice as fast as international trade, as companies seized the opportunity to be more efficient. But the container revolution is now complete, and so the growth difference will ease.

Regional trade will grow – and global trade will slow

Ten years ago, many global manufacturers were stampeding to move factories to China and other parts of Asia to save costs, while banks were shifting call centres and IT support to India. Several years ago I predicted that outsourcing would go into reverse, which has happened. Asia is becoming more expensive. Long supply chains are easily disrupted. Cultural gaps, tariff barriers and varying exchange rates can be troublesome. Local demand in Asia is growing.

So we will see more clusters of regional suppliers, delivering components to make products to be sold in the same area. That is why 'south to south' trade will grow significantly (e.g. India to Brazil, China to Malaysia, or South Africa to Tokyo). Such trade doubled from 12 to 24% of global trade from 2000 to 2011, and will increase to more than 40% by 2030. Half of all trade in Asia is already within the region.

A significant amount of offshoring is already being replaced by nearshoring or reshoring of manufacturing – 'jobs moving back home'. Jobs are also moving around Asia. So Intel has built a new $1bn chip factory in Vietnam, just a few miles from the border with China where labour is twice as expensive. Samsung switched almost all manufacturing of electronic goods out of South Korea to many other lower-cost locations within Asia.

How to save money on logistics

It is a scandal that 30% of trucks on the road in the EU are empty, transporting just air over 150 million kilometres a year. Tens of thousands of journeys a year are wasted carrying identical end products, components or raw materials in opposite directions from different producers, factories, warehouses – literally passing each other on motorways. Expect new websites to sort out waste, and become money-spinners.

We will also see great efforts to speed up shipping. Automated cranes can already unload a giant container ship and reload it in 24 hours, re-sorting containers on the dockside as the Post Office sorts letters and parcels.

Every day counts. An average delay of a week on the shipping time can mean a loss of up to 25% of trade. It is often 20% more expensive to trade with a low-income country than a middle-income country, because of lack of infrastructure, red tape, slow customs, form-filling and maybe pressures for bribes to keep goods moving.

Paperwork and customs delays still account for over 10% of all shipping costs in many countries. We will see huge efforts by the World Trade Organization and governments to solve this with secure electronic bills of lading and other freight records, together with wider use of electronic tags on every item. Expect experiments with blockchain and other secure ledgers to make this more efficient and safe. Many emerging economies will also invest in combined rail, road and port facilities. Mexico has spent over $220bn on such a super-hub in the past eight years.

3D printing – overhyped yet revolutionary

Custom manufacturing will grow – whether personalised clothing or high-speed development of prototypes using 3D printing. However, 3D printing has been much over-hyped. Less than 3% of all homes in developed countries will own a 3D printer by 2040, and such devices will have almost zero impact on sales of pre-manufactured products.

3D printers are limited in the kind of materials they can print with, and in the size of what they can make. Next-generation printers will use raw materials that can be 'fired' in a microwave or domestic oven.

That said, 3D printing is already a very important technology to prototype new engineering parts for an auto company, or for dentists to create false teeth. For example, with a 3D printer, Airbus can make a new bracket for an aircraft door using 90% less titanium.

Robots taking over the world – rather slowly

Despite all the talk of robots taking over most menial jobs and putting tens of millions out of work, the growth of robots in factories has been slow – up from 92,000 to a mere 387,000 a year from 2000 to 2017. A third of that increase was in 2017. Compare this to the growth of smartphones, for instance, and the pace is still snail-like. Sales of such robots are likely to increase by around 10 to 15% a year – mostly confined to the auto industry, which owns most robots in America. Robots will become cheaper and more intelligent, but smaller models will still cost over $20,000 each in 2020.

Expect rapid growth in military robots – with tens of thousands of drones owned by the Pentagon alone, raising the prospect of swarms of small, semi-autonomous flying robots being thrown into the air above a major battle zone. Mass-produced 'suicide drones' will soon be available on the open market, able to fly 80 miles an hour, to detonate explosives at any target 40 miles away. They will be used by terror groups and insurgents, as well as by traditional military forces.

Domestic robots are already here, of course – cleaning floors, for example – but other uses will be hard for consumers to justify, apart from control devices in things like heaters or fridges as part of smart homes. The biggest personal use of robotics will be in cars – self-drive will be almost universal. The only question is by when.

Robots as personal servants or friends?

The greatest nonsense of all has been the notion that within a couple of decades, in most homes, you will find a walking, talking cyborg-type robot that smiles, tells jokes, does a range of household tasks, or helps with personal care, and becomes a close friend. The truth is that it will be many decades before such machines become cheaper, better and more acceptable to people than real human beings.

Yes, it is true that sales of complex life-size robots as sex machines are growing among affluent men, but it is also true that real, consenting human beings are 'free' and more enjoyable. Robots will face a lot of competition for such roles. There are also ethical questions: if someone is in a relationship, and then has sex with a robot, are they being unfaithful?

However, we will see major advances in devices that think 'intuitively', able to infer meaning from things. Google has led the way in 'Semantic Search', for example, which goes beyond keywords to try to understand what you are really thinking about.

We are still a long way from being able to have a sophisticated conversation with a robot, on a wide range of themes, where you cannot tell if a human is replying or if it really is just a machine. Expect many more experiments, with far more realistic conversations by 2025.

Future of Asia – global growth engine

When historians look back in 500 years' time they will record this period as the 'Century of Asia', built on manufacturing and cheap labour.

China and India will completely dominate our globalised world by 2050, with a third of world population, and relentless economic growth, driven by low-cost labour and emerging middle-class consumers. More than 85% of all the world's new graduates in science, technology, engineering and maths (STEM) over the next two decades will be from Chinese or Indian universities. Expect to see the same pattern in software development, medical research, business studies and accountancy.

Asia already represents over 40% of the world's GDP on purchasing power parity (PPP) terms. It is the world's factory, with complex regional supply chains, smelting 76% of the world's steel and emitting 44% of global pollution. However, apart from giants like Toyota and Samsung, the region still has relatively few truly global players. Expect this to change rapidly, especially in areas such as Chinese e-commerce, or Big Data companies in India, or biotech in South Korea.

Expect joint action by China and India on a growing number of issues from 2025, acting together as an increasingly powerful force in global politics, carrying the moral strength of a third of humanity. India's growth will be held back by poor infrastructure, while China will be burdened by its ageing population. Both countries will start experiencing severe shortages of highly trained managers, engineers, scientists and other groups, which will be reflected in a salary inflation of more than 20% a year for the fortunate few. Both nations will also continue to be affected by corruption.

China shifting from exports to ownership

By 2040, China will dominate global markets of every kind. China already has the world's largest banking assets of $42 trillion, and is the world's largest economy in Purchasing Power Parity. It is the largest manufacturer, the largest exporter, the fastest growing consumer market, world leader in digital innovation, high-speed rail and green tech, generates 40% of all global e-commerce transactions, and files more patents than any other nation. Yet despite all this, a shocking number of business leaders talk down China's capabilities, and are out of touch with reality.

China is a 'nation of nations', with eight languages, a huge middle class, and one of the best-educated workforces in the world. China is evolving rapidly towards a fully 'developed' nation, and for many globalised corporations, manufacturing in China is already an old-fashioned idea, because wages are becoming so expensive.

This will all be part of a transition from an export-led, manu-facturing economy to a more balanced economy serving Chinese consumers. As a direct consequence, global trade in the renminbi (RMB) will rise. It has already overtaken the euro as the world's second most important currency for trade after the dollar.

Expect consumer spending in China to continue to grow by 7% on average each year for the next 15 years, with occasional dips in the adjustment process. By 2025, China's consumer market will be three times larger than Japan's.

President Xi Jinping is the most powerful leader that China has seen since Chairman Mao, with popular agendas such as stamping out corruption, breaking up state monopolies, faster economic reform, greater equality, and the aim of developing China into the world's most powerful nation. He will run China strongly and efficiently, to a grand master plan with bold, visionary investments for China's future, while also respecting ancient Chinese philosophy.

Expect many more bold decisions that will impact global markets.

China's leadership will do all it can to maintain economic growth above 5–6% a year for the next two decades, to satisfy the aspirations of the people, and to reduce the risk of civil unrest. It is likely to succeed. The memory of revolution is recent, strong and unsettling. Every adult in China aged 65 today has vivid memories of life as a young adult under the Red Guards and the Cultural Revolution led by Chairman Mao.

The workforce in China

As we have seen, at least 300 million more Chinese people will migrate to cities over the next 25 years, from poorer locations, seeking better lives, providing extra labour to compensate for the ageing workforce. A further 600 million middle-class people will expect better lifestyles, more personal freedoms, and will be increasingly strong in their private opinions about how their region should be governed, about pollution and corruption, the size of their families, or the future well-being of their children. For example, social media stories about contamination of rice led to consumer boycotts, and huge purchases of European powdered milk and baby food. The government restricted imports, but tens of millions continued to get relatives and friends abroad to send supplies, creating huge logistical and supply issues in Europe.

Expect China to further develop its own form of democracy,

allowing regional voting for candidates with different policies, even if technically as part of a one-party state, within the limits of national policy.

China will continue to age as a society because of the one-child policy. Shortage of younger workers has been partly hidden by migration from rural areas. An additional challenge for China is that many families over the last 30 years have chosen to have a boy as a single child – either by selective abortion or in some cases infanticide. There is now a significant gender imbalance – 50 million women may be 'missing'. More Chinese men will look for a lifelong match with someone born outside China, using dating agencies and other means.

China will relax further its one-child policy, worried about the falling population of those of working age. Birth rates have risen 8% in a couple of years, but that will not be enough to supply all the workers that China will need.

Regionalisation within China

There is more than one China: culture, tastes and fashions vary hugely from one part of the country to another, together with what is permitted locally. Over 400 million people do not speak Mandarin. Expect large companies to decentralise decision-making within China rather than concentrate leadership in a city like Shanghai or Beijing. Expect more localised product development, branding and marketing.

Freedom of speech, religion and fertility in China

As we have seen, Chinese is already the dominant language of the web, and many of the world's greatest online companies over the next two decades will be born in China – now the centre of global, digital innovation. Expect the government to continue to walk a narrow line between embracing the freedoms of the virtual world and wanting to control it.

Senior government leaders recognise that major unrest could be triggered not only by lack of jobs and lower economic growth but also by anger over corruption, inflation, inequality, pollution, over-zealous censorship and lack of religious freedom. The government also fears wider contagion from regional unrest in places like Xinjiang, among Muslim Uighars, and also in Tibet.

Stamping out official Chinese corruption

Expect rapidly growing numbers of arrests for corruption. Many global suppliers of premium retail such as watches, perfumes and hotels have been hit by an absolute ban on expensive business gifts and extravagant lifestyles by public officials.

The fifty wealthiest members of China's National People's Congress are said to own more than $94bn. Expect many more probes into how and where leadership wealth was made. Over a million officials have been prosecuted, removed from office, disciplined or punished in other ways in five years.

Renewable energy will improve China's environment

We are already seeing three times America's investment into renewable energy each year, especially wind power, to reduce air pollution in major cities (and seize the global market in renewables). Expect far-reaching measures to reduce water pollution and food contamination. China now requires 15,000 enterprises to publicly report their air pollution levels, water use and heavy metal discharges in real time – until recently such matters were government secrets.

From export-led growth to domestic-market dominance

China's image as the factory of the world will change, as costs of manufacturing in China continue to rise. China will lose jobs to nations like Vietnam, Cambodia and Myanmar – even to Europe, Mexico and the US. China's future economy will be driven more by domestic demand from its own growing middle class, and by investment in new technologies such as high-speed rail, wind energy and biotech. Growth of retail spending in China is likely to exceed GDP growth by 3 to 5% on average over the next decade, as middle-class consumers save less, and draw down their assets.

China will rapidly buy up the world's assets

China's four sovereign wealth funds are already worth over $1 trillion, invested in government debts in other nations or ownership of global companies. China will go on buying up assets in Europe, America, Nigeria, DR Congo, Indonesia and other emerging markets – whether land, mineral rights, utilities, infrastructure, factories or service companies. In addition, China's largest corporations will seize majority stakes in major competitors across Europe and America over the next 15 years.

Back home, expect booms and busts in Chinese real estate, with risks of a severe banking crisis due to poorly controlled lending and accumulated bad debts, particularly in the state sector. Such a crisis could be large enough to destabilise and depress global markets for a decade.

We will continue to see bold, visionary moves by the Chinese government, resulting in giant nationwide industrial enterprises and breathtaking infrastructure projects. China will continue to spend between 6 and 8% of GDP on infrastructure for the next decade.

Territorial disputes and armed conflicts

China will expand its regional influence, largely through economic means. China is unlikely to be as territorially or militarily ambitious as other superpowers have been in the past, except in the case of sparsely populated islands, which would enable it to extract new energy or mineral resources. China will have challenges managing all the territory it already controls, including Tibet.

As with Russia, events from the Second World War are likely to continue to overshadow foreign policy, in particular the relationship with Japan. This particularly relates to alleged atrocities that are downplayed by many Japanese leaders.

Expect ongoing complaints by many global businesses and smaller investors that business is difficult in China. Expect some multinationals to pull out altogether, blaming a wide range of barriers to business, including corruption, red tape, hostility by government to companies that take profits out of China, careless attitude to intellectual property, ruthless self-interest, lack of transparency in business dealings, and so on. Revlon, L'Oréal (a Garnier brand) and Yahoo were among the first to abandon China. Many governments will continue to worry about IT contracts with Chinese companies supplying telcos or other infrastructure with equipment that could potentially be hijacked by the Chinese government for spying or other hostile purposes.

Chinese companies to watch

Alibaba – world's largest e-commerce platform, specialising in business to business sales.

Lenovo – bought IBM's computer business, now world's largest PC maker, bought Motorola's smartphone business, and IBM's server business. Third-largest smartphone maker after Apple and Samsung.

Huawei – second-largest telco equipment company in world, banned from US and Australia public sector contracts over fears that its equipment could be used to spy on behalf of the Chinese government.

Xiaomi – China's Apple – smartphone and tablets; threat to Samsung.

Tencent Holdings – 650 million users of messenger app, fifth-largest internet company in the world in 2014 after Google, Amazon, eBay and Facebook. Highly innovative.

Baidu – main search engine in China, with 66% of market, fits in with government rules.

ZTE – one of world's ten-largest smartphone companies, also telco network equipment. Expect huge success for their ultra-low cost smartphones.

China's economy will be three times the size of India's in 2025, but India will close that gap in the longer term.

Future of India – growth of global services

Alongside China, India will become a dominant world leader, as a highly globalised nation of nations, the largest democracy on earth, and already third-largest economy in the world in terms of PPP. India has a key advantage in international trade and service delivery because English is a national language, alongside Urdu and many other languages, unlike in China where English is hardly spoken.

Expect India's economy to grow 5–7% on average over the next decade. However, just as China is becoming too expensive a location for many multinationals in terms of outsourcing manufacturing, India is becoming increasingly expensive for outsourcing of services. Salaries are rising three to five times faster for senior managers in some sectors than in Europe or America. And as in China, India's long-term future will depend on the growth of its own internal markets.

A single state is larger than most nations: Andhra Pradesh, with over 200 million citizens, of which 75 million speak Telugu. The Minister for Health oversees no fewer than 114 medical and pharmaceutical colleges, while the minister for education has 15 universities, 131 engineering colleges and 600 industrial training institutions.

Young and highly ambitious, well-educated workforce

Half the population of 1.2 billion people are under 26, and this single fact will drive economic growth more than any other over the next 30 years. More than 66% of the national wealth is generated by India's 646,000 towns and cities, and this will increase rapidly with the arrival from rural areas of a further 300 million people over the next 25 years. Population growth is also the reason why income per head has remained much lower than in China, despite national economic growth – more wealth but more mouths to feed.

India's central government will continue to exercise far less national power than in China, and this will mean fewer large-scale national programmes for energy, infrastructure, industrial parks, and so on.

That said, India has already taken world-shaking decisions at high speed to demonetise the economy and enforce biometrics. In a single step, 80% of all bank notes were withdrawn, causing chaos, and forcing massive take-up of online payments. And in another single step, 850 million citizens had biometric data registered on a government record system, as the basis for secure payments and access to full financial services, even by those who cannot read and write. No other nation on earth apart from China could have driven such a profound digital revolution in such a short time, providing a massive boost to India's own IT sector.

Most important of all, India is a nation of industrious, well-educated and highly ambitious entrepreneurs, and is exceptionally well connected globally, with hundreds of millions of people in its diaspora, often in highly influential roles across the world.

Despite outward signs of busy chaos, India will remain one of the best places in the world for business leaders to make things happen fast. This is a country that is able to deliver from an empty concrete shell with no facilities a complete working call centre with trained staff and 24-hour video links to Europe, less than 12 weeks after signing a contract.

Religious caste and corruption in India

India will continue to be a highly tribal and religious society, with many internal tensions, particularly between the majority Hindu, Muslim, and to a lesser extent Christian, communities. Expect frequent outbreaks of ethnic mob violence and lynching in local areas, stirred up by social media accusations against people from other castes or religions, or against politicians, particularly at election times.

Discrimination based on caste has been illegal since India's independence, but many social, workplace and religious barriers remain, as caste has been fundamental to Hindu tradition for more than 3,000 years, and last names usually indicate which caste someone belongs to. The whole system will look even stranger in future to those from very different cultures, in nations that embrace absolute equality of every human being.

Corruption will continue to hold India back, despite popular anger and calls for reform. It is institutional, and at every level – some estimate that politicians and government officials may be pocketing bribes of more than $3bn a year.

India's global status

Expect India's national profile and military power to grow rapidly. Indian influence and culture will also be strengthened by more than 200 million Indian managers, executives, health professionals, teachers, lecturers, lawyers and accountants working around the world. India's voice is still missing at the table of the permanent members of the UN Security Council, at G7 leadership summits, and so on. This is unsustainable, and will change by 2030 as part of a restructuring of the UN and other bodies, to fit the realities of Asia's rise.

America declines in future power

America will decline in importance and influence globally, as emerging markets grow, representing 85% of humanity.

'Make America Great Again' was the powerful election slogan of President Trump, repeated hundreds of millions of times in homes, business meetings, churches and government agencies. Such slogans connected with fear that America is being seriously weakened by other nations, and by other threats, and is not the noble giant it was.

Yet America will *still* be the only superpower in 20 to 30 years' time, and many of America's multinationals will *still* dominate some global industries in 2040. While China has been a natural base for global manufacturing, and India for many global services, America will endure for several decades as a dominant 'home' location, with 128 of the world's largest 500 multinationals, accounting for 70% of all global trade. China is rapidly catching up, with 95 already.

America will remain rather isolated and strongly nationalistic, compared to all other developed nations over the next 15 years, rallying citizens around the American flag and other symbols of

American loyalty. At the same time, America is the most globalised nation on earth, and will continue to be a premier destination for well-educated, highly skilled migrants. America's future will be redefined by the emergence of nations such China, India, Brazil, Indonesia, Malaysia and the recovery of Russia.

America will take more than a generation to adjust to a more modest world status, as further global superpowers emerge. It will still be the case in 2025 that most US citizens do not own a passport. This will mean that most of the new generation will also lack experience of how people think and feel in other nations, which will result in lost opportunities, and will reinforce isolation.

Oil and health revolutions across America

As I predicted, America is now the world's largest oil producer, due to the vast boom in shale extraction, with a related boom in shale gas – all part of a national security objective, since 9/11, to be independent of other nations, such as Iraq, Iran, Saudi Arabia or Russia, for its energy. The impact of the US fossil fuel boom on global markets will last for decades, having also damaged growth of green tech by lowering prices for carbon (see p. 252 onwards).

America will continue a step-by-step transition to health care mainly funded by the state (already the case today), despite much hostility to the concept of free care. As we have seen, the US spends 30% more per person on health than any other developed nation – around $750bn, of which up to 10% is lost because of fraud.

America will continue to be a gun-loving and violent society, compared with Europe. America has the world's third-highest murder rate per million people – beaten only by Honduras and Venezuela. Guns are used to kill around 10,000 people a year, almost twice that number commit suicide using a firearm, and mass shootings are frequent. Ordinary citizens own over 300 million non-military pistols, rifles, shotguns and machine guns – more than the size of the entire adult population.

Influence of race and religion on future US life

America will also continue to be deeply challenged at times by issues of racial equality and prejudice, and by the fact that 45 million voters now speak Spanish as their first language.

Over 11 million people in the country are illegal residents, and have been there for an average of 13 years. America spends $2bn a year keeping illegals in detention, more than on the prison service, and the nation spends more on immigration control than on all federal law enforcement. Expect steps to be taken (eventually) to formally recognise most of the remainder as members of American society, while also stengthening the border with Mexico.

Despite a rapid decline in church attendance, America will remain deeply influenced by religion. Six out of ten Americans believe that God heals people in response to prayer. Four out of ten believe that God created humans just 10,000 years ago, and six out of ten oppose (almost) all abortion. Churches in America will tend to become much larger or much smaller, with a decline of medium-sized congregations, and will continue to be mainly right-wing, conservative politically.

Legacy of President Trump viewed from 2050

By the year 2050, President Trump will be viewed by historians as an eccentric, autocratic and controversial leader, who was able to attain office (preceded and succeeded by more traditional presidents) primarily through social media and large rallies, both of which enabled him to reach millions of supporters, exploiting their fears with simple, emotional messages. At every level, yet more secret Russian efforts at helping Trump into the White House will be exposed, as well as numerous actions by Russia to then undermine his credibility and paralyse his administration, as part of a wider strategy to weaken US and NATO leadership.

Indeed, Trump's presidency has already been severely damaged by long and embarrassing investigations into Russian links, and by the president's very hostile reactions to investigators, to the great advantage and obvious amusement of Russia.

As a conspiracy theorist, appealing to the masses with dark warnings of threats to America from China, migrants, terrorists and the Deep State, Trump successfully eroded trust in the judiciary,

FBI, CIA, State Department, most journalists, broadcasters and media outlets. He used the powers of the presidency to attack the credibility and influence of institutions and individuals that tried to hold him or members of his family to account. However, this will not be enough to enable him to deliver his political agenda, even if he survives impeachment efforts and is elected for a second four-year term.

His actions mean that it will be easier for presidents to ignore ethical codes on conflicts of interests, and misuse of executive powers. Trump will also be regarded as the first post-truth president of any developed nation, freely making up or exaggerating facts, while dismissing corrections as 'fake news'. His methods will be studied by autocratic leaders for generations.

He will be regarded by 2050 as an ineffectual president who often damaged American interests; lacked focus; failed to understand how to make things happen in government; could not build cross-party consensus; and was further weakened by high staff turnover. But Trump's lifetime appointments of many Conservative judges to federal courts will have a very long-term impact on ethical issues, civil rights, environment and government regulations.

As with all successful autocrats, Trump will continue to be a strong influence among his own followers, long after his presidency ends, however it does so, harnessing his talent for creating news.

Well beyond the tenure of President Trump, America will continue to polarise over migration, outsourcing of jobs, China's rise, abortion, global warming, environment, and military adventures. Future presidents will also struggle to navigate these issues, and to integrate America back into a closer relationship with the rest of the world.

President Trump's election and departure will raise more questions about the electoral process, including campaign funding, with powerful ties to business interests and even foreign governments. But these will not be enough to reform rules on funding.

(For a discussion on the reasons why all elected presidents have diminishing powers to make things happen, see Chapter 5, p. 237.)

Globalisation of retail and e-commerce

National and regional retailers are being hit by a wide range of global customer trends, each of which could destroy them in their present form. Indeed, every single trend in this book will affect retail to one degree or another. Just one of them is e-commerce, with Amazon alone now responsible for 5% of all retail sales in America. At $500bn a year, Walmart has hit back, with 40% growth in online sales in a single year, 1,000 pick-up locations and free delivery on all orders over $35.

Mega-chains will dominate retail growth

In many EU nations, over 70% of all retail spending is in just four or five retail chains, and across the EU as a whole, 50% of all food sales take place in just ten chains. In Germany, 37% of all food retail is now in budget stores like Lidl or Aldi. Expect to see a similar unstoppable trend in every other nation, driven mainly by global or regional retailers, unless governments pass laws to halt these semi-monopolies.

As a result of all this consolidation, national food and drink markets will be dominated by very small numbers of central buyers, setting national prices for milk, or bottled water, or other basics. This will be a very tough period for local farmers.

National price wars will become regional price wars. Big regional chains will push some national food industries against the wall, because they are able to import huge volumes of lower cost (and possibly lower quality) alternatives from other nations.

Sales by chains in the EU have grown rapidly – by up to 25% over the last 14 years, but floor space has often grown at twice that rate, so productivity has fallen. And the value of total EU food sales has also fallen over the last decade or so. One reason is, of course, that more people are eating out more often, and this trend will continue.

Too many new stores

Across every type of retail we have seen more shopping centres and other new outlets built, but for every square metre of new retail space, another metre needs to close and will close. Therefore, we can expect pressure on rents for commercial retail space, and see the demise of huge numbers of smaller stores, as well as some hypermarket outlets. And that is without taking into account the growth of online sales. No surprise, then, that in 2019 over 200 UK shopping centres were at risk of bankruptcy, a trend that is spreading across much of the developed world.

Many large out-of-town grocery stores will close across Western Europe over the next decade, as middle-class shoppers shift away from large weekly purchases, to buying food several times a week from local stores, open 24 hours a day, also owned by large chains.

Buying food 'just-in-time'

Around four out of ten adults in the UK have no idea by 4 p.m. what they are going to eat later that evening. Impulse, grazing, and exploring are part of the daily leisure routine.

Each community is different, and the most successful chains will use Big Data to predict different product combinations to stock in each local store for maximum sales. Over 60% of their trade will usually come from people who live less than 700 metres away.

Price, quality or brand?

Competing on price alone will mean a savage fight to the bottom on profitability. Only the largest and most efficient retailers will survive such a contest, and many will experience huge profit losses in the battle.

Apart from scale, the only other reliable way for retailers to compete on price will be to stay very *small*, with tiny overheads, trading from local market stalls, on street corners, or using virtual equivalents such as eBay.

Future of supermarkets and food retail

Hypermarkets, supermarkets, convenience stores, corner shops, niche outlets – all will be faced with similar challenges when it comes to selling food.

There are seven key things that each will offer but it will be almost impossible to score highly on all of them, and still make a profit.

PRICE – SPEED – CHOICE – QUALITY –
EXPERIENCE – INSPIRATION – TRUST

So a convenience store will focus on speed and experience, while the hypermarket offers lower prices and better choice, and the premium niche store goes for quality, experience and inspiration. The middle market in groceries is going to be squeezed further by discounters as well as by premium outlets. But they will all need to focus also on trust. Without trust a food store has nothing to sell, which is why reputation is vital in this industry.

Touch – smell – feel

One of the most important reasons that people shop physically rather than online is because they want to inspect what they buy. But many supermarkets are still wrapping most fruit and vegetables in tightly sealed plastic packaging. Expect more stores to direct fumes from their in-house bakery into the store entrance, or offer tasting sessions with regional cheesemakers or wine experts.

Improve the customer journey through the store

Many superstore layouts are specifically designed to confuse customers, so they take longer journeys that are constantly interrupted by special offers; designed, that is, to encourage impulse spending but guaranteed to frustrate and slow down a considerable number of people. As we saw in Chapter 1, customers are becoming very, very impatient and every second counts.

These kinds of errors may have worked in the past, and supermarkets may think they are being rewarded with additional sales, but in future they will find they are more likely to annoy and alienate customers, with more switching to smaller stores.

Smart offers at great prices

Every large store will use Big Data to create clusters of special offers, vouchers, discounts, sent to customers at home or on email or in SMS, based on things it 'knows' they will like.

Expect more retail chains across Europe and other nations to print price comparisons on every receipt, showing every customer how much their total bill would have been at three or four other main competitors. If they have spent more than they would have done elsewhere, the store will print a voucher equal to the amount they are 'owed'.

Specialist food retail outlets – many opportunities

We will see the return of the small specialist food store (at least in higher-income areas), satisfying customers who are looking for expert advice and inspiration from retailers who really know about their products – e.g. premium coffee, tea, wine and cheese.

Many niche stores of all kinds will be very successful (not just in food retail), offering specialist ranges of products to highly selective consumer groups for a premium price. The best stores will be run by a single owner-buyer-retailer with similar tastes, interests and style sense to its customers.

Street markets

Street markets will continue to be popular: providing buzz, energy, 'street atmosphere', local variety and niche experts. Expect larger chains to experiment further with market-stall atmospheres in parts of their retail areas, all in response to the greatest challenge of all to traditional retail grocery – boredom. Same products, same look and feel, same experience. Customers want consistency, but they also need to explore and to be excited.

Global e-commerce more than $5 trillion by 2025

Online sales are an even greater threat to traditional retailing than large chains or budget warehouses. Global online sales will roar ahead to more than $5 trillion by 2025, from more than $2.6 trillion in 2018, with most transactions taking place on mobile devices.

Over 30% of all UK shopping apart from groceries is already online, growing at 10% a year, mostly via mobiles, and more than twice the level of sales per person as America. E-commerce is growing at 30% a year in Asia. It all adds up to the biggest change in retailing for a generation, and will mean huge pressure on all physical stores in mature markets like the EU. And as physical retail declines, so we will see lower tax revenues from business rates.

Forget about shopping online or offline – both have merged into one activity. In most nations, online shoppers are almost entirely mobile: placing an order on a train, while sitting in the park, watching a film, or in a boring meeting at work.

Already one of the most common places for people in certain nations to do some of their online shopping is inside a traditional store – maybe comparing prices, researching, looking at customer reviews, perhaps ordering from the store's own website.

Expect new waves of disintermediation – where whole tiers of business get wiped out by technologies that allow people to go direct. An example is estate agents or travel agents, many of whom have already been swept aside by websites that allow buyers and sellers to connect at the speed of light. The best will survive, but only by offering specialist knowledge and excellent websites.

Counterfeiting and pirating of goods is already a $1.2 trillion industry and will continue to grow rapidly because of e-commerce, as it is less easy for consumers to detect before buying, less easy to assess the integrity of the seller, and less easy for police to track and prosecute, especially across borders.

Global premium retail

With over 500 million new middle-class consumers over the next 20 years, expect a boom in premium retail sales – whether of luxury handbags, fashion accessories, perfumes, gadgets, jewellery, lingerie, watches, fast cars or yachts.

The majority of middle-class consumers in emerging markets will continue to chase premier European or American consumer brands for the next decade. While we can expect several new global superbrands to emerge from India, China and Latin America, most will struggle to engage top-end consumers in developed nations before 2030.

Some consumers will react against endless premium malls and airport retail areas, with identical collections of boring outlets for global brands, and favour niche premium brands instead.

Threat from your own online store

Most stores will be strongly tempted to stick with the same prices online as offline, risking future growth. Some retailers will experiment with setting up a completely new online channel to run cut-price sales separately from their own brand. Others will face the risks head-on and invest heavily in online discounting.

Google and other large players like Amazon and eBay will sweep up huge sales with instant displays of 'unbeatable' offers, matched to web pages recently looked at by customers. Many shoppers will never get past the first display line of a Google search. The same is already happening to the travel industry.

Future of Amazon, Alibaba and similar retailers

Amazon is now the world's third-largest retailer after companies like Walmart, Carrefour and Tesco, with $232bn of sales a year. Amazon's assets are a global superbrand, with a simple website, and highly efficient warehousing and distribution, shifting a billion items a year.

Amazon's greatest *hidden* asset is its ability to provide any small business with its own e-commerce pages, created in minutes, with instant payments, cheap warehousing and fast delivery. Amazon already lists over 230 million items for sale in America alone – 30 times that of Walmart.

Four million businesses already sell on Amazon. This is likely to double by 2022. Most will sell exclusively through Amazon, especially where those businesses are able to shave a little off competitor prices. Amazon's revenues will also be boosted by pay-as-you-go cloud storage – already $25bn a year of sales.

Websites like eBay will create a new generation of young entrepreneurs, whose entire careers since junior school have involved buying and selling bits and pieces online – whether used toys, bikes and cars, or old china, camping equipment or spare solar panels.

Expect a boom also in micro-facturing – tens of thousands of home-based entrepreneurs who are making, marketing and shipping their own products, some using the most expensive 3D printers to fulfil orders.

Why home delivery is unfit for the future

In the UK, over 2 billion online products are delivered each year to homes – time-consuming because so many are not in when the delivery van arrives. We will see a boom in click-and-collect retailing across every developed nation. Order online and decide where to collect: local garage or coffee shop.

As I predicted, same-hour delivery is becoming the new norm for people in many cities, for a premium price. It means a more sustainable alternative to the online mega-warehouse. A customer places an order, routed to the nearest local store. Staff immediately order a taxi and get the package ready. The taxi uses an App like Uber to guide them to the customer, whether at home or work or in the local gym. For longer distances and higher-value products in rural areas, commercial drones will make the delivery.

Expect huge consolidation of home delivery services by online companies, aiming to make the last mile more efficient, which is where much of the cost remains. Product returns will be stream-lined, too – many people keep less than 50% of the clothes or shoes they buy online.

Retail in emerging economies

From Uganda to Congo, India to Vietnam, we will continue to see an almost identical retail experience. Despite all the trends noted above, almost all shops in the whole world will continue to be roughly the size of a single shipping container – never much wider or deeper or higher. One outlet next to another for mile after mile.

Such shops, typically with brick walls and tin roofs, are often living rooms of families who own them, and bedrooms at night. Lit by a single light bulb, such stores have an almost identical range of products as ten or twenty other similar shops within a few hundred metres. We see clusters of clothes shops, clusters of metal-working shops, clusters of furniture shops. The most important rule in retail location has always been co-opetition. And this will be as true in the slums of a megacity as on the streets of Paris or New York. Jewellers will continue to cluster, fish sellers will cluster. Such clustering will dominate physical retail globally for the next 100 years.

Malls will take off in all emerging markets

At the same time, expect growth in top-down mass retailing in emerging markets, despite e-commerce. Big companies will invade a completely new area where there has never been a single store a fraction of the size before. The first mall in a new area will usually be relatively informal, not air-conditioned, housing smaller shops. And then premium malls will follow, identical in many ways to malls in Europe, Singapore, Beijing and North America.

Boom in informal retailers

Alongside container-sized outlets, shopping malls and open markets, expect hundreds of millions of informal retailers for many local products such as water, soap, rice and flour – selling at traffic lights, on the pavement and from bicycles or small stalls. The key for every maker of lower-cost products in megacities will be these informal networks.

Manufacturers will divide more products up into tiny packages or bottles, to use for a single day or week, for those on very low incomes (bottom of the pyramid). Hundreds of millions of informal retailers on the street will be children in 2025 – street selling will often be their only means of survival. This will cause moral outrage in tourists from wealthy nations located many thousands of miles away, who think that all child labour should be banned.

Retail in Latin America heads online

Latin America is also experiencing an online revolution with more than $80bn of sales, including $26bn in Mexico, growing 40% a year, and $23bn in Brazil. In Mexico 58% of adults have online access compared to 46% in Brazil, 67% in Argentina, 59% in Chile and 34% in Peru.

Most consumers in the region are very uncomfortable about buying online, because they do not trust the payment system, but that will change fast. Most online sales are still on websites owned by traditional retailers but the big threat from pure online retailers will soon be felt.

Few people have credit cards or bank cash cards, so newer types of payment will take off. PayPal, for example, is already used for most online sales in Mexico. A hundred million people in Latin America are likely to move straight into a PayPal or mobile payment world, having never had a bank account or plastic card before.

Future of financial services, banks and insurance

Many predicted the death of banking as we knew it, following the 2008–2013 crisis, but our world needs strong banks just as it needs hospitals and schools. Banks are fundamental to every civilised society.

Trust is the most important thing a bank has to sell

Without trust you have no bank. You could say that trust is the only thing a bank really has to sell. The fundamental issue for many banks is how to rebuild trust after scandal upon scandal. This will require a revolution in culture and day-to-day behaviour – we will look more closely at this in Chapter 6.

Banks and their shareholders have been punished, mocked, blamed by societies. Owners of banks have lost huge amounts of money. But the main owners of bank shares are of course pension funds, so all of us have been affected. Expect more global regulations to force banks to hold more capital, with lower limits on the levels of risk-taking. But if regulation is too severe and returns on investment fall too low, no one will invest in banks, banks will be poorly led, bad to work for, with old technology, vulnerable to hacking, and providing last-century levels of service.

Rise of third millennial banking

Investment banking risks have already been separated from retail and corporate banking. We will see further regulations. But we can also expect to see some regulations relaxed by 2025. New types of banking services will also evolve, with ingenious work-arounds, enabling better investment returns with better managed risks.

Many predicted the decline and fall of the City of London as one of the world's dominant financial centres. As I said at the time, this was overstated. Whatever the final terms of the trading relationships between the UK and the EU after 2025, the City will continue to be one of the world's most important communities of the smartest and most experienced financial experts, from over 100 nations. The City will also continue to be one of the greatest generators of GDP in the UK.

Retail banking will become far more mobile, automated and highly competitive. As we will see later, banks will become telcos, and telcos will become banks, along with a string of new non-banking competitors who have all applied for banking licences in Europe and elsewhere.

Revolution in peer-group lending

Expect rapid growth of peer-to-peer lending, social lending or crowd-funding websites. Costs are less because connections online are short between lender and borrower, with no people in the middle taking big fees, and no banks involved. A huge advantage is that large numbers of small lenders can club together to share their risks in a single loan transaction.

China saw a massive boom from 2015 to 2018, with an astonishing $217bn of loans issued, but some investors lost huge sums and 300 companies went out of business following new regulations.

Brazil, India, Indonesia and Israel are passing new laws to facilitate safe expansion. Some $4bn is lent each year on such platforms in the UK alone, with average savings of at least 1% on interest rates from banks. The loans are mainly between 18- to 34-year-olds. Peer-to-peer lending is just a small fragment of the rapidly growing 'shadow banking' industry, and regulators are slowly catching up. In the past, such lending has been by individuals to individuals, but hedge funds and other financial agencies are piling in to provide lending capital.

Linked to this movement is crowd investing, which will also

boom: this is where large numbers of small investors club together to back an entrepreneur. Crowd-funding platform Kickstarter alone has raised over $4bn a day for entrepreneurs since 2009.

Boom in micro-loans and savings associations

One of the most radical and exciting innovations in banking is micro-loans. I have seen at first hand across different parts of India and Uganda the extraordinary impact of micro-loans on the poorest of the poor. There are now over 10,000 micro-finance institutions worldwide, growing 15–20% a year, and serving an estimated 200 million people, 25 million of whom are in India, with a total of over $50bn in loans/savings. Consider that in India alone over 190 million people have no access to banking. Globally, that figure is over 1.7 billion. Typically, over 97% of all micro-loans plus interest are repaid on time. These loans are used to start small businesses.

Micro-loan schemes are usually profitable, popular with many governments and are a gateway into traditional banking as well as micro-insurance products. Millions of savers have now been through two or three loan cycles and are proving creditworthy to traditional banks. That is why many investors are entering the market.

Future of corporate banking

High-end corporate banking will remain people-based, including treasury management, global money flows, advice on mergers and acquisitions, multi-currency, and multinational deals. Low-end corporate banking will go the same way as retail, moving to mobile, with a wide range of web-based portfolio management tools.

Future of private banking

Private banking used to be mainly wealth management for older, typically female, customers (because women live longer), with whom private bankers often had a long-term advisory relationship. New private banking clients will typically be younger, hyper-connected global citizens, micro-managing their affairs and with highly complex and rapidly changing business needs, demanding responses day and night at the speed of light.

A rapidly growing area for private banking will be philanthropic advice. Private bankers help make wealth for their clients faster than most can spend it, which creates a problem, since most clients are worried about spoiling their children or grandchildren, and cannot invent enough new ways to use the money themselves (see pp. 311–312).

Impact investing and social enterprises will be the fastest growing area of new investment in private banking over the next 20 years. Future generations will regard it as bizarre and irresponsible for someone who already owns $1bn or more to invest their money in commercial projects that do *not* result in a more sustainable future.

Why cash has such a long future

Despite predictions by bankers and 'digital gurus' about a cashless society, cash has never been so popular in many parts of the world. Many people love cash: for its anonymity, convenience and speed – and because it is invisible to the tax authorities. Cash use will continue to grow in the EU until around 2025, despite huge handling costs for retailers and banks.

Between 10% and 20% of all earnings across the EU are untaxed, depending on the country. Such informal cash transactions in the so-called shadow economy are now reflected in official estimates of the size of each nation's economy, along with revenues from illegal drugs and prostitution. (The latter is worth at least £4.5bn a year to the UK economy alone, out of more than £150bn total in the 'shadow economy'.)

EU nations with the largest 'shadow economies' include Belgium, Spain, Italy and Greece. The higher the tax burden on employers and workers, the more widespread tax avoidance tends to be. India's untaxed earnings percentage is at least 20%, if you include 85% of all workers who pay no tax. China's is probably around 10%.

Expect rapid growth of virtual cash: untraceable, anonymous

units of value such as Bitcoin, but more energy efficient, traded across the internet. Virtual cash will be hated by most governments, because it underpins the dark web, and is used to trade drugs, buy arms, pay ransoms, hire assassins or fund terrorists. China and South Korea have already banned or severely regulated Bitcoin and we can expect other nations to follow – while the rest will seek to regulate or tax its use (which will be difficult). However, every government will have to come to terms with cryptocurrencies, blockchain and related technologies, and embrace them.

Sweden leads the world in cashless payments, but China has the highest growth in cashless payments in the world. As already mentioned, India abolished 80% of all bank notes on a single day. Expect further bold moves towards a truly cashless society, coupled with huge expansion of services based on biometric identity. India already has the world's largest biometric database, but the big question is how to use it to make a positive difference to the lives of ordinary people.

Cryptocurrency booms and busts – reality check on Bitcoin and blockchain

Whenever a new technology emerges, it tends to attract money from two kinds of people: tech people who are close to the innovators, who really understand what it does, how it works and the global potential, and members of the public who are fascinated by the hype. And history shows it is usually the latter who are most badly burnt

The key to Bitcoin is that each Bitcoin is registered online to its owner, in a completely secure and anonymous way. Ownership can be transferred online to any other anonymous owner, and each transfer is recorded in a way that is (probably) impossible to tamper with. So Bitcoin exchanges are a radical alternative to traditional money: untraceable, uncontrollable, untaxable – hence the huge attraction to criminals or tax evaders.

Bitcoin prices rose from around $800 to $15,000 in a year, and fell from around $15,000 to $2,700 in the following year. Very few people on earth really understand the technology, and even fewer are able to work out genuine Bitcoin business from fraudsters and fools. Many people just invested in buying Bitcoins themselves, winning or losing vast sums in a form of digital roulette.

A single Bitcoin transaction uses as much electricity as your home for a week

Here are some facts about Bitcoin that will limit its future:

◆ Bitcoins have no actual value – the price people are willing to pay is based on what people think they may be worth in the future.

◆ Bitcoins are made by solving a complex digital puzzle. It takes a lot of computing power to create them.

◆ It takes 94,000 kilowatt hours of energy at the time of writing to produce a single Bitcoin.

◆ Bitcoin 'mining' uses more power globally a year than 180 whole nations put together.

◆ That's more power on this experiment last year than 2 billion of the poorest people used – 1 billion of whom have no access to a national grid.

◆ Power consumption is already equivalent to 25% of the UK's entire energy output.

◆ That's also equivalent to the entire power used by 4.3 million homes across America.

◆ That's the same as 24 megatons of carbon dioxide or 1.2 million transatlantic flights.

◆ A single Bitcoin transaction, logged in a blockchain, burns up as much energy as your home for a week – so forget about using Bitcoins as a global day-to-day currency.

◆ If Bitcoin mining and transactions continued to grow at the frenetic pace they did in 2017–2019, the total power consumed would be more than the whole world uses today for all of human existence, by 2022.

◆ Millions of computers have been hijacked by Bitcoin miners to create more Bitcoins for free – slowing the processors down and running up extra power bills.

◆ Bitcoins are fixed in number and as each of the remaining Bitcoins are found, the complexity of the puzzle increases even more.

◆ The limited number of Bitcoins, and the potentially unlimited ways in which they might be used in future, led to a frenzy of speculative investment, and then to catastrophic losses.

◆ Although Bitcoin transactions are in theory recorded forever on a blockchain register, Bitcoin trading exchanges have been hacked with losses of hundreds of millions of dollars.

It is astonishing that so much of the world's energy has been wasted on an experiment to produce digital tokens that no one in the world knows the real value of. What is more, such tokens are used today mainly by criminals to pay for drugs, arms, assassinations, or by ordinary people to pay ransom when kidnapped or blackmailed. Considering all the global challenges we face, and their urgency, and considering that a billion are hungry or lack clean water, mining Bitcoins hardly justifies the amount of carbon dioxide produced, even if people can afford to do it.

So here is the question, given that there are many ways of paying for things in the world, and Bitcoin is just about the most expensive, wasteful and inefficient, and prices are so volatile because based on no real asset: why would we attempt to build a global payments system on them?

So what about blockchain, which has been widely praised as the answer to all kinds of secure record systems – whether for large bank payments, logistics and supply chains, recording real estate transactions and so on. Blockchain is just an ultra-ledger, originally designed to support Bitcoin and other currencies. What is the point of a secure currency if you cannot record safely which coins have transferred ownership? The trouble is that blockchain is also affected by similar huge energy consumption challenges, and this is likely to be the case for some years to come.

E-payments will be dominated by China and India

In comparison to Bitcoin, traditional e-payments are almost free, take place at the speed of light, are easy to set up, easy to track, easy to audit and relatively easy to tax.

Global e-commerce transactions are set to grow by 13–20% a year, and will be worth more than $6 trillion by 2023. China's e-commerce market is already worth more than $1 trillion, more than twice the next largest region, which is North America, driven by Alibaba and JD.com, as well as Alipay and WeChat Pay.

A third of all e-commerce payments today are on smartphones, but this proportion will rise to at least 70% by 2025. As we have seen, most e-commerce transactions in the UK and many other nations like Vietnam are already on mobile devices.

Until recently, most small retail payments on mobile devices were taking place not in Europe or America but in Africa. And for several years, most m-payments in Africa were in Kenya, where over a third of GDP is already traded each year using M-Pesa alone. Around 25% of the entire population of Africa already has a mobile money account of some kind – compared to only 2% in Latin America. Africa has redefined retail payments, and Asia will be next. Take Singtel, for example, which has around 430 million registered SIM cards in its customer base, including partners. Of that, maybe 150 million are unbanked, with no access to financial services. I expect that up to half of these will carry out their first m-banking transactions over the next five years.

Free smartphones from your bank

As we saw in Chapter 1, the cost of providing free smartphones, tablets, web data, video calls and so on is falling rapidly towards zero. The cost of biometric ID is also falling, and it will soon be impossible to buy a smartphone without finger print recognition.

At the same time, revenues that can easily be captured by mobile payments are increasing fast. As a result, many payment companies will offer free smartphones, video calls, voice calls, mobile computers, broadband, perhaps even free movies – on condition that customers only use their smartphone for payments.

But that spells the end of traditional phone contracts, and the end of traditional retail banking. The most important and urgent question for every large bank or telco is this: who will 'own' the customer relationship?

As we have seen, the most important thing to know about any mobile customer is their location, which is the greatest single predictor of their next action. But banks are blind to location. Credit card and current account data only tells them about the past. Phone companies can predict the future: they handle every web page, every search term, every text, know which apps are down loaded, who the person calls and when. That is why banks will be forced to collaborate with telcos to offer next-generation financial services, within limits of privacy regulations such as GDPR.

Fight to own the new global standard

As we have seen, scale is everything in a global world, so there will be very few winners in global payments. Qualcomm has dominated mobile phone technologies for 2G, 3G and 4G for years, and up to 70% of its costs are legal, defending their patents. In a similar way, there will only be room for two or three truly global mobile payment systems.

Expect a huge fight among consortia of banks, telcos and IT companies – whether based in China, India, Europe or America. The prize will be tens of billions of dollars in royalty payments, from every financial institution, retailer and telco, for at least two decades.

A key complication, however, is that if a telco seeks to become a bank, it immediately becomes subject to all kinds of limitations on the amount of capital it uses, its reserves policy, and so on, in places like Europe and America. This means that the most radical innovations in mobile payments are likely to be in emerging nations, as they are today.

Why most banks are far too small

You could say that banks are primarily IT companies, trading payment data, plus a few financial experts and advisors. The primary vulnerability of banks, therefore, leading to loss of reputation and trust, will be IT failure or attack: lost confidential data, hacks into bank accounts, total systems failure including 'denial of service' attacks.

IT complexity and vulnerability has raced far ahead of IT budgets. In many banks, most efforts by IT departments are still spent trying to get very old 'legacy' systems to talk to each other. Each merged bank brings its own IT history, usually with unresolved mess from other legacy systems.

Not a single person understands all banking code

In all large banks that are more than two decades old, there is not a single person alive today who has a full grasp of all the IT systems, and how they inter-relate. Bugs may exist that no one understands, in areas nobody knows about, in languages hardly anyone uses now. Inter-dependencies are often overlooked. It usually takes up to seven years to sort out the mess from a merger, trying to get two old systems working together – paralysis instead of agility, while customers continue to change rapidly, leaving banks far behind.

Security costs and compliance costs are soaring

To make matters worse, cybersecurity costs are rocketing, and banks have many new compliance requirements. Large banks are being attacked ten times more often than five years ago. They are also dealing with huge numbers of customers who have been tricked by phishing attacks, using rogue bank web pages and other schemes.

Then along comes a highly innovative, customer-focused software company like Salesforce.com, with a development budget of $8.3bn a year, spent mainly on cloud-based call centres, that can set up in a matter of days. Using their system, a bank can transform customer experience overnight.

One must conclude, therefore, that a bank with a total IT budget of – say – only $900m a year, of which $820m is spent on legacy systems and security, is not likely to survive the next generation of mobile banking. Their IT innovation budget is far too small to keep pace with customer expectations.

Retail banks will need to collaborate to grow faster

But how will banks grow, achieving the right economies of scale in IT innovation, without being completely overwhelmed by yet more legacy problems? Many will form partnerships, either with FinTech companies or with other banks in non-competing territories. Expect all kinds of alliances between – for example – banks in Europe and Asia.

Some banks are dumping all their existing IT systems for retail, migrating customers onto new platforms, where new products can be added as simply as installing an App, with fewer complexities and unknown horrors for hackers to exploit.

Future of shadow banking

Our world needs efficient banking, with easy flow of money between lenders and borrowers. When regulations are tightened, then more lightly regulated forms of banking are soon developed. And so it is that shadow banking has grown.

Shadow banking (which describes a loose collection of companies providing financial services to other companies and very wealthy individuals in novel ways) caused the last financial crisis, and is likely to cause another. Shadow banking may include reselling packages of loans or unusual types of assets in private arrangements, hedge funds, private equity funds, brokers for state loans, virtual trading (where people bet on rises and falls of stocks or currency without owning any assets), and so on.

Because these groups are very hard to track, identify and define, they are hard to regulate. New types of financial products can emerge online in days or weeks, with offerings so complex that few understand them.

Governments have been less worried about regulating shadow banking than conventional banking, since major losses are more likely to be suffered by a few large investors rather than a million retail customers.

Future pensions and fund management – mis-selling

Much of the world's stocks and shares are owned by pension funds, which hold over $47 trillion of assets, most of it invested by fund managers via the world's stock exchanges. Fund management is likely to trigger a new mis-selling crisis at some point over the next decade, with fines and lawsuits likely to be so large that they will break some of the world's largest investment banks. Expect global reforms of fund management and the pensions industry.

This is an industry with awesome global power. Black Rock alone has $6.3 trillion of directly controlled assets, and oversees a further $20 trillion through their Aladdin Artificial Intelligence trading platform, carrying out 250,000 trades a day. Over 17,000 investment managers and traders around the world are influenced by Black Rock's analytical models to guide their decisions. A further $20 trillion of assets are run on SimCorp's Dimension platform. So the two platforms are handling around 40% of the total value of global equity. A single technical error by one of these robotic systems could trigger a massive cascade of automated responses by much of the rest of the market.

A 12-year survey of 2,846 mutual funds in America, overseen by 1,825 fund managers, showed that even managers who remained in the industry long term (presumably with the best performance) had no ability to beat the market on a risk-adjusted basis. All these fund managers use the same sources of information in most cases, and tend to focus on the largest stocks, so they find it hard to out-do each other (unless they break the law by insider trading).

Fund managers hate investing in actively managed funds

I have spoken to audiences of hundreds of fund managers over the years, with up to $1 trillion under management in a single event. Only a small minority would ever dream of recommending their own actively managed funds to their own friends and family, because they know very well that these funds usually destroy wealth, compared to ultra-efficient, low-cost computer trackers. This is a major moral issue, which is likely to call the integrity of the whole industry into question. If a fund manager is aware that their own active fund is likely on balance to deliver less than an equivalent tracker, then selling that active fund to investors could be regarded as unethical.

Considering all this, it is shocking that 89% of the value of global funds are still controlled by fund managers: too many funds, too many fund managers, duplicating research and decision-making. We will see more legislation in many nations over the next decade, enforcing transparency about all charges, capping fund management fees, and imposing additional compliance costs so that smaller funds become less viable.

One thing is certain. The total number of fund managers will fall rapidly, and the value of funds that they each manage will grow. Only the best performing will survive, and most smaller funds will be forced to merge.

New models of investing

We will see more boutique services allowing smaller retail investors to manage their own portfolio of investments online, in tax-efficient ways, right up to full pension provision, with live reporting data. Charges for such services will be low.

Younger high-net worth clients will invest less in large institutional funds and will use their own family offices more to manage their wealth, making many decisions themselves, particularly where investing in new technology, startups, or social enterprises. Family offices (small teams of advisors and staff, supporting the business interests of very wealthy individuals) now control $4 trillion of assets, more than hedge funds, equivalent in value to 6% of global stock markets.

Pension funds are likely to invest more heavily once again in hedge funds, but complexity will continue to create new risks. Pension funds will focus on hedge funds that are more easily understood. Expect a severe public backlash against hedge funds if we see failures of several more over the next few years.

Death of national stock exchanges

We are likely to see many more stock exchange mergers, across national boundaries and regions, to reduce technology costs, share marketing and increase liquidity, and more platforms trading 24 hours a day. It is curious that major stock markets still have fixed opening and closing hours, when the companies they list are often completely global, in every time zone, and traders want to trade without restrictions.

On some days, up to 85% of all individual trades on Wall Street are not 'real' trading decisions at all, but are made by robots/Artificial Intelligence trading machines owned by just 2% of 20,000 trading firms, reacting automatically to all kinds of data, sometimes with strange results. At times over the last few years, up to 70% of US trades on some days have been very high-frequency buy–sell actions by robots, holding stocks sometimes for just a few seconds. Only 30% of assets in US stock markets are still actively managed, with dramatic growth of tracker funds and other automated platforms.

High-frequency trading also drives up to 30% of EU trades. The new trading kings are mathematicians who fine-tune such algorithms.

Speed will be everything. Robots will continue to fight against robots to get trades executed a fraction of a millisecond before each other, which will require constant upgrades of ultra-fast cabling by trading companies, and many other techno-tricks. For example, some companies are using microwaves to transmit orders faster than other traders, who are still using old fibre-optic cables.

Subtle attacks will be far more common: for example a hypercritical report on a particular company, based on false data, promoted widely on social media by someone who has just taken a huge short-term bet on the share price falling. Such actions are nothing other than investor scams, designed to steal from real investors. The writers don't have to convince a single human being on Facebook, Twitter, LinkedIn or any online investor forum in order to win (although the online buzz is helpful) – all they have to do is trigger over-reactions by robots.

Expect all kinds of regulations in some nations to make highfrequency trading less profitable, and less easy to carry out. But this will not prevent the fact that we will continue to see a megashift from active fund management, with decisions made by very expensive teams, to passive fund management, where the fund is automatically adjusted to reflect the changing composition of the stock market.

Growth of spread-betting

We will also see rapid growth of 24-hour spread-betting websites, where individuals or companies bet on a share price movement taking place, without owning any shares. A million people in the UK alone have spread-betting accounts, with bets usually placed by smartphone, encouraged by full tax relief on all 'winnings'.

Billions of dollars of bets are already being made on the future price of any share, commodity, fund or currency. Many people will win or lose huge amounts in this global casino, as gains and losses are highly leveraged. A single £10 bet could win or lose £1,000 if not capped. All these kinds of 'derivatives' will create strange price movements, which at times will be very violent, confusing and destabilising. Expect many nations to regulate this industry, with new rules to cap losses.

Future of insurance industry – huge growth

Insurance is as fundamental to a stable and prosperous society as banking, hospitals and schools. Yet more than 3 billion people have never heard of insurance, do not know how it works, and have no idea how to get hold of it.

Expect rapid growth, therefore, of basic insurance in emerging markets, targeted mainly at the emerging middle class. Health insurance will lead the way, after insurance types that people are forced by law to buy, such as motor insurance. Expect a boost in many nations in sales of life or health products, encouraged by tax rebates, especially where they are structured to contain an element of saving. Many who are unbanked today will gain their first insurance cover using a smartphone, or through micro-loan groups and savings associations.

EU retail insurance dominated by home and motor

Most insurance sales in the EU will continue to be cover for homes or vehicles, with travel and life insurance following behind. Expect savage online competition from so-called aggregator sites that display competing quotes for the same risks from up to 300 different companies.

Price comparison sites of various kinds are now being used by 85% of all people who use the web in the UK. These sites are already seizing over 40% of the general insurance market in countries like the UK and we can expect a similar pattern in many other developed nations by 2020. Insurers will be able to win sales without offering the lowest price, but only by persuading customers of the value of a 'favoured' brand, one that will pay out when there is trouble, and handle a claim rapidly and sensitively.

Price comparison means huge fines for loyalty

Aggregators will provide a very precise mathematical tool for marketers to measure their own brand value. If the cheapest quote from an unknown company is $150, but the customer selects the third one down the list, which is a well-known brand offering a price of $230, then we know that the 'added' value of the brand to that person is precisely $80.

European insurance companies often offer very low prices for new customers, making their profits in following years by increasing prices for their most loyal customers. Expect growing numbers of customers to switch companies every year in response – to whichever insurance company is the most willing to throw money away with such unsustainably low pricing, until such a flawed pricing and underwriting model is abandoned.

Why many insurers will detach from banks

Many banks experimented a decade ago with their own insurance companies, hoping to 'cross-sell' insurance products to existing customers, but in most cases the results were disappointing. Most insurers will remain independent of banks, with partnerships and syndicates, but all held at arms' length. This is even more likely in future with different and complex regulatory requirements for each.

Re-insurance will be a vital part of the future of all large insurers, backed by huge corporations like Swiss Re and Munich Re. These companies will be taking views on every trend and Wild Card in this book, how they interact, what it all means for, say, business disruptions over the next decade in a particular industry, or for the risks of New Orleans being hit by another huge hurricane, or Russia invading Latvia. (For more on insurance, see pp. 219–220.)

Future of the travel and hospitality industry

Along with manufacturing, retail and banking, the travel industry will be a fundamental engine of future globalisation. Human beings are genetically programmed, as hunter-gatherers, to travel, and have an irresistible urge to explore. Therefore, whatever happens to the global economy, and in other world events, we can expect the number of people travelling each day to grow dramatically as wealth increases, and as real costs of transport continue to fall.

The greatest growth in travel will be within Asia, and in people from Asia visiting outside their own region. We will see a rapid increase in the number and size of regional airports, high-speed rail networks and new roads.

Future of rail – faster speeds, long distance, hyperloop

Twenty-four nations have already built high-speed rail links, and the length of high-speed track is doubling every decade. At present 98% of all trains running faster than 195km/hour are found in Western Europe or East Asia (90% in China, France, Japan, Germany, Italy, the UK and Spain combined), but high-speed rail will become more widespread.

In less than 15 years, China built over 25,000km of high-speed track to become the world leader, and is laying 7,000km a year of new rail, of which half will be high speed. Much of this was imported technology, with trains from companies like Siemens. However, the next wave of expansion will be almost entirely Chinese, and Chinese rail expertise will be exported globally. This is part of long-term Chinese government strategy to dominate high-tech industries globally.

Future investment in high-speed rail will be held back in Africa by unrest, in Russia by economics, in the UK by planning restrictions, in China as the backbone of a national service is completed, in Latin America by economic uncertainty, and in the US by a culture that prefers planes and cars.

Expect a boom in low-tech, rapid transport in cities, with automated 'light railways', or trams, or buses on special concrete tracks. These will be built rapidly, at relatively low cost, on pillars above streets, as tracks weave their way around cities.

Numbers of rail travellers will grow much faster in most countries than growth in capacity, so trains will become longer, double-decker, more crowded and more frequent.

Expect more experiments with hyperloop travel – carriages suspended by magnetic forces, travelling along tunnels or tubes from which air has been extracted to reduce friction. However, most of these projects will fail to make money, and will only progress if backed by huge amounts of investment by ultra-wealthy people as vanity projects. The fact is that air travel is convenient, easy to organise, and low cost. And high-speed rail is also a mature technology. Hyperloop's advantage is being able to deliver passengers right into the heart of a city at the speed of a plane, but tunnelling is extremely costly, and placing airtight tubes above ground, so that they cannot be attacked or damaged, is also very costly. And that's before you levitate carriages, and so on.

Future of aviation and air travel

Expect boom-time for aviation – with short-term blips caused by recessions, regional conflicts, threat of viruses, rise in fuel costs, or other adverse events. The number of journeys each year has grown more than ten times over the last 40 years to over 4.6 billion. Expect this to grow by an average of 5% per year for the next decade, and to double to over 9 billion by 2038, to exceed the entire global population. Chinese airlines alone carried 600 million passengers in 2018, up from 440 million in just five years. More Chinese people will take to the air than Americans by 2022, which is why the country will open 136 new airports by 2025.

Most growth of aviation will be in Asia, and the least in Europe / North America. Europe will see huge growth in long-haul visitors arriving from Asia, particularly from China and India. Some 200 million Chinese tourists will fly to visit other nations in 2020, and their spending on vacation will triple, especially on luxury goods.

Despite severe safety problems with 737 Max, Boeing has a seven-year backlog of orders for 5,000 planes worth $400bn, while Airbus has orders for 7,577, worth even more. Engine-maker revenues alone will be more than $1 trillion over the next 20 years. Over 70% of engines today are made by GE or CFM, GE's joint venture with Safran in France, another example of monumental scale in a globalised world.

Britain is the second-largest aerospace manufacturer after America, with 17% of the global market, and is home to 30% of Europe's Eurospace firms – Rolls Royce engines are used in half of all the world's new wide-bodied jets, BAE makes fighter jets, and AgustaWestland makes helicopters.

While virtual working, video calls and other technologies will grow, they will not be enough to prevent growth of business travel, as I predicted a decade ago. Business budgets will be capped, however, or cut, forcing business travellers to hunt for bargain flights, flying economy as a general rule unless long haul.

Cheaper flights in real terms

Flying is 60% cheaper today in real terms than it was in 1995. The aviation industry was changed profoundly by new budget carriers, who completely reinvented the process of selling tickets, filling and emptying planes. Expect all major budget airlines to offer premium features copied from traditional airlines by 2025, such as allocated seats, a free drink in-flight and free luggage allowances. This will attract increasing numbers of business travellers.

European budget airlines will carry more than 50% of all air passengers by 2030. As a result, all traditional airlines will be forced to radically alter how they work. Expect mergers of national carriers, and new global mergers, which will reduce costs.

Flying on less fuel – but planes will look the same and carbon will be taxed

New planes will become more efficient, and will fly with fewer empty seats. Flights will use less fuel per passenger because of: smarter air traffic controls (including 'free routing' to allow pilots to fly directly from A to B, saving 10 minutes per flight on average, and continuous tracking of all planes anywhere in the world using satellites); more direct flights using medium-sized planes, rather than huge jets feeding people into big airport hubs; shorter circling times around busy airports; better aerodynamics; lower weight; more efficient jet engines; and flying at higher altitude where air is thinner.

Expect a growing number of nations to impose carbon tax on aviation fuel, which is now responsible for 2% of global emissions. When road vehicle fuel is taxed at 70% or more, it makes flying far cheaper than it should be, in a world looking to encourage low carbon use. The 2020 UN cap covering 75% of aviation emissions, signed by 72 nations, will simply result in more carbon trading, offsetting their growing emissions by cuts elsewhere in the world. Electric-powered planes will be confined over the next 25 years almost entirely to vertical take-off, drone-like air taxis with limited range (see below).

Planes will outwardly look almost identical in 35 years' time, limited by the laws of physics and efficient air flow, passenger comfort and easy freight-handling. Indeed, flying has gone *backwards* in some ways since the launch of Concorde in 1969, flying passengers between 1974 and 2003 at supersonic speeds of up to 1,334 miles per hour (2,140km/h), at a maximum height of 60,000 feet (18,300m). Most aircraft today are slightly slower than they were in the 1960s.

But the pilot's own experience will be very different, with most of their work fully automated including most take-offs and landings. The result overall will be even greater air safety, but some of the worst crashes will be caused by major robot errors, machines fighting against desperate human crew for control of the plane.

Air passenger experience will hardly change at all over the next

30 years, apart from far better mobile messaging, ticketing and virtual passports, which will help streamline travel.

Most planes built in the last 40 years have a life expectancy of more than 30 years, or more than 30,000–40,000 flights. So most passengers in 2030 will be flying on planes that were already in use in 2015, maybe designed decades earlier. Jumbo jets were first built in 1969, for example, and some of the 1,435 that were built will still be flying in 2025. But seat width will increase because of growing numbers of overweight passengers.

Expect a new generation of carbon-fibre, supersonic passenger planes by 2028, with less nuisance from the usual sonic boom, although all will need to convince regulators that they can be permitted to fly above the speed of sound over populated areas.

In all developed nations, the average age of fliers will rise, together with the number of people with severely restricted mobility. This will provoke redesign of duty-free areas, instead of forcing everyone to walk three times as far as necessary to board a flight.

Future of cars: cheaper, faster, cleaner, smart

More than 1 billion cars are on the roads today. But we would need to see that rise to 4 billion for the whole world to have the same level of car ownership as America. By then, almost all of them will be electric-powered, and the majority driven entirely, or assisted, by robots. Inevitably, roads will be very congested, especially in city centres, many of which will ban private vehicles most or all of the time by 2030.

Most new car owners will be in emerging markets over the next 50 years. Chinese people are driving 230 million cars, more than any other nation, 8% of them owned by 40,000 car rental companies. Private car ownership in China jumped from 1% to 21% from 2002 to 2019, with more than 24 million new cars now sold a year.

Around half the population in the Philippines and Indonesia do not yet own a car, compared to only 3% in Malaysia, where 53% of households own more than one vehicle. In Thailand and Indonesia 80% of consumers hope to buy a vehicle in the next two years, and in most cases this will be the first car they have ever owned.

On the other hand, in many developed nations, car ownership will fall, as a younger generation refuse to follow the 'unsustainable' ownership patterns of their parents, preferring to rent as they go. This pattern will be accelerated by driverless cars, which will be more expensive to buy, and may feel ridiculous to actually own. We are already seeing the impact of the sharing economy on the number of households in many nations who are opting not to own a second car.

Mobile Apps will make it even easier to hire and drop vehicles for long and short journeys, at very short notice, and easier to hire a car with a driver (despite legal challenges to taxi Apps like Uber). We will also see more tax breaks, traffic lanes and other incentives to encourage car sharing by commuters as well as more car leasing.

Fuel efficiency of all fossil-fuel engines will improve, with use of nanotech coatings for all moving parts, and many other advances in engineering, as well as lighter vehicles. These gains will slow down (but not halt) sales of pure electric vehicles.

Electric cars have taken off more slowly than many manufacturers and governments hoped, held back by expensive batteries. New types of battery will be lighter, cheaper, more efficient, with faster charging and longer life. Tesla cars already have a range of 400 miles and 600 miles will be normal by 2025. It's to do with scale as well as innovation: Tesla's new battery factory will have a greater output than the entire world's battery production today.

Most sales of electric vehicles over the next decade will be smaller models designed for city use, encouraged by tax breaks for owners and subsidies for manufacturers.

But the greatest push towards electric cars will come from several European governments who are set to ban all sales of carbon-fuel cars within the next 15 to 20 years. As a result of this shift, and tremendous pressure from customers, every car manufacturer in the world is already switching most of its innovation budget to electric vehicles.

However, traffic jams in many larger cities will be a growing nightmare, especially in emerging nations where car ownership is growing far more rapidly than road construction. Drivers and passengers spend 90 billion hours a year in traffic jams. In some cities, a third of all fuel consumption is used simply in trying to find a parking space.

Self-diagnosing and self-repairing cars

In many nations it is already impossible to buy a car that is not online all the time, able to summon rescue, police or ambulance automatically in the case of accident or breakdown.

Brazil will soon require every new car to have a built-in tracking device to prevent theft. America's highway agencies are working on proposals to force all new cars to have the ability to network with each other (Vehicle to Vehicle or V2V). Expect all large car makers to adopt the technology from 2021 onwards, well before legally forced to do so. Revenues from services, devices and infrastructure for online vehicles could be worth more than $200bn by 2025.

All new cars will self-diagnose problems before they happen, with sensors across vehicles to monitor tyre pressure, brake pads, piston compression, battery condition, gas emissions and power use. We will see more head-up displays, with speed and fuel indicators, and a wide range of informatics including navigation and messaging.

Cars will also watch driver behaviour, so that insurers can price each day's premium on yesterday's driving patterns for that particular driver. This will help people to drive better and at lower cost, because insurers reward good behaviour. Police will argue that they should be able to get access to the same data.

Who owns the driver?

Drivers will expect new features for the basic price, so manufacturers will be stuck with more costs. As in banking, the key issue will be: who owns the customer? Indeed, who owns the vehicle? Manufacturers will try to hit back with a one-stop solution. So, for example, they will send details of breakdowns, faults or accidents directly to their own dealers, rather than to local garages.

Car manufacturers are already offering a far wider range of ownership, as motorists move from traditional 'buy and keep'. Telcos, makers of networking devices, producers of apps and V2V services will build their own clusters of technologies. They will try to push back manufacturers into more limited roles.

Semi-automated cars will soon be almost universal

Apple and Google both want to control car information. The vision is that cars will constantly exchange useful information without bothering the driver. Live traffic information, common mechanical problems, best fuel prices, updates to maps. V2V communication will eventually mean the end of traffic lights in some cities, as each vehicle perfectly times its approach to every junction.

Self-driving cars – with legal issues

Several companies will soon be selling 100% auto-drive vehicles, but they will not be widely used outside European cities, America and Asia until 2030, because of fears about safety. Expect rapid growth in robotic farm tractors and industrial vehicles, for example in open-cast mining. But in cities, it will only take some high-profile deaths of child pedestrians to slow down the introduction.

The question is this: if a robot kills a pedestrian or an occupant in another vehicle, whose fault is it? Who goes to prison? Vehicle owner? The manufacturer? Software company?

More than 1.3 million people die in road traffic accidents a year (more than deaths from malaria or TB) and 50 million are injured. A key argument will be this: robot drivers make fewer mistakes, so even if some people are killed by robots, fewer will die than if humans drive.

Once insurers recognise that accidents are fewer when robots drive, expect a discount for every mile on 'robot' mode, and extra costs to drive on 'manual', with normal rates for 'assist'. By 2035 it will be considered by some to be selfish, antisocial and dangerous to insist on driving yourself. In the meantime, robot drivers need to be more efficient – self-driving cars consume 20% more energy because of the computing and sensors involved.

Homeless cars, car trains and flying cars

In the world of driverless cars, you will step outside your home to find the car roll up. You don't own it but it feels like yours. A variation will be 'car trains' where many cars are in convoy on motorways, metres apart, to save 20% energy.

So-called flying cars will still be rare and expensive in 2030, owned only by the super-wealthy, or rented per trip by premium taxi/air transport firms, but only permitted in most nations outside major cities, partly because of noise pollution. The most common technology will be drone-like rotors offering stable computer-driven, battery-powered flight for one or two passengers over short distances.

Space travel and colonies on other planets

Space tourism will grow, with at least three companies carrying up to 1,000 passengers a year into space on short flights by 2035, despite tragic accidents. This will be yet another example of an increasingly bizarre world, where risk-seeking ultra-wealthy people play in orbit, while 1 billion people still lack clean water or food.

We will see a new Space Race, dominated by China and Russia, with some American and European action, aiming to colonise the moon, and then Mars (one way ticket at first). Expect a small residential unit on the moon by 2030–35, with no useful economic purpose. America's space budget will focus on defence. An important new justification will be threats from comets, with an increasing number identified across space, each of which could devastate the earth.

Most spending on space to 2040 will be satellites for better geo-positioning and bandwidth. Space will become a potential battle zone, with hundreds of space drones. These will be used to repair, capture, interfere, hack or destroy satellites – and destroy drones from other nations.

Most will be owned by America, Russia and China. America spent $98bn in a decade researching ways to knock out intercontinental ballistic missiles, with little success – even more difficult when any satellite can be a drone in disguise, and any low-orbit satellite could contain a nuclear missile.

A major space hazard will be tens of millions of pieces of space debris, orbiting at huge speed, from accidents and military tests. A single attack on one satellite could create enough tumbling debris to damage other spacecraft for a decade or more.

Future of hotels and holidays

The number of people taking more than one annual holiday will double over 20 years, with soaring numbers enjoying city breaks. Half the UK takes at least three holidays a year away from home.

Expect many more culture holidays, exploration holidays, learning holidays and activity holidays. Expect growing popularity of holidays involving risk, excitement, tests of endurance and unique experiences, offering extremes of hot and cold, ranging from the United Arab Emirates to Greenland, the North Pole or Iceland, with strong emphasis on eco-aspects or sustainable tourism. We have already seen that medical tourism will also be a booming sector (pp. 110–111).

Older travellers look for new experiences

Middle-aged and older travellers will look for unusual experiences – deep-sea exploration, travelling to the Antarctic, learning to sail a yacht, fly a glider, climb a high mountain. So many people will try to climb Everest each year by 2025 that numbers will be strictly rationed.

Cruise ships will grow in number and size, carrying over 45 million passengers a year by 2028, compared to 26 million today, in a market already worth $46bn. These ships will be based mainly in the Caribbean and Mediterranean, with some growth in Asia and to exotic locations such as the Antarctic. Many ships have become destinations in their own right, with over 6,000 passengers and 2,500 crew. Larger ships are already restricted in ports that can cope, so we will see a boom in mega-cruise docks.

The average age of cruisers is likely to fall by five years over the next decade, as more families try the experience, offset in the following decade by more older people with money to spend. Expect growth in smaller, specialist, themed cruises for the retired who want culture, history and expert learning, or to learn new skills such as painting.

Impact of web on hotels, travel agents and airlines

Websites like Airbnb will continue to transform the hospitality industry globally, by creating a vast informal market for people who want to rent out a room or their entire home, matched to others who want low-cost, personal alternatives to hotels. This will erode growth of budget hotels, but they will still expand worldwide, offering 100% more rooms in a decade, as the total number of nights away from home globally continues to rocket.

Traditional travel agents are in free-fall, and will be almost wiped out in many parts of the world by 2030, except for niche specialists. Everything they offer will be available online at the same or lower prices, and they will be unable to earn as much in commission.

Many package holiday companies will face meltdown, driven to the wall by online tools that assemble complex combinations of hotels, flights and car hire, at unbeatable prices.

However, the best tour companies will do well: offering expert insight into poorly known destinations in exotic places, specialist guides, well-constructed journeys and extraordinary experiences.

Future of education – new ways to learn

Over the next three decades, education in many nations will start at a younger age than it does today. Education outside the home for three to five-year-olds increased by 10% to 85% in OECD nations in the decade to 2016. This will be driven by parents in two career households, and by research showing how important early learning is to later success.

School and college is all about preparing a new generation for their future. In many cases, we will be educating for jobs that have yet to be invented, but most teaching is locked into the past, training for tasks that no longer exist.

Take examinations: how absurd to force young people to scribe indelible symbols onto pieces of paper, and to lock them into rooms without access to their digital brains. Cambridge University is considering allowing students to write exam papers on laptops, partly because examiners can't read their terrible handwriting.

Many other universities already allow exams to be written on computer if people have a disability that means that writing is difficult or impossible. Yet handwriting in exams will still be the dominant mechanism for proving student knowledge by the year 2030 in almost every part of the world. But work means using keyboards, not pen and ink.

The whole basis of education will be questioned. For example, what you can remember is now less important than it was. What really counts is understanding how to make sense of streams of data, picking out patterns, seeing context, and knowing what sources to trust. Skills that really matter are: search/collate/ interpret/analyse/summarise/conclude/decide. Of course we also need memory, on which we base all experience, but not in order to regurgitate facts.

Radical change to teaching methods will be needed

Classroom teaching has hardly changed in 50 years, apart from the introduction of digital whiteboards, digital image projection, and the use of personal devices in class. As we have seen, young people's brains are being profoundly altered by digital tech, and that includes the ability to concentrate on learning, and the ability to reflect.

Around 60% of 18- to 34-year-olds in America think that four-year college education offers bad value for money, and universities have seen six years of falling enrolments. In lectures with 70 or more students, 51% complain that they can't hear what is said, 41% find it hard to read what is on the screen, 34% are distracted by noise outside, 50% are distracted by their digital devices, and 45% are distracted by what their neighbours are up to on their own devices.

Expect rapid expansion of new educational tools, including short, interactive video, designed to fit the curriculum. But the basics of communication will also need to be fixed.

In education, one of the worst crimes has been plagiarism: where a student copies paragraphs from another source. But in business, if an executive has to assemble a report very rapidly, about an area they know little about, the issue is not whether the whole report is *original*, but whether that report is *accurate* and *useful*. Expect educational skill teaching to adjust to this reality.

Tougher rules for schooling

Expect a return to single-sex schools in many areas where co-education has resulted in tens of thousands of boys dropping out. Expect persuasive arguments that single-sex education for both sexes means sharper concentration and fewer distractions or showing off, especially with the age of puberty falling to eight or younger in some girls.

Expect a complete rethink about punishment and discipline, with recognition that a no-touch policy isn't working in many nations. In many schools, the playground culture can be threatening, bullying and very violent, not only to pupils but also to staff.

A high percentage of teachers in state-funded schools across the UK have been threatened with violence or attacked at school, while pupil stabbings and shootings outside school have become far more common in inner-city areas, linked to turf wars, drugs and gangs. Expect strident calls for teachers to be able to teach without fear of attack by pupils or parents.

Expect greater powers to suspend or expel pupils for antisocial or violent behaviour. Expect growing expenditure on special needs schools for the most disruptive pupils. Despite the trend to try to integrate the worst behaved with the best behaved, most schools will not be able to keep their most disruptive pupils, as emphasis grows on getting results. Expect continued ghettoisation, with people choosing a state school in a 'nice area' and then working out which home to buy nearby.

Future of universities – big shift to Asia

University education will be dominated globally by India and China, who already each produce more high-quality graduates in many disciplines than the rest of the world all together. Despite this, many of the best Asian students will head for top European or American universities, to broaden horizons and forge networks.

Free lecture videos – so what are you selling?

All universities will be faced with a huge dilemma – along with every business school. Do they record lectures by professors and other faculty? And, if so, do they place those lectures online for students on the closed university intranet, or make them publicly available? And if they do go down this route, will anyone still want to attend the physical lecture?

Universities like the Massachusetts Institute of Technology (MIT) have recorded lectures for 15 years, giving them away online for free, and others will follow. I have been doing the same for two decades.

Some business school professors fear that their material will be 'stolen', but experience shows that offering free online access makes business sense, as well as being the 'right' thing to do. As a result, we will see vast growth in the quality and range of free education, available online in every nation. Of course, it will put extra pressure on any lecturer who never alters their material.

All of this will be a great challenge for paid distance-learning courses, which offer password access to videos and course materials, video tutorials, plus someone to mark essays and perhaps a residential week or two.

As we have seen in other contexts, people want to breathe the same air and learn from others in groups. Group experiences have great power to change people profoundly, especially when a group is together for a year or more of study. So physical tutorials, workshops, seminars and lectures will continue to be important.

Videos are great for *information* but useless at *transformation*. Online videos are no substitute for a shared learning experience in the classroom. Universities and business schools will focus increasingly on *personal transformation*, interactive learning (rather than groups just listening to experts) and on building educational tribes, in order to survive.

Education gets longer (and longer, and longer)

Despite the growth of informal online education, most people will spend even more time in formal education by 2030. We have already seen how parents are hot-housing their children from their early years, while job markets are so competitive that students are forced into second or third degrees, in many cases because their first degree was useless for the workplace.

However, most first, second or third degrees (including MBAs) are poor substitutes for a year or two in a stretching business. And as the cost of degrees soars, with less government subsidy, even more people in developed nations will question the value of a degree. Four-year college degrees may cost up to $160,000 in the US, including food and accommodation, but the real cost is more than doubled by losing four years' earnings.

In the UK, government grants hardly exist, while student debt has soared to the point where, as we have seen, 10% of female students are selling their bodies for sex, pole dancing, doing escort work, or stripping off in front of webcams in order to survive (see p. 154). This is hardly a sign of a civilised society. Expect a policy rethink.

Countries like South Korea and Malaysia will rapidly expand engineering and biotechnology courses, reflecting strong government commitment to expand industries in these areas. Numbers of students for courses such as music technology or anthropology will fall rapidly in countries like the UK, as more statistics show disastrous employment records for post-grads.

Consulting, accounting and law firms

There are very few global consulting and accounting firms, and this is already causing big problems for regulators, unhappy when the same companies audit the same accounts for years. We should be worried when auditors are from the same organisation as consultants, when huge companies find members of their teams on both sides of complex deals. It is hardly surprising that so many audits of multinationals have turned out to be so misleading to investors.

Arthur Andersen disappeared almost overnight as a result of the Enron scandal, and it will take only *one* more such event to create a crisis, because only three global firms would remain. Expect further regulations about companies needing to change their auditors every few years, and more restrictions on conflicts of interest.

Auditors will be strictly audited

Auditors will increasingly be held legally responsible when banks or insurers or other types of company fail spectacularly, soon after a clean audit. It is outrageous that global auditors have been able to walk away without penalty, from large companies that collapse, only days or weeks after being paid hundreds of thousands of dollars to vet them for accounting irregularities and risks.

Auditors will be called more strictly to account for such appalling failures in their own processes, for giving false and dangerous assurances, based on too narrow a view of the business. Auditors will no longer be able to hide behind 'standards of compliance' in their audits. They will be expected to probe for *truth*, to ask the difficult questions, and to place their own reputations (and existence) on the line in the robust assurances that they give.

Legal services move to mass-market budget retail

Global law firms provide clusters of legal experts who are able to take a view on highly complex issues, particularly across territories. Few are structured in the right way to support the future needs of global companies, often led as they are by senior partners who are professionally expert but may be incompetent in a global CEO-type role. The most important question for a global law firm to answer is this:

If we were building a large firm from scratch, would it look like us? And if not, how can we fix it?

Expect rapid change in how smaller-scale legal services are delivered, with a growing trend to 'retail legal' teams, operating out of call centres, shopping malls, and so on, or completely online using simple questionnaires to generate a huge number of highly complex, completely customised legal documents in seconds at very low cost.

Many kinds of standard legal practice will be automated

– including aspects of employment law, consulting contracts, buying and selling property, making a will, divorce proceedings, personal injury claims, and so on. One-off legal advice will increasingly be offered online, either using chat screens or email, or video calls. We will also see more outsourcing of basic legal services by larger legal firms in developed nations, to teams in countries like India.

More countries will follow Australia and the UK in deregulation, to allow non-legal firms to offer such services, and teams of legal experts to raise capital in the markets. We will see many new companies offering expert legal advice, in a highly efficient, rapid and customer-friendly way, breaking with all the familiar ways of doing things.

Law itself will change profoundly over the next two decades, influenced by every global trend. For example, False Memory Syndrome will continue to feature in legal actions that rely on uncorroborated accusations or confessions, especially over sexual behaviour – false memories can be implanted easily and unintentionally during conversations.

Future of diversity and innovation – for global insight

To manage in a universal world, we need universal teams, but corporations are often too tribal. Most large companies are monocultural: dominated by nationals from one country.

While this brings strength – loyalty, team spirit, better communication and faster decisions – it also carries huge risks, with such companies more likely to miss investments or partnerships in new territories, and more likely to make major mistakes. What is more, monocultural teams are very unattractive for people from other nations to join.

Key to innovation will be more diverse teams

Among CEOs of large corporations, 85% say that diversity is the key to innovation. More diverse or universal teams find more ways around problems, and better alternatives. Diverse teams are better connected across markets and communities, less likely to have blind spots, more able to see opportunities, have wider skills and experience, and are more likely to draw highly talented people. Diverse teams are more likely to understand diverse customers.

More women, ethnic minorities and foreign nationals in senior positions

In many developed nations, girls outperform boys at school, and women outperform men at university. Most new doctors in many countries now are women. And in many business schools most of the best MBAs are female. Yet few board members are women, and women leave corporations every year in significant numbers. Expect a wide range of measures to change this, some forced by regulation, for example gender quotas on boards, as have been imposed on corporations in Germany.

But the focus needs to broaden beyond gender. Take senior management in the UK, for instance, which is almost entirely white, even though a growing percentage of the population is Asian, African, Afro-Caribbean or from other non-white ethnic groups.

Repeated surveys prove how many barriers there are for ethnic minorities. These are often caused by subconscious but strong racist attitudes, often in 'decent', 'tolerant' people who would be horrified to think they were in any way biased.

Most white people have very limited insight into the number of such barriers in their own workplaces, communities or nations. Children are often exposed, from birth, to negative messages, whether from neighbours, from playground taunts, unconscious or conscious facial expressions, half-hidden comments in shops, railway stations, airport lounges or law courts. And, when you add ethnic, gender and age discrimination together, the impact can be overwhelming.

This whole issue will matter more in future, not only as an issue of caring and justice, but also for customer insight and marketing. How can you provide world-class support to a customer group that you do not properly understand? How can you underwrite risks accurately in a community you have never been a part of? Increasing diversity, therefore, will be one of the most important ways for leaders to grow their companies, stimulate innovation, reduce risks and increase customer loyalty.

★

So, then, we have looked at a fast, urban, tribal and universal world. To many people, the picture may seem reasonably complete, but two more Faces of the Future remain. A world driven by radical agendas and ideologies, where every decision will be influenced by a rethink about ethics, values, personal motivation and spirituality.

Chapter 5

RADICAL

AS I PREDICTED 20 YEARS AGO, radical, revolutionary forces are sweeping across parts of our world, bringing new kinds of leaders to power in unfamiliar and disturbing ways, and will continue to do so. A cluster of 'democratic' revolutions swept away the Soviet Union from 1989 to 1991. For a while, Western governments talked about a peace-dividend as they cut military spending.

The collapse of communism left an ideological vacuum, with no balance to a Western narrative of capitalism, materialism, free speech, human rights and free market thinking. Only one superpower remained, a self-appointed policeman of the world. This helped unleash new radical forces, many of which continue to be deeply resentful of and intensely hostile to America and all it stands for.

Dot.com delusions of an age of global tolerance

A decade later, at the height of the dot.com boom, many technogurus made false and naive predictions that global access to the web would make our world more tolerant. It would democratise society, undermine dictators and contribute to global harmony. But they forgot the dark power of tribalism linked to emotion; how easily the web amplifies the most radical and extreme voices; and how rapidly social networks can create new movements.

They also failed to see how easily groups like Islamic State could restrict web access in territories they controlled, broadcast terrifying propaganda on social media, torture and kill hostages, discourage journalists from entering the region, and make it almost impossible to know what was really happening.

At a time of so-called universal media access, this was shocking and a big wake-up call. After all, if a relatively informal and small group like ISIS could do this, what about a national dictator, or highly autocratic leader, abusing all the tools of a digital super-state? As we have seen, control of the web is strengthening every day across entire nations such as China and Russia, affecting more than a third of humankind.

Rise of radical activism and extreme ideologies

For almost two decades I warned about the growing impact of radicalised activists and how they would change politics in many nations by 2020. Activists driven by extreme religious ideologies, by hatred for a people or a country, or by single issues such as climate change, immigration, abortion, animal rights, religion, ethnicity or nationalism.

Radical ideologies will feed future terrorism

Terrorism has always been the radical edge of political activism. So if you want to see future terrorist agendas, look at the fringes of political movements. As in the past, most terrorist groups will continue to be relatively small, tribal, informal, fragmented, mobile and short-lived. Most will be local rather than globalised, using any means to frighten, sabotage and attack for the sake of a cause, seeing themselves as moral freedom fighters.

Much of the recruitment to terrorist movements is fuelled by a narrative about rich versus poor and freedom from oppression, a narrative that is often anti-Western in nature, all of it amplified by social media, and by growing inequalities of wealth and opportunity.

Terrorist groups tend to be on the margins of society, seeing themselves as agents for radical change – and they usually lack significant resources. Terrorists, therefore, are driven to maximise efficiency: always looking for the greatest possible impact from each action, with an eye on what will capture the most social media attention.

That means school shootings, bombs in shopping malls, random stabbings, driving cars at pedestrians, flying drones with sharpened blades into the faces of children or politicians, and a host of other local atrocities. Every home has a kitchen knife, every licence holder can hire a car – so such acts need neither group support, nor big finances, nor much planning.

In that sense it is perhaps surprising just how rare such types of violent attacks by individuals actually are, since most are so easy and cheap to carry out, and impossible to prevent.

The reason for their rarity is that such acts require overcoming a powerful human instinct to protect others from harm. Many who commit such appalling acts over the next decade, therefore, are likely to be towards the psychopathic end of personality spectrums.

We will also see more economic and anti-corporate terrorism directed at things and not people, because these are easier, psychologically, for 'ordinary' people to justify to themselves: spiking food products in shops; cutting optic cables; damaging huge satellite dishes; or launching computer viruses. And there will be more state-sponsored terrorism as conventional wars become more difficult and expensive.

Tomorrow's larger terrorist groups will also try to buy or steal things like germ warfare weapons that can threaten a city yet be carried in a briefcase.

One in 350,000 risk of death from terrorism

Despite the impression we might get from watching the news, actual numbers injured or killed in terror attacks will remain almost insignificant compared to all other causes of death. Lifetime risks of witnessing a single act of terrorism will remain effectively zero in most parts of the world. So the real vulnerability to terrorism will come *not* from physical threat, but from *irrational fear*.

Deaths from all terrorist attacks globally are less than 20,000 a year, mostly in Iraq, Afghanistan, Pakistan, Somalia, Yemen, Syria, Lebanon, Libya and Nigeria. Globally, that is an average risk of 1 in 35,000 of being killed each year, the same as being struck by lightning at some point in your life. But if you live outside the most troubled parts of those nations, or in other parts of the world, your risk falls to 1 in 350,000 a year.

Thus the greatest challenge in future will be for government and community leaders to help restore a sense of reality, so that people can go about their normal lives without exaggerated fears, based on common sense, rather than social media hysteria and nonsense.

The only way to ensure future terrorists cannot win

Eventually, it is likely that the public hysteria portrayed in the media over individual acts of terror will subside, evolving into a more rational and pragmatic response, in recognition of the fact that the greater the reaction, the greater the win for the terrorist.

Media of every kind provides protest groups and tribal factions with huge coverage at zero cost, allowing them to hijack national agendas and disturb the well-being of tens of millions with an act as slight as attempting to stab a single tourist. Placing stories about terrorist acts routinely on the front page or at the top of TV news bulletins will be seen as counter-productive and antisocial, because it gives terrorists exactly the reward they desire, and encourages more of the same, especially if they or their causes are named.

History shows that all communities hard hit by terrorism go on to develop psychological resilience, so that each new terrorist act causes less impact, and is no longer considered particularly *newsworthy*. As we have seen in Iraq, under the most terrible of circumstances, in cities where car bombs are a daily reality, most people decide that life must go on. They drive to work and shop in the local market.

In other nations, we have seen the same. By the end of the Second World War, 25% of all houses in London were damaged or destroyed, mostly by random bombs raining down from the sky – but life went on. It was the same in German cities that were hit repeatedly by RAF bombing raids.

During the height of the IRA terror attacks in the UK, daily life also continued. One bomb was so close to our home that it shook our windows. Another missed killing our eldest daughter by minutes. But none of us changed our daily routines – as a matter of absolute principle. Why let terrorists win?

Why democracy is in deep trouble

Only 40% of the world's population lives in nations with free and fair elections, and many democracies have moved towards autocracy over the last decade. Examples include Russia, Argentina, Venezuela, Ukraine, Turkey, and Belarus – all hold regular elections, but have strong controls on the media and on opponents. South Africa's ANC has become increasingly hard to challenge. In Bangladesh, Thailand and Cambodia, opposition parties have refused to accept election results, or have boycotted the process. President Trump has been the most autocratic leader of America for a hundred years or more, attacking both press and the judiciary on almost a daily basis, and questioning election results.

Very few nations have long experience of democracy

Surprisingly few developed nations have long democratic traditions. Democracy began only in 1978 in Spain, in 1975 in Portugal, in 1946 in Italy, in 1918 in Germany (with interruptions under the Third Reich), and, following its ancient Athenian invention, in 1956 in Greece, although the army soon took over.

New democracies fall apart for many reasons. One is that the first free election leads to a government being formed that blocks further such elections – for example, election of an Islamic party that promised that its first democratically mandated action would be to form a theocracy, with clerics in power 'forever'. And in new democracies, the party that is elected often fails to realise that it cannot ride roughshod over the wishes of those who didn't vote for it.

In America, a strong system of checks and balances often produces gridlock, leading to what can become an annual budget crisis. And in Western nations generally, faith in democracy has been weakened by a combination of government scandals, blatant leadership lies and lack of authenticity, paralysis, political in-fighting and self-seeking, by bloated government spending and debt, and by unpopular military adventures.

Trust in elected politicians in many nations has never been lower. Huge lobbying budgets and immense campaign spending will continue to feed worries about whether entire democratic systems are being corrupted by business or (in discreet ways) by other governments, all seeking favour in exchange for their huge financial or practical support. For example, there are 20 lobbyists for every member of Congress in America, and spending in the last US presidential race alone was more than $2.4bn, $6.5bn for presidential and congressional elections combined. (President Trump also benefited from around $5bn in free media coverage reporting on the unconventional or shocking statements that he made.)

Within the European Union, Italy and Greece were forced in 2011 to replace their own democratically elected leaders with technocrats, who were more obedient to the rule of Brussels.

At the same time, countries like China have proven that a nation can grow in a stable way, generating huge economic growth, without democracy. In 2013, 83% of Chinese nationals were very satisfied with the direction of their nation, compared to only 31% of Americans.

Democratic governments will rapidly lose power

Across the world, democratically elected presidents and prime ministers are finding that their own power to make big things happen is vanishing – for ten reasons. As a result, it will be much harder for them or their government ministers to deliver on future promises, as President Trump discovered. Many national parliaments will also weaken, and confidence in democracy itself will be undermined further.

1. **Privatisation.** In the past, governments owned and controlled electricity, gas and water companies, national airlines, post offices, railways, health services, telecommunications, and so on. In every part of the world, many state-owned companies have already been sold off. In the old days, politicians could

make bold promises; today, in many areas they have to defer to corporate power and the markets.

2. **Regionalisation.** Regional trading blocs take freedom from member nations, who agree to be bound by agreements. The European Union, in particular, is set to take even more power from member governments, and will impose thousands of new regulations over future decades.

3. **Decentralisation.** A total of 160 national governments have made their own central banks independent of government – up from just 20 in 1980. At a stroke, all these governments gave away control of interest rates and other aspects of monetary policy.

   Elected governments across the world have also given added powers to local government and city mayors. This process will be accelerated by separatist groups, immigrant communities, independence movements and religious activists (some of whom want to impose their own laws, e.g. sharia law based on the Koran).

4. **Unelected civil servants.** One of the greatest causes of inertia and paralysis in governments will be the civil service. Governments come and go, but almost all publicly paid employees remain. They often have natural resistance or even hostility to policy shifts, and may have powerful loyalties of their own. To make matters worse, the civil service in many nations no longer attracts top-calibre graduates in the way that it used to, and this trend will continue.

   Many government leaders will shake up the civil service by controlling more of the most senior political appointments, as in America. However, this will mean that senior civil servants will increasingly find promotion blocked, making lifetime civil service careers even less attractive.

5. **Globalisation – big firms gain powers.** As we have seen, in a globalised world, governments are unable to impose higher rates of tax, or strict labour laws or tough environmental controls, without the risk that global corporations will move elsewhere. The same applies to entrepreneurs.

Web companies find it particularly easy to shift profits to low-tax nations. For example, Google cut tax by $2bn by routing earnings through Ireland, Bermuda and the Netherlands.

Many super-corporations are larger in economic weight than entire nations. They can dictate terms to governments, set agendas for commerce, and form global monopolies, dominating local markets. This is a major reason why nations like India, China and America have been so reluctant to allow foreign multinationals to own majority stakes in key national companies.

6. **Lack of capable and experienced leaders.** And while remuneration packages for CEOs in industrialised nations remain so much higher than for prime ministers or presidents, many political parties will find themselves crippled by a lack of brainpower and talent. Once elected, many national leaders find themselves surrounded by low-quality political activists who have never led large organisations, are ignorant about the wider world and how government works, and are unable to master complex briefs, lead large teams, build consensus, communicate vision or transform their departments.

Surveys show that very few of the brightest and most talented leaders would dream of wasting their lives in 'democratic politics'. Why enter a profession that is (almost) universally despised, has no real power, no job security and is badly paid compared to what could be earned elsewhere?

Why on earth would they want to be president of the US, or of France, or prime minister of the UK? Especially when they can expect their private lives to be taken apart in the media on a daily basis. The pressures on those in public office have never been greater, with lifetime security risks for them and their families, unrealistic public expectations, 24-hour social media criticism, ever-present reputational risks from false accusation, and all on top of the tremendous complexity of leading a nation.

So the best leaders are almost all choosing to run

corporations or non-profit foundations, rather than pretend to run countries. As a result, many democratic governments will continue to be led by slow, feeble-minded, ignorant and incompetent teams.

Lack of talent among politicians is the greatest single threat to healthy democracy today, and this will feed further public contempt of the entire system.

In contrast, government posts can be extremely attractive in autocratic states, where leaders enjoy far greater powers to get things done, are subject to less scrutiny, have greater privileges and higher salary, and greater job security (if you keep in favour). But even autocratic states are increasingly challenged by global market forces.

7. **Activism and social media.** Non-government organisations are more numerous, better funded, and are better at campaigning, using social media. Social media lobbying, together with street demonstrations, can rapidly overturn policy announcements, disrupt law-making, reverse budget decisions and paralyse government. Expect many more campaigning websites like change.org, which allow people to create instant petitions – some of which attract hundreds of thousands of supporters in weeks.

8. **Crisis of trust in politicians.** What is the point of voting when you cannot believe the words of a manifesto? In the UK, 62% of voters say that politicians 'tell lies all the time', a view shared across the European Union. So what was so new, then, about an America president like Donald Trump? 'They are all the same anyway so maybe he's not so bad.' Who cares about well-used cliché phrases such as 'big society' or 'public service'? Only 1.6% of the UK population still belongs to any political party (mainly Labour), down from 20% in 1950, while 27% of EU voters in seven nations say that they have 'no trust in government'. In 49 democracies around the world, voter turnout in elections has fallen 10% in the last 25 years.

As I described in my book *The Truth about Westminster*, despite the constant political fights in the news, the fact is that most politicians agree broadly on most things, in private or when they are out of public office. That is why it is so rare for a new government to reverse legislation that they bitterly opposed before they got into power. So there is a significant lack of integrity in most political media debates.

9. **Small majorities or unstable coalitions.** In many democracies we see instability and weakness, where no single party has a large enough majority to lead strongly, or where a president is blocked by a Parliament or Congress majority formed by opposition parties. Even worse, sometimes it is only possible to govern at all by cobbling together two or more political groups with very different agendas. For example, coalition governments in Italy have often collapsed in the space of just two to three years, while UK decisions on Brexit were gridlocked.

10. **Individual politicians elected by minority of voters.** When there are many different candidates, a member of parliament can be elected by only a small minority of voters, which means that they lack moral authority for strong action. Yet such an individual may end up making all the difference between a coalition government continuing or collapsing.

These ten factors also raise serious questions about what government is for. What is the role of government leaders in a world where so little power remains? We can expect a great debate about this in many nations over the next decades: big government, small government, virtually no government, centralised or decentralised government, and so on.

When faith in ideology and parties dies, trust in the person is all that's left.

As I predicted over 20 years ago, *leaders rather than policies will continue to be more important with every passing year, over the next three decades.* Emotional speeches, appealing to mass prejudices, will win elections, often overcoming logical arguments about policies. This is especially the case in communities that distrust journalism, who dismiss investigative 'factual' reporting as hopelessly biased, and who rely instead on friends or strangers on social media.

Expect many more political earthquakes, where a firebrand politician with a really odd set of ideas is elected because so many people trust that leader to make the right things happen. Voters will be more likely than in the past to elect charismatic personalities, people with spontaneity, conviction and authenticity – sweeping away career politicians with scripted speeches. But for all the reasons above, such eccentric or extreme leaders will also face major frustrations after they get elected, and voter disappointment.

Future of dictatorship and one-party states

Benign dictatorships can serve many emerging nations well. Autocrats have the powers to get things done that elected politicians only dream of. One-party states often embrace elements of the democratic process, as we have seen in regional Chinese elections for many years. Therefore, for all the reasons above, democracy will turn out not to be a one-size-fits-all solution to the political problems of the world.

As history reminds us, dictators only survive long term by popular consent, or with the support of the army and secret service. And at some stage they usually crave the international status of being elected, even when many observers dismiss their election as fixed.

Dictators are becoming weaker

Dictators who use oppression and brutality to impose their will on their people will increasingly find that capital, investors and talented people flee; their currency and the economy will eventually collapse.

However, there will be a cushion for dictators or autocrats who are sitting on huge mineral or oil wealth in places like the Middle East. And it is in the Middle East, therefore, that we can expect the most radical experiments over the next 30 years in theocratic dictatorship (by clerics), propped up by oil revenues, in defiance of the rest of global market forces. In most cases such theocracies will simply be the replacement of one form of dictatorship by another.

Impact of single-issue campaigns on companies

The boards of all high-profile companies will meet single-issue activists at annual shareholder meetings on a regular basis. CEOs need to know how to handle people hanging from ceilings, or running naked down the aisles, shouting and asking very awkward, well-researched questions.

But single issues will also be harnessed by CEOs to build sales and market share. In a world where almost all products and services are converging in price (falling) and quality (rising), the only way to differentiate is with your values. *Cause-related marketing* means selling to people who believe in the cause more than the differences in the product.

I am not talking about ticking boxes as part of so-called corporate and social responsibility (CSR) in the Annual Report. Such compliance exercises are nothing to do with total business transformation around a vision to make the world a better place.

In the US, 93% of consumers prefer companies that are really helping the community (up from 84% in 2010) and 90% are more likely to buy products linked to causes they really care about, assuming price and quality are equal. Staff also want to be proud of who they work for.

Expect tens of thousands of new partnerships between businesses and charities to market products or services for mutual benefit, with commitments to give away a percentage of profits and so on.

Many more companies will switch a large proportion of their marketing budget to spend on community action or sustainability partnerships, strengthening their brands and generating huge amounts of goodwill and media coverage.

There is a triple win, which helps explain why companies that score high for social responsibility, often score high for business growth.

More customers →   ↑ Profits

More motivated teams → ↑ Productivity

More investment →   ↑ Price of shares

Most middle-class consumers are loyal to responsible companies

Globally, over half of all middle-class consumers say that they are willing to pay more for products and services from companies that are committed to positive social and environmental impact – up from only 10% in 2011. In America, the figure is 42% across the whole population, compared to 7% in 2011.

Institutional investors are also adding their own pressures. Indeed, in nations like the UK, they are required to; pension funds have to show that they are investing in ethical ways, which has boosted shares in the so-called FTSE4Good Index.

This is a momentous and long-term change, which has been under way for 20 years, although there was a partial reversal in the 2008–2013 economic crisis.

As a response to all this, large companies now spend almost $2bn a year on different causes, sponsorships, and so on – aiming to 'do well by doing good'. Expect this to more than double over the next decade.

A growing percentage of new companies will give away *all* their profits. An example is Thankyou, founded by Daniel Flynn in Australia as a social enterprise selling bottled water, nappies and personal hygiene products. Since 2008 it has grown at astonishing speed and given away $6m to fund water, hygiene and food production in 15 nations. Their breakthrough came from massive social media campaigns, where consumers demanded that major chains stock the products – culminating in a helicopter flying around supermarket HQs trailing banners. The supermarkets soon caved in, but the greater gain was national media coverage.

Abortion will continue to be a big issue in the US

Abortion is an example of a single issue that has become more powerful than the law itself. Abortion is now almost impossible in some US states, despite being legal. The church-dominated anti-abortion movement in the US is now bigger than the civil rights movement of the 1960s, and was a significant factor in President Trump's election.

From 2008 to 2011, the percentage of doctors willing to conduct an abortion fell from 22% to 14% as a result of campaigns against clinics, despite most people in America supporting a woman's right to legal abortion. In one state, it has been hard to identify a single doctor still willing to conduct abortions. Tens of thousands of activists have been arrested, cautioned or imprisoned, while many pro-abortionists have been threatened, assaulted or murdered.

In late 2018, after fierce campaigning, Alabama and West Virginia passed new laws to restrict access to abortion if the 1973 'Roe v Wade' pro-abortion ruling is ever overturned by the Supreme Court – which is now more likely after several anti-abortion judges were appointed for life by President Trump.

Vision for theocracy – God-centred government

We will continue to see huge differences between radical Christianity and radical Islam in their visions for government, and in how they get involved politically. Many Islamic groups have the goal of theocracy: entire nations run under God's authority, according to His rules for all humankind, imposed on believers and non-believers alike. Such groups will often accept lower economic growth and cuts in living standards in order to achieve this ideal.

In such theocracies, sharia law will be overseen by Muslim clerics. Forced 'conversions' will continue to be common, with death threats often received by those who convert to another religion, or by those who seek to convert them. Thus, many Islamic societies will continue to rely on fear and the force of law as important tools to encourage religious obedience. This will be different from the situation in most other nations, which will continue to promote the rights of all people to participate freely in whatever religion they truly believe in.

Christianity will focus less on government and more on policy

Almost all Christian groups since the 1950s have been driven by a relatively non-governmental mission: to recruit willing followers, who desire to live lives that are in keeping with Jesus's example and teachings. They will continue to celebrate compassion, unselfish love and kindness as outward signs of inner religious obedience.

Their theology contends that, as individuals are touched and changed by the love of God, so too are communities changed, towns and cities are transformed, and whole nations and governments are revolutionised. Social action will therefore continue to be a major element of this tradition, whether running food banks, health care for the poor, or shelter for the homeless.

While many Christians are likely to engage in politics in future, almost all will encourage democracy, rather than attempting to impose theocracy. However, most will support activist campaigns rather than joining a political party.

Peace will overcome religious violence eventually

As history proves, where you have two groups of radical zealots – one promoting hate, fear and violence, the other promoting love, respect and peace – the violent often gain power in the short term, but lose moral force eventually. Societies built on fear are ultimately unsustainable, and therefore unusual.

Extremely violent, intolerant, Islamic militants will continue to be a poor advert globally for their religious brand, and in the long term they will damage wider (voluntary) acceptance of Islamic religion, except to small minorities of people who are attracted by such behaviour, and by the comfort of dogmatic creeds. The same applies to extreme Christian groups.

Expect support to peak and wane for the most ruthless and violent groups in any religion – and militant Islam to decline in aggression, as more moderate followers of Islam grow rapidly in number over the next 50 to 100 years, fuelled by large middle-class families, and by extra finance generated primarily from Middle East oil over the next four decades.

Moderate Muslims are likely to be increasingly repelled by 'medieval' atrocities, committed in the name of Islam. As is the case with all fanatical groups, Islamic militants are likely to realise eventually that their dreams will never be achieved by terrorist acts, but only by winning the hearts of people.

Radical forces in the Middle East

Radical ideologies and tribalism will dominate the Middle East for the longer term, with constant risk of more regional conflicts. One of many contributing factors is the arbitrary nature of country borders, imposed as lines in the sand on nomadic Arab peoples, by Western powers many decades ago.

The Arab Spring was in many ways a reaction to corrupt autocracy and inequality of wealth, but resulted in greater tribalism. Autocrats, such as Saddam Hussein and President Assad of Syria, kept a lid on tribal tension with brutal repression, fuelling further conflict, the impact of which will endure for several generations.

Pressure on ruling families

We will see instability across the region from time to time over the next 40–50 years. A number of Arab nations ruled by ultra-wealthy royal families may become very vulnerable. New generations of violent activist groups will seek to bring about inter-connected theocracies as part of an Arab-wide Islamic region.

Sunni and Shiite Muslims will continue as distinct communities well beyond 2050, with ripples felt across the entire world. Such conflicts will be stoked by atrocities, as well as by regional interests.

The civil war in Syria is likely to further destabilise and then reform the entire region, over several generations. It will take at least 15 years beyond the signing of a peace agreement to rebuild the nation and resettle over 4 million refugees, and a further 15 years for bitter memories to begin to fade.

Centuries-long vision for the region

A potential flashpoint for the next century will be Saudi Arabia, the heart of Islam, protectorate of the Two Most Holy Places, with immense oil wealth, and great aspirations for its large, young population. Saudi Arabia will remain a major target for Islamic revolutionary forces over the next 20 to 30 years, and the royal family is likely to make concessions to help maintain stability, including further crackdowns on corruption, and measures to distribute oil-derived wealth more equally. As part of this we will see further major investments in education, job creation and affordable homes. But at the same time, there will be pressures in some parts of the community for liberalisation.

Saudi Arabia's oil revenues will decline

We cannot be sure when Saudi Arabia's oil revenues will start to decline permanently as reserves dwindle, and as our world shifts from burning carbon, but at some point in the next 40 years, oil revenues will no longer sustain the national economy. This issue will have a very significant impact on most of the Middle East, and will drive rapid investment in alternatives such as solar power, as well as biotech, nanotech, infotech, medtech and pharma.

Major social shifts

Countries like Iran are experiencing hidden social revolutions that are quite liberal, in contrast to their public image or official policies. For example, a government survey reported that 80% of unmarried women in Iran have boyfriends, and many are sexually active. In addition, 17% of 142,000 students in the survey said that they were homosexual.

Turkey will experience great pressures for stricter Islamic laws, with unstable borders to Iraq and Syria, while pulled in the opposite direction by many middle-class citizens who look West, rather than East. Turkey will continue to risk being overwhelmed by events across its borders, with 1.6 million refugees arriving from Syria in just three years. Turkey will also experience tensions with Kurdish peoples to the east. Expect autocratic leadership to continue, with stronger media controls than in the EU, all of which will make joining the EU very unlikely for the next 20 years.

Future of Palestine and Israel

Another flashpoint will, of course, be Israel and Palestine. I realise that many readers may have strong feelings about what *should* happen, but this book is about what it is reasonable to expect *may* happen. Here is a 'common sense' view, based on the current situation and long-term factors.

Israel is a tiny nation of 8 million people, packed into a narrow strip 263 miles long and up to 71 miles wide. If the entire Arab world of 366 million people starts to focus on Israel instead of inter-Arab conflicts, it is obvious that the entire nation could be overrun, unless Israel resorts to major threats, including some kind of nuclear device. But against what nation would such a device be used? Especially if the forces raging against their borders on all sides are diffuse in origin, in some kind of hybrid conflict, with tens of thousands of informal militia volunteers gathering on the borders, from more than 40 countries? And what if an Arab nation with a nuclear device threatened to retaliate?

Pressure likely to grow for autonomy in Palestine

Israel seems likely to continue to resist external efforts to broker a lasting settlement for 4.4 million Palestinian people, who are living in densely packed areas with limited freedoms. New generations of freedom fighters, militants and activists are likely to grow up in these communities, deeply hostile to Israel, finding common cause with wider movements across the Middle East.

Arabs are likely to outnumber Jews in Israel and occupied territories, as a combined total, at some point in the next decade. Israel will not be able to have all of the following: a strong Jewish majority, all of the land and full democracy. Either it will have to sacrifice land to form two states, or sacrifice a Jewish majority in a 'bi-national' state, or lose global recognition as a proper democratic nation.

The future well-being of the Palestinian people is likely to remain a fundamental issue of justice for most Arab peoples as well as for a growing number of non-Arabs around the world. A total of 135 nations have now officially recognised Palestine as a country.

If America chooses, at any point in the future, to fully defend Israel's borders, it is likely that American troops will be drawn into a long-distance, bitterly contested, very costly and potentially lengthy land battle. Such action could be ultimately unwinnable, if this enrages the entire Arab world against America and Israel for generations to come.

Despite these threats, Israel seems likely to try to pursue similar strategies as they have in the past for the next 15 years – hit back hard when attacked, keep a constant military alert, and weaken the Palestinian people with oppressive actions including the building of new Israeli settlements on land that was inhabited previously by Palestinians.

However, Israel will need to adapt its strategy rapidly to the new world of asymmetric tribal conflicts. Like America, Israel is very ill-equipped for hybrid wars – multidimensional, informal, urban battles, sweeping across several of its borders at once, as a movement of people on a collective suicide mission, rather than structured as a traditional military campaign.

Sustainability will be a dominant theme for 300 years

Expect far greater concerns over the next 30 years about sustainability and what kind of planet will remain in 100 years, including worries about shortages of water, food and other resources and major threats to other forms of life.

A quarter of all 4,000 known mammal species are likely to be extinct by 2035 without aggressive action. One in eight plant types are also threatened. Stocks of large fish in the ocean have fallen by 90% over the last few decades. Sea-water acidity has risen by 25% since the Industrial Revolution, because of rising levels of dissolved CO_2, altering chemistry of trillions of sea organisms.

Numbers of insects, a key indicator of global ecology, have fallen globally by 45% in 35 years, because of insecticides and other chemicals used in farming, as well as changes in land use. Farming impacts entire ecosystems: insects have fallen 75% in German nature reserves, and insect numbers have also collapsed in Puerto Rico's rainforests. Preserving biodiversity will be a growing priority in almost every nation.

Concerns about global warming will intensify

China is now producing almost twice as much CO_2 as America, more than any other nation. On current trends, China alone will emit more CO_2 from 1990 to 2050 than the entire world produced from 1750 to 1970. But how much does this really matter?

The science of global warming is just a 'best guess' about what life will be like in 2100, and about the contribution of carbon emissions to what is happening now. But by the time we have proved whether the science is right, it will be far too late to respond, if the consensus of almost all climate experts is correct. In the meantime, emotional reactions to climate change data are what will matter most in predicting the shorter-term impact of global warming trends on business and government.

Most people in the world are becoming more aware of risks from climate change, and more concerned that human activity may be contributing to it. Expect these concerns to grow, except where nations are temporarily distracted by other crises. This will mean more laws, international agreements, carbon taxes, and so on.

What of the long-term future? My own view is that there is a very significant risk that our world will become warmer by at least 2.5 degrees centigrade, as a result of CO_2 emissions, by 2060. But even if you think that risk is as low as 5%, in other words very unlikely even by 2100, the potential consequences could be so huge that by the time we know for sure, the damage will have been done. And that argument alone will guarantee vigorous action, with an increasing sense of urgency over the next 40 years.

Despite growth in green tech, we will struggle to stabilise CO_2 emissions over the next decade, depending on speed of growth of the global economy. Thereafter, expect year-on-year declines.

Expect continued debate about rising sea levels. We know that the oceans rose 17cm in the last century and rose a further 3.2mm a year on average from 1993 to 2010, double the rate from 1901 to 1990. On that basis alone we would expect a minimum rise of 24–30cm by 2100. But this does not allow for higher emissions over the last 15 years, nor for melting highly reflective polar ice on a large scale, exposing land and sea to further rapid solar warming.

A rise of half a metre would affect most of the largest cities in the world in a significant way, since they are all built around sea ports. Over 3 billion people live within 100 miles of the sea, a significant proportion of whom will be affected in some way by rising sea levels, for example, by higher taxes to pay for coastal protection.

We will also see changes in agriculture and fishing, as some areas become more arid, and others are flooded more often. Warmer air will mean greater sea evaporation and greater rainfall with major changes in where it falls.

So what will be the scale of global response? The answer is that it is likely to be gigantic, eventually, once governments across the world become convinced, together with their populations, that global warming is something approaching a global emergency.

In times of war, a very significant proportion of national economies is spent funding military costs. It is easy to imagine 1–2% of global GDP being diverted to decarbonise the world, capture and store carbon dioxide, which would give a government budget equivalent to around $1 trillion a year. Such spending will also stimulate economies. That expenditure compares with $3 trillion spent on renewable energy globally from 2014 to 2018 – mostly by companies and individuals to save money, in a process that will accelerate.

Unstable oil prices will create chaos for energy companies

We have already seen how 40-year energy policies can be over-turned by a single 40-second event, and why energy markets will continue to be very unstable at times. We should expect a number of oil price peaks and slumps, created by over-production, stop-start investment, economic cycles, decarbonisation of energy production, carbon taxes, and regional conflicts.

Oil prices are likely to swing below $40 and above $180 per barrel at various points over the next three decades. Prices fell from over $140 to below $40 in a few weeks in 2008, and to below $20 in 2001. Such extremes will continue to cause chaos and pain for oil and gas companies, as well as for green tech.

However, it is likely that the *average* oil price will be above $75 a barrel for much of the next 30 years, which will help drive transition to a carbon-less future. Indeed, many oil-rich countries need to achieve above such a price to balance their budgets. And it is hard to see how we can transition as rapidly as necessary to a low-carbon existence without such an average price.

Whenever oil prices fall below $75 a barrel, huge damage is done to green tech investment. Fund managers can easily lose confidence. Businesses and private individuals delay energy saving measures. And green tech companies can rapidly run out of money if they cannot sell energy at a high enough price.

Future oil prices will depend (among other things) on whether low cost producers hold back production, since a nation like America or Saudi Arabia can easily flood the world with oil for years, and still make a profit at prices of less than $45 a barrel. But they cannot do so for long without squandering limited oil reserves.

Theft of oil from pipes in emerging nations will continue to be an issue, with loss of around $7bn a year of revenues. Long pipes are impossible to protect. Expect further tragedies as low-income farmers in remote rural areas or slum townships continue to make holes in pipelines to fill containers, risking massive explosions and fires.

Truth about peak oil – global supplies

There have been many wild predictions over the last 30 years about how oil and gas would soon run out. However, from 2008 to 2013 alone, energy industry estimates for global gas reserves went up from just 60 years to 200 years at current rates of consumption, just because of shale gas innovation. And every year, proven oil reserves also continue to rise, while only a third of geological formations that could contain oil have so far been explored.

Every time energy prices rise, more carbon can be extracted. Around 65% of oil in most wells had to be left underground in the past, being too hard to extract. Until oil prices collapsed in 2014–2015, companies were routinely drilling around 10km below sea beds to extract oil, because technology had improved and because they expected future oil prices to make their effort worthwhile.

Frozen methane and other untapped carbon reserves

We have not even begun to explore extraction of frozen methane, which is one of the world's largest carbon stores. Energy stores under the ice caps or oceans are probably as large as all proven oil, gas and coal reserves today. One of the most worrying risks is that as the ice caps melt, frozen methane starts to bubble up in an uncontrolled way leading to runaway global warming. No expert on earth can be sure of the impact of this. It's already started: there are now many places above the Arctic Circle during the summer where you can hit the ground with a stick and ignite a flare of methane gas leaping into the atmosphere.

Expect the Arctic to become one of the world's most important new areas for extraction of fossil fuels, iron ore, uranium and other resources. The Arctic probably contains up to 30% of the world's undiscovered natural gas and 15% of the oil. Expect $60bn of Arctic investment by 2025.

We will see growing geopolitical tensions over who has rights to what is under the ice – with Canada laying claim to the North Pole, and Russia increasing its military presence in the region. We will also see similar disputes over ownership of tiny islands and surrounding sea beds across South East Asia, to secure drilling rights, with growing risks of regional conflicts, especially involving China, but with the potential to involve many other nations, including America and the UK, through all kinds of military alliances.

Carbon reserves will never run out – carbon consumption will fall from 2025

The truth is that carbon reserves will never run out, because there will always be more that can be extracted, if the price goes even higher; because there is more carbon available than it would be wise to burn; and because it will eventually become illegal to extract more than a limited quota in many nations.

Renewable energy is growing so fast that it will supply all growth in annual power consumption globally by 2025, which means that fossil fuel consumption is likely to fall year-on-year from peak consumption in that year.

Indeed, our world is likely to take steps to ban use of more than 40% of the reserves we have *already* discovered, unless we find better ways to capture CO_2 emissions from power stations, and store them back underground.

And of course we can already convert any form of carbon into more or less any other form: gas to a coal-like substance, energy to gas, rapeseed oil to petrol, coal to gas, wood to oil, waste CO_2 to petrol, and so on. We can also use wind power to manufacture methane or hydrogen gas as a way to store energy, or transmit it over long distances in pipes.

Quick route to reducing emissions

The fastest and cheapest way for any nation to reduce carbon emissions in the short term is to switch from coal to gas. Replacing five coal power stations with gas is the equivalent of installing 9,000 megawatts of wind power. In America, emissions fell by 12% from 2007 to 2013, primarily because the shale gas boom drove more than 50 coal-fired power stations out of business.

Gas will still be widely used in power generation in 2060, as a rapid and flexible balancer between sources like nuclear and wind or solar, and will be a central element of national power management. This is not because our world will need so much gas power by then, but because of legacy gas power stations owned by large utility companies, built decades previously in a rush to replace coal.

Fracking will become far more widely accepted, partly encouraged by national security fears in the EU, threatened by the thought of unreliable gas supplies from Russia. Fracking has revolutionised the energy market in America, which overtook Saudi Arabia in 2018 as an oil producer. But fracking has brought hidden environmental costs, in particular because the process requires up to 10 million gallons of water per well, which is then contaminated with dangerous chemicals, and can also result in contamination of underground aquifers.

Nations like Russia and Saudi Arabia will be negatively affected as fracking becomes more widespread, and we can expect official and covert initiatives to try to slow the fracking industry down, including funding activist groups, and flooding the market with cheap oil.

We will also see rapid investment in facilities to ship liquid gas around the world, partly to handle the glut of American shale gas, and also to reduce dependence in Europe on Russian gas. Expect huge investment in ports, ships, pipes, gas storage and infrastructure.

Everything connects to everything

The shale gas boom meant that gas prices in America fell dramatically, and many smaller gas companies went bust. At the same time, coal power plants became uncompetitive and in a single year over 50 went out of business, so global coal prices fell. As a result, the Vietnamese began building very large coal-fired power stations. Coal-fired power generation jumped 5% globally in 2012 alone as a direct result of low-cost shale gas. So what was the final carbon saving in the world?

$50 trillion in green tech investment

Over the next 30 years we will see over $50 trillion invested in green tech. Investment in renewable energy is now greater than all investment in coal, gas, oil and nuclear combined.

Some 25% of global power generation is already from renewable sources, and is expected to rise to over 40% by 2040, mainly as a result of government-driven decisions. We will need a similar revolution in cutting gas and oil heating for buildings, and for transport.

When oil prices are above $85 a barrel, even the greatest climate sceptics become converts to energy saving. And as we have seen, an additional driver is government fear of dependence on rogue states for energy. So cost saving, national security, protecting the environment – whatever the primary motivation, the outcome will be a frenzy of green tech innovation, even if it is held back sometimes by short-term falls in the price of carbon.

And even if we see *zero* green tech innovation for the next 50 years, we already have all the tools we need, at affordable cost, just by scaling up what already exists.

Tackling climate change at low cost

Much of this will cost nothing. Take the normal process of replacing old fridges, cars or gas boilers. In real terms you will probably spend less than last time you bought one, yet the new model will be more energy efficient. So, just by replacing things when they wear out, your energy consumption at home or when driving will fall rapidly over 10 to 20 years, probably by more than 30%.

There are many other ways to save energy that repay costs in five years or less. For example, some companies are offering free upgrades of heating and air conditioning for 15-year-old offices and hotels, on condition that the owners continue to pay the company the same as they used to in energy costs, for a limited period.

The green tech company takes out a loan to pay all their own design and installation costs, and it also pays all the energy bills over the first four years. At the same time, each month the owner pays the company the amount it would usually pay to the utility company for gas or power. But the energy consumption is of course greatly reduced, once the new systems have been installed. The cost saving pays off the loan, and provides enough extra cash to fund the entire installation, plus profit on top.

We are seeing similar schemes for city-wide street lighting, which is 5% of all energy used in many nations. Replacing lights can more than halve energy use, with payback in four years, saving up to 3% of the entire national energy bill.

A great way to save energy in buildings is to make them last longer. Around 30% of the lifetime energy used in a building is in putting it up and 10% is in pulling it down. Future generations will think it a scandal that most offices built over the last decade were constructed only to last 30 years, or 40 at most. Yet most private dwellings in developed nations are constructed to last for 100 years or more.

Technology	Energy saving	Cut in global energy use	Payback period	Speed of introduction
Low energy streetlamps	60%	3%	4 years	1–10 years
Aviation efficiencies	35%	1.5%	3–10 years	1–15 years
Vehicles	35–70%	10–20%	5 years	1–15 years
Building controls	35–70%	4–5.5%	4 years	1–15 years
Insulating homes	5–50%	6–8%	3–15 years	1–15 years
Heat pumps	25–50%	6–8%	10–15 years	1–25 years

How to save 30–40% of today's global CO_2 emissions at 'zero cost'

Some $300bn a year is already being spent on energy saving by companies and governments in just 11 nations – and we have only just begun.

Nanotech coatings for every moving part in a car engine will alone save at least 5% of fuel costs. Condensing gas boilers save 30% of fuel. The list is endless, with hundreds of new energy-related patents filed every day.

Cost of solar panels will fall towards zero – by 12% a year

Solar panels will continue to fall rapidly in cost, by up to 12% a year. They typically convert only 18% of sunlight to power – but expect this to double over the next 15 to 20 years. The cost per watt has fallen to $3 for domestic panels. But very large-scale projects in America are generating at 6 cents per kilowatt hour, without any subsidy, lower than the cost of coal or gas power.

The latest silicon-based panels are already so cheap that they can be bought by a home owner with a bank loan, and will earn money from the first day without government subsidy. This is the case in Australia, Germany, Italy and the Netherlands. Germany already leads Europe in solar panels, because of generous subsidies, but this is nothing to what we will see in the future. Next-generation solar panels will be twice as efficient.

Over 600 gigawatts of solar panels have already been installed around the world – and at least the same again will be installed *every three years* from 2025, equivalent to five times the entire energy consumption of the UK. Around 8% of Italy's power already comes from sunlight. We can expect lift-off on a gigantic scale by 2025, and solar power is likely to become the world's largest source of electricity by 2060.

Most solar panels will be installed in places where there is no connection to a national grid – serving over 1 billion people who are currently off-grid. Solar power installations are expensive to put in, but running costs are zero and they last many years.

Imagine a world where the cheapest roofing material is solar panels, when energy generation is included. We can see how vast this solar boom will become, with solar cells covering cars, factories, walls, roofs, airports, fields, lakes and deserts. Owners of lakes in some countries are starting to cover part of the surface with floating solar panels – which do not disturb wildlife too much. Farmers across Europe are covering land with solar panels. Research shows that biodiversity is often higher in fields with panels than it is in ploughed fields.

Deserts could power all America and Europe

We will see enormous arrays of desert mirrors, reflecting light onto tubes containing gas, to drive steam turbines. These have already been built in Spain and the UAE, but will be overtaken by silicon panels as costs fall. A single solar farm just 50km by 80km, in the Nevada desert, could in theory generate enough energy to supply most of the US, assuming a smart grid, as well as large-scale battery storage during the day for use at night (time differences will help spread load). India has already built a 2 gigawatt installation and is planning another to generate 5 gigawatts. One of the greatest challenges is dust: in Spain vast areas of such panels need cleaning only once a year, but in the UAE they need to be cleaned once a week.

Wind, waves and tides

We will also see huge growth in wind power between 2020 and

2050, especially offshore in the shallow seas of Western Europe, and across China. Average blade length will continue to grow. The longest blades already dwarf the size of the largest wings on passenger jets. Efficiency will improve, with hardly any moving parts, and better blade design. Optimisation will soon be reached for blade size and other components, and wind innovation beyond 2030 will be less than solar.

Expect 250 gigawatts of installed wind capacity in the EU alone by 2025. China will dominate this global industry, with more turbines already than any other nation. We can also expect opposition in many places to more wind farms from people who consider this a 'visual pollution' of the landscape.

We will also see more energy generated from waves and tides, with most of this from tidal barrages, which has the potential to generate 15% of UK energy by 2050. However, such projects require gigantic investment and are likely to look less attractive in future compared to solar, wind and other sources. We will see more tidal turbines in places like Scotland and Brittany, where tidal currents are strong. But wave machines will prove very expensive and disappointing compared to solar or wind.

Smarter grids

The windiest and sunniest places on earth are often far from cities, so we will need new ways to transmit wind and solar power without high power losses. We also need to connect hundreds of millions of home-based power generators, so that their own solar panels and wind turbines are part of the national grid.

Supergrids will carry power over many thousands of kilometres, across entire continents, with almost zero power loss. Supergrids use high voltage, direct current rather than alternating current, so power always flows in the same direction, which means very little power is lost into the atmosphere as electromagnetic radiation. Expect over $10bn to be spent globally on building supergrids.

Germany alone has been planning to build 6,400km of supergrid, as part of a €100bn European investment, but cost and impact on the landscape will be big issues, and are likely to slow construction down. Whatever happens, Europe will be far more joined up energy-wise in future.

Energy prices turn negative – energy stores to manage demand

We will see huge investment in low-cost energy storage, to the point where it is no longer considered a major problem, using a wide range of existing tech and innovations that have yet to be developed. Up until now one of the most common ways to store surplus energy at night was to pump water from one dam, uphill to another. One approach that will be more widely used is salt caverns – natural spaces underground that are gas-tight, into which air is compressed using surplus power. When power is needed, compressed air is combined with natural gas to turbocharge gas turbines.

We will use the batteries of hundreds of thousands of electric cars as additional power stores, as they will be plugged into the national grid most of the time. Car batteries will act as power donors at times of peak demand, with the agreement of their owners who will be paid to participate. We will also see many mega battery banks, like those being built by Tesla to serve entire cities or regions. Tesla's 100 megawatt battery in Australia has been earning back 33% of its cost every year, replacing very expensive power stations that were previously used for only a few peak days a year.

When you add all these things together, the combined impact will be extraordinary. For example, in June 2013 there was so much sunlight and wind in Germany that the national grid was threatened with meltdown. Energy companies were forced to contact some of their biggest customers to persuade them to burn up more power, by any means. They were paid four times the normal cost of electricity for every unit they were able to burn up. So energy prices actually became negative. Expect many more radical upsets in green tech energy markets.

Nuclear boom despite a meltdown

Despite the Fukushima disaster in Japan, we are about to see a global boom in construction of new nuclear power stations – except in Japan and Germany. Global spending on nuclear reactor pressure vessels alone is around $16bn a year, with 48 new nuclear power stations being built across the Asia-Pacific region and a further 22 in other parts of the world.

The only thing that will slow this down would be another major nuclear accident, say in France, spreading radioactive dust across Western Europe.

We are likely to see a new generation of nuclear power stations by 2060–2070 (or possibly earlier) based on nuclear fusion, which is a radically different technology from splitting the atom (fission) and involves fusing two different atoms together to release energy, with far less radioactive waste. The EU, America, Japan, China, India, Russia and South Korea are jointly building a 23,000-ton, 500-megawatt experimental fusion reactor in France that is likely to cost more than $30bn, and with first plasma experiments scheduled for 2025.

Meanwhile, the global aerospace company Lockheed Martin claims to have built a small working prototype, and hopes to have a commercial-scale device by 2025. They say it will be small enough to fit on a truck and could power 80,000 homes using 20kg of fuel a year.

While the Chinese are also exploring the use of thorium as a new fuel, there is no shortage of uranium, which forms around 3% of the cost of a new reactor. If uranium prices treble, which would still be quite affordable, we can start to mine uranium from sea water, even using today's Japanese technology. We could supply the world with uranium for over 10,000 years at current energy levels, from sea water alone.

Those that worry about very long-term consequences of nuclear waste products, and risks of radiation leaks or explosions, will argue for solar and wind for safety and cost reasons. But some governments will say that such sources need supplementing with constant and reliable non-carbon energy.

Germany will follow an anti-nuclear path

In contrast, Germany is quickly phasing out nuclear power as part of their policies to transfer to renewables – so quickly that even the meteoric rise of solar and wind power across the country will barely make up for the loss. As a result, Germany's use of carbon will change far less dramatically over the next two decades.

Germany achieved its green tech boom by offering very generous government subsidies. The money for these subsidies is clawed back from all energy customers in a special green energy tariff which is added to normal energy prices. So the result of the green tech boom has been a jump in energy costs.

Energy prices paid by industry in Germany are now projected to rise to around $150 per megawatt hour, almost three times that in America, by 2020. This is a major risk to 75% of its small- and medium-sized industrial companies. Energy-hungry companies like BASF, SGL Carbon and basi Schöberl are complaining that they may be forced to relocate production out of Germany as a direct result, possibly to America, where shale gas prices are likely to remain much lower.

Germany spends $20bn a year on green subsidies, working out at over $200 to prevent a ton of CO_2 from being emitted. At the same time, carbon credits are being traded between companies for only $20 a ton of CO_2, so some strange market forces are operating. It will be at least five to ten years before carbon pricing settles to a more sustainable level. The entire carbon trading market will be restructured.

Carbon emissions trading will be very important in future. Some 15% of global emissions are already capped, equal to around 7 gigatons of CO_2. So companies or nations needing to exceed a cap need to buy a carbon permit from companies that have made reductions – effectively funding the decarbonisation. The original carbon market was flooded by over-generous allowances during the 2008 economic downturn, and these were then traded, as companies made simple energy savings.

Hydrogen and fuel cells – some false promises

As I forecast some years ago, hydrogen is very unlikely to become a major global fuel for cars, trucks or planes, for several reasons. First, it is an inefficient fuel to transport in tanks, as it produces less power per litre than a carbon-based gas. Second, the gas molecules are very small, so leaks are harder to prevent. Third, battery technology is improving rapidly as well as the efficiency of petrol and diesel engines. It is impossible to imagine a national hydrogen gas grid running across America, for example – too expensive to even consider. But we will see growth of hydrogen-powered vehicles in cities – for example buses.

Expect further improvements in fuel cells that produce power directly from carbon fuel. However, like hydrogen, such fuel cells will face severe competition over the next two decades from next-generation batteries.

Biofuels – expect a radical rethink

Future generations will regard it a crime against society to burn food in vehicles, or to convert crops from farms into other forms of carbon, instead of growing food to feed the world. By 2015, *40% of all corn grown in America* was already being converted to biofuels. In Europe, all drivers are forced by law to burn food in their petrol or diesel cars or trucks – 5% of all petrol or diesel sold in the EU is from food, rising to 10% by 2020.

The American government encouraged use of biofuels to help the nation become energy independent, but even if every ton of grain were converted to petrol or diesel, it would not be enough to keep more than 25% of the auto industry on the move, so the impact is insignificant on energy policy.

To make matters worse, up to 92% of theoretical savings in carbon emissions are lost because of energy used in fertilisers, CO_2 emitted in transporting biofuel to factory, energy used in the making of biofuels, and in trucking the fuel from rural areas to cities. Biofuels are often grown on deforested land, especially in nations like Brazil, which further undermines their environmental benefit.

Biofuels are also expensive in terms of subsidies. For example, the EU is paying €1,200 per ton of CO_2 saved by biofuels, which is six times the average subsidy paid by Germany for a wide range of green tech to reduce CO_2 emissions.

Impact of biofuels on farming

Biofuel production is taking over the countryside in many nations. Within the EU, an area of farmland the size of Belgium was recently being used to grow biofuels for EU use, and a similar land area outside the EU is also needed. Biofuel farms in the EU were recently using more water than the entire Seine and Elbe river flows combined. And then Argentina stepped in, flooding the EU with low-cost biofuel, produced from their own farmland, bankrupting many EU biofuel producers.

At a time when 840 million are hungry, the EU *alone* is burning enough biofuel calories in vehicles each year to feed 100 million people. And importing food as fuel is no better. It still impacts global food supply and the use of fertile land.

Twice over the last ten years we have seen prices of some foods soar by more than 50%. And each time, influential bodies like the UN have said that up to 70% of these rises have probably been caused by burning food in vehicles. So it may be that over 30 million people in the world today are starving as a direct result of biofuel policies. And as we have seen, the real issue is not necessarily the facts (which may be disputed), but how people around the world feel about it all.

Food and oil prices will be locked together

One thing is clear: the moment we link food and energy together in this way, we create a single food-fuel market, so oil prices and food prices are now locked together across the world, which is a risky situation. It means that land prices, farmland prices and woodland prices (because woodland can be cleared to grow grain) have also become linked to energy prices.

So a Middle East oil scare produces a food price spike. If the price of oil doubles over the next decade, prices of some foods may double too. Some counter that while this may apply to biofuels from food, it is different when you are converting biomass (non-edible crops). But biomass still comes from the land. So we are seeing farmers devote huge areas to crops that count as biomass, while reducing the land area they use to grow food.

Biomass has certainly become a very fashionable concept in energy. One of the UK's largest coal power stations, Drax, has been converted to biomass. The only trouble is that this monster is impossible to feed from the UK alone, so bio-waste has been transported to Drax in containers shipped from Brazil – yet another sign of global madness.

Some claim that biofuels are a natural form of carbon capture – using sunlight to take carbon from the air to make fuel – but capture is only for a few weeks, and overall carbon impact is zero. Growing food does the same thing.

Some biofuel crops do grow very fast, capture more carbon than food crops, and can be grown in areas unsuitable for traditional farming, and may, therefore, be more justifiable to use in this way, but as I say, this whole area is likely to become more controversial, and such crops will compete for natural wilderness, wetland areas and forests as well as for normal farmland.

Carbon capture will be widely used – eventually

An obvious way to reduce emissions of CO_2 is to capture chimney gases from gas or coal power stations, and bury them underground in old gas fields, which of course have been proven to be gas-tight for millions of years. The process is still experimental, but expect rapid growth.

Carbon capture, utilisation and storage is an industry already worth $3bn a year, growing by over 20% a year.

A simple way to do this is to use some of the power station electricity to extract oxygen from the atmosphere, which is then pumped into the power station to burn gas or coal. The only chimney gases are then water vapour (condensed to provide local water), a very little sulphur dioxide, and pure CO_2 to be pumped underground.

The world's first large-scale capture and storage plant was opened in Canada in 2014. Over a million tons of CO_2 are being pumped into an oil field, which will also help further oil extraction. We are likely to see more such projects in the US, Canada, Saudi Arabia and Australia. In America, growth will be accelerated by a tax credit of $50 per ton of CO_2 buried underground, and $35 per ton used in other ways – not quite enough to cover all costs yet.

Imagine a world with free power

As we look beyond 2100, it is easy to imagine that 'free' electrical power will be part of normal life for hundreds of millions of people. Indeed, this is already the case for people who have owned solar panels or wind turbines for some time, whose costs have already been paid long ago through savings on their fuel bills. They will go on experiencing free power until those devices break down. The same applies to any farmer fortunate enough to have a small water turbine working off a local stream or river.

The lesson, therefore, is that electrical power in future will become more a question of capital investment than fuel consumption.

Sustainable cities, green manufacturing and IT

Every architect, builder and city planner will be expected to focus on sustainability in future, and this will be a key aim of Smart Cities, using next-generation connectivity to cut energy use and improve efficiency. Many European nations will require a percentage of new homes to be completely carbon neutral, so that all emissions are offset by green energy that is sold to other consumers.

It's not just a question of carbon emissions but also of air quality, especially in megacities such as Delhi where research suggests that average life expectancy is now being reduced by up to ten years because of pollution.

Many manufacturers will reduce the energy they use per unit of production by at least 50% over the next 20 years, as happened in the European petrochemical industry over the last two decades. By

2040, many factories will produce much or all of their own power from green sources.

Web represents 5% of all global power use

The IT industry will also come under a lot of pressure to be more energy efficient, to save costs as well as the environment. At least 5% of all global energy is consumed in powering the web, including all browsing on local devices. And as we have seen, this does not include 1% of all global energy that could soon be spent mining Bitcoins and other cryptocurrencies, or on transactions using those currencies.

Farms of tens of thousands of web servers are already wasting enough heat to power small towns, which is why so many will be located in future in very cold parts of the world – to cut cooling costs. In some cases the heat generated is already being used to heat homes in cold places, but in most cases 100% of the heat is wasted.

Further growth of $500bn recycling industry

One of the easiest ways to save energy, forests and raw materials is to recycle. A $500bn industry is assisted by subsidies and public goodwill, and will grow rapidly over the next three decades, especially in emerging markets, mainly as a result of new laws. Around 34% of all copper used in factories is already from recycled sources; 500 million tons of steel is recycled in America each year; and 20% of all steel production is recycled, in a process that saves 75% of energy in that industry.

In America alone, the business of recycling corporate waste is worth more than $80bn a year, growing 1% a year, and creating 450,000 jobs. But over 2,000 landfill sites are still taking waste and only 10% of solid waste is recycled. Every American produces 2kg of waste a day, or 64 tons over an average lifetime. America throws away 2.5 million plastic bottles every hour. As I predicted, the Chinese government has now banned most imported plastic and paper waste, which means that 40% more American and European household waste will be processed locally.

Around 400 million tons of plastic is already in the oceans, and on current trends, the weight of marine plastics will be greater than all the fish in the sea by 2050. Micro-particles are now found in just about every marine creature, as well as in millions of people. Expect thousands of new regulations over the next decade globally, to force rapid action on this problem. Part of this will involve a big rethink about polyester clothing and how washing machines are designed – a single clothes wash can release 700,000 microplastic fibres.

A single recycled plastic bottle saves enough energy to run a 100-watt light bulb for four hours. From a carbon emissions point of view, plastics are a very long-term method of carbon capture: they are inert, and carbon molecules in almost all plastics will not convert to carbon dioxide for thousands of years – unless they are made of biodegradable polymers, a relatively new market that will be worth $6bn by 2023.

We will see many innovations in collecting and sorting domestic refuse. Car breakers' yards in the EU are already achieving 100% recovery. Entire cars are cut into small granules of 18 different materials, separated automatically in a continuous process.

The same technology is already being used for domestic and commercial waste in countries with high labour costs, sorting tens of millions of tons a year without human beings involved. But emerging nations will continue almost entirely to sort by hand.

Closed loop recycling is the future

Most recycling is really downcycling: high-grade products end up as low-grade raw materials. So for example, plastic water bottles end up as insulation in new homes, or face tissues end up as newsprint.

True sustainability means closed loop recycling: for example, water bottles are collected, melted down, and recast into new water bottles, repeatedly. Anything else is destructive. Expect huge investment in closed loop technology – indeed entire economies will be built around this. Governments will introduce this rapidly because it costs them nothing to sign a regulation requiring it, voters like the idea, and the technology is proven and is falling in cost.

In Germany, the percentage of plastic drink containers that are rescued and re-formed into new drink containers has leapt from less than half to over 90% in five years – just some of the 35 billion drink containers that are collected by machines made by just one manufacturer, Tomra, in exchange for tokens or cash. But 1.4 trillion drink containers are thrown away each year so we have far to go.

And as raw materials rise in price, expect many old waste dumps to be mined by recycling machines.

Safeguarding water supplies will be a key challenge

Water is one of the primary needs of humanity and we are facing a serious global shortage, especially near megacities. By 2025, two-thirds of humankind will live in areas where there are water shortages, up from one-third today. While nations like Brazil have a surplus of clean river water, most nations are already facing water deficits.

Globally we now use 35% of accessible supplies. Farming uses 60% of all the world's pumped water, even though only 1% of the world's fields are irrigated. An additional 19% is used to dilute pollution, sustain fisheries and transport goods. Thus the human race already uses around half the planet's supply. But water use has quadrupled since 1950 due to a larger and wealthier global population, more intensive faming, and climate change. So, then, it is clear that water demand will increase by at least 40% in many emerging nations by 2040. And pressures will be even greater in areas of hot countries frequented by tourists, with soaring demand for water in popular holiday resorts.

To make matters worse, warmer sea and land temperature means more rain in some places but less in others. Underground water levels are falling in many of the world's most important crop-growing areas, including the western US, large parts of India and north China, where water tables are dropping a metre a year. In some areas of the US, water levels have fallen significantly because of fracking oil and gas. We will see longer pipelines across countries and continents, balancing supply and population. These will create new opportunities for trade, political demands, and sabotage by terrorists or hostile governments.

Water and electricity industries will be even more closely linked in future, as water management uses a lot of power. In addition, as we will see, power can be used to make fresh water from the sea.

Many rivers semi-dead in Asia

Over-irrigation means that many rivers already die for part of the year in Asia. These include most rivers in India, among them the mighty Ganges, a principal water source for south Asia, and China's Yellow River.

With the number of urban dwellers set to reach 5 billion by 2025, steps are being taken to switch water from farms to cities. Three hundred Chinese cities are now experiencing water shortages.

Almost all households in industrialised cities will be affected by 2025, with widespread water metering, 'grey water' systems (for example, bath water stored for watering the garden), and a shift in culture to viewing all water as a limited natural resource. Expect as many regulations on the use of water as on energy conservation.

Thirsty world by 2030

By the year 2030, virtually all of the world's economically accessible rivers will be required to meet the needs of agriculture, industry and households, and to maintain lake and river levels. This is based only on current trends with no allowance for climate change.

The death of the Aral Sea is described by the government of Uzbekistan as one of the most serious ecological catastrophes in the history of the human race, and took place in a single generation. Originally one of the world's largest lakes, its shores are now far from their original location, and mineral levels have risen dramatically.

Coupled with this is coastal pollution. While half the world's population still lacks basic sanitation, 80% of all local sea-water pollution is from contaminants carried there by fresh water.

Ensuring future water supplies

Humanity will find many ways to manage water more efficiently. Here are some ways in which shortages will be dealt with – the first two alone will make a huge difference in most developed nations, and in cities of many emerging nations.

◆ water meters for every user, and charging more per litre

◆ stop leaks – 25% of London's water is lost from ancient pipes

◆ drip irrigation and growing drought-resistant crops

◆ shift water-hungry agriculture to wetter areas of the world

◆ better local water management with small dams for farmers

◆ large dams – also used for power

◆ collect rainwater, e.g. roofs into cisterns

◆ cut water use by washing machines, dishwashers and toilets

◆ recycle waste water or 'grey' water for uses other than drinking, washing or food preparation

◆ increase use of nanotech-coated surfaces that are sterilised or cleaned without using much water, e.g. in urinals.

Desalination will fall in cost and become widespread

Production of fresh water from the sea will grow by at least 8% a year for the next 20 years, and produces around 1% of the world's fresh water today. Expect huge innovation in desalination technologies, with increasing efficiency of new types of membranes, and falling energy costs as green tech becomes far more widely available. Around 50% of Israel's water is already produced this way at 58 cents per cubic metre (ton). The Middle East and Africa are already spending $8bn a year on desalination.

Our world has unlimited sea water and vast amounts of wasted solar energy, so expect integrated facilities that convert light into fresh water, mainly in very hot desert areas, close to the sea. Expect other water sources with lower salt content to be used by desalination plants, like the one installed in East London, which takes tidal waters from the River Thames.

Risk of water wars

Over a decade ago I warned of water wars, and that water would become a national security issue. We then saw this in Syria and Iraq. Rivers, canals, dams, water treatment plants and pipelines all became military targets. Entire cities in desert areas were placed under siege with little or no water.

We could see water wars between nations, quarrelling over, say, how much water flows into a country down a long river, or how much one country is allowed to pollute another's water supply. In 2006, there was a drought in East Africa which caused the levels of water in Lake Victoria to fall. The Ugandan government took a decision to reduce the amount of water flowing out of Lake Victoria through their hydroelectric dam into the source of the River Nile. This was in open defiance of a 1929 treaty under which Egypt had exclusive rights to 80% of the Nile's water. Uganda's action also threatened a crisis for Sudan, a country that similarly depends on the great river.

Germany and Austria were sued by Black Sea states through the EU for polluting the River Danube. Algae blooms in the Black Sea killed millions of fish, and completely wiped out 40 species. Expect many more rows between neighbours up and down river, whether farmers, villages, towns, cities, nations or regions.

Dams will be bigger and more controversial

Controversy will continue to grow over vast dams like the Three Gorges Dam of the Yangtze River in China, which created a lake 600km long, drowned a city of 250,000, and displaced 1.3 million. Three hundred new large dams a year will force up to 4 million people a year to leave their homes around the world, often ancestral lands.

In theory dams are a wonderful idea: offering free power, irrigation, flood prevention, tourist attractions, water sports, fish farming and drought protection. They create jobs, are national status symbols, and prevent global warming. For example, the Congo River at Inga could supply half the energy needs of the whole of Africa, and only 10% of Africa's potential hydroelectric capacity has yet been harnessed.

Daily water use per person (EU)

Europeans use 4.6 tons of water per day, according to Water Footprint Network. But around 3 tons of this is virtual water. For example, every time you eat a single tomato, you are indirectly consuming 13 litres of water, because that was what was needed to grow it. Cotton farming is a major consumer of water. Many different organisations have calculated that around 10,000 litres of water are needed to harvest a single kilogram of cotton fibre.

Cotton wool ball	4.5 litres
Tomato	13 litres
Sheet of paper	13.6 litres
Slice of bread	50 litres
Orange	58 litres
Egg	146 litres
Pint of beer	170 litres
Burger	2,400 litres
Cotton T-shirt	4,000 litres
Leather shoes	9,600 litres
Pair of jeans	11,000 litres

But dams also change environments. Constant irrigation brings salts to the surface, so that farmland is increasingly infertile. Silt that used to be carried by floods clogs up reservoirs, and fish cannot swim upstream.

800 billion cubic metres of virtual water

Nations will look to save water by virtual trading. For example, it takes *a ton of water to grow a single kilogram of rice*. To grow a 40kg bag of rice requires 40 tons of water, and a single 40-ton lorry loaded with rice is the equivalent of importing 1,000 lorries to a water-starved nation, each carrying 40 tons of water – the same as a small ship. You would need 25 such ships to carry enough water to make a single ton of rice, so it is madness to grow rice in a desert. Water-deprived nations like Egypt will be able to save huge amounts of water by producing more goods and growing less food.

Our world is already trading 800 billion tons of virtual water a year, equivalent to all the water flowing down ten rivers the size of the Nile. If all food tariff barriers on shipments to America, Europe and other parts of the world were removed, the amount of virtual water traded would double in a short period of time.

How the world's forests will be saved

Deforestation is the largest cause of greenhouse gas emission, responsible for 23% of the total – more than all cars, trucks, trains, aircraft and ships combined. Every year 13 million hectares of forest are cleared, the equivalent of 50,000 square miles, which is four times the size of Belgium. And illegal logging is continuing on a gigantic scale in nations like Brazil – an industry worth $100bn a year.

Forests produce oxygen, store carbon, increase rainfall and prevent flooding – so we will see rapidly growing efforts to protect and expand them in future. The carbon stores of the world's forests are equivalent to more than 40 times the world's annual global carbon emissions.

Protecting forest also encourages biodiversity. Almost half the world's land species are in Brazil and Indonesia. Expect special efforts to preserve the habitats of these countries.

At the same time, tree planting is taking place on an extraordinary scale. Across Europe, the amount of forest has grown by 15% over the last 15 years – by an area the size of Greece. Every year, the area of new forest created in Europe is growing by the equivalent of 1.5 million football pitches.

Globally, 12 billion trees have been planted in the last 5 years alone, with 2.5 billion planted in 2009 as a global UN initiative – 1 billion more than planned. America recently planted 30 million trees in a single campaign. More than 70 million trees were planted in Spain over two years, 11 million in Romania and 5 million in France. It costs only $5 to save a ton of tree wood from being burnt. Expect many more forest trading schemes that protect or manage vulnerable forest in exchange for carbon credits.

Encouraging and important though this is, planting trees will have limited impact on global warming for the next 50 to 60 years. It's far more important not to cut them down in the first place. A new forest tree may capture a ton of carbon over six decades, but most of that happens in the final 15 years. Almost all the carbon in a mature forest is in living trees, and little is stored long term. When trees die, fall over and are left on the forest floor, their carbon becomes food for organisms ranging from fungi to insects.

Hardly anything remains from a fallen tree after a decade. To prove this, go for a forest walk where trees have grown for 200 years. Dig with a spade to see how deep you go before you hit soil with very little carbon content (for example, yellow sand rather than compost-enriched black soil). The answer is usually no more than a third of a metre. Carbon is only stored for any length of time when biodegrading fails, perhaps because of acid bog or some other unusual factor. So, unless that tree falls into a bog, the only way to keep the wood carbon from returning fairly soon to the atmosphere is to use the timber in buildings or furniture, protecting it from decay or burning.

Paper and cardboard industries can be 'green'

Expect a boom in cardboard consumption from the growth of the global economy; the growth of e-commerce (more packaging for home delivery); and the reduction of plastic by many companies (due to consumer pressure and new laws).

The paper and pulp industry is often condemned for killing trees, destroying forests and wasting energy. However, such activity can actually result in more forest rather than less. The key is in balancing old and new trees. If a new paper mill arrives in virgin forest, cutting down many square kilometres of mature trees, then even with the most active forest management there will be permanent loss of carbon in that forest. The only way for such a company to claim full balance is to plant new trees on at least twice the area as the one they cut down.

Paper and cardboard packaging are in many ways far more eco-friendly than plastic, especially because cellulose from tree fibre is a natural, harmless substance that many organisms digest as food. Imagine a situation where every tree is replaced with several saplings, and all paper or cardboard is recycled at least twice before being burnt in a power station as biomass, or being composted to help grow food. Such an industry can be truly sustainable, and efficient, even more so if – say – woodchips and other tree waste are also used to generate power.

Transcontinental smog – linked to forest burning and coal power

In the next decade, we will continue to see transcontinental smog: whole sections of the surface of the planet where the air on the ground is unhealthy to all and lethal to some. Smog kills by aggravating asthma, bronchitis and a host of other lung conditions and by directly increasing the risk of heart attacks through carbon monoxide exposure. In a city like Calcutta that could mean up to 25,000 additional deaths a year. Across a whole region or continent the results can be devastating.

In 2013 dense smog developed over a million square miles of South East Asia, affecting 300 million people – the worst for 15 years. Indonesia was forced to apologise for its forest burning to grow food. In 1998, Malaysia declared regional smog a national disaster and schools were shut throughout Sarawak because of forest fires in Indonesia. Some estimates suggest that such fires release as much carbon dioxide as Europe produces in a whole year. More recently, West Coast America has been impacted by bad air from China, India and other Asian nations.

Carbon rationing will create tension

Carbon caps and taxes will cause international tension and conflict between emerging and developed nations, unless applied fairly – but that will be almost impossible. We will see many more global energy summits end in deadlock. However, this will not prevent rapid evolution of a wide range of green technologies across the world.

China will be the world's largest investor in green tech over the next three decades – mainly solar and wind – to improve their environment, and as a major export industry. At the same time, other nations will continue to criticise China as the world's largest carbon emitter.

In order to be fair, carbon rations would have to be a fixed allowance calculated for a nation, based on a rate per person per year, perhaps sold on the open market as a tax on all carbon consumption, with subsidies for the poorest and most vulnerable. But such a system would mean that villagers could no longer cut their own trees to make charcoal for cooking, and it would condemn the poorest nations to a relatively carbon-free existence forever.

Emerging nations will continue to insist that they should be able to have their own carbon-based 'industrial revolutions', and that developed nations must accept responsibility for the largest contribution to the mess the world is now in, since this has arisen mainly from their own industrial activities over the last 200 years.

It will be argued that even though the wealthiest nations have reduced their carbon emissions to some extent, they have continued to ransack the earth's limited carbon supplies, and they therefore need to make far more radical cuts in emissions. The UK, for example, was responsible for almost 100% of global carbon emissions in 1790, following its industrial revolution, which was based on coal and steam power.

Enough food for 11 billion people

One of the greatest concerns I hear is that we will be unable to feed a world population that could reach 11 billion by 2050. The good news is that we could probably feed many more, but only with radical changes to land use, food tariffs and other trade barriers.

Food production is the world's largest industry, worth 10% of global GDP, or around $8 trillion a year, if you include farming, food packaging, restaurants, and so on.

According to the UN, 840 million people are malnourished and often go hungry. Although this number has fallen by 160 million in ten years, this statistic is one of the most shameful trends in this book, particularly as it is relatively easy to deal with. We will look further at the ethical implications of global hunger in the next chapter.

Today, we already grow enough food to feed 9 billion. But we waste at least 40%, worth $3 trillion – in fields, storehouses, factories, warehouses, shops and domestic rubbish bins. In some nations, 25% or more of what is grown is lost in harvesting or while stored on the farm, or damaged when transported. And in many EU nations, more than 30% of food purchased is thrown away. In America, 60 million tons of food is thrown away a year, worth $160bn. With advances in agriculture, better infrastructure, larger farms, better types of crops and livestock, and less food waste, there is no doubt that we will be able (in theory) to feed everyone on the earth in 50 to 100 years' time. Will we see an end to hunger then? Maybe not – because of local issues such as drought and crop failures, civil conflicts and refugee crises.

We will see more genetically modified crops in many regions, with crops resistant to disease, needing less fertiliser, less water, and able to grow in salty soil. Such crops will mean fewer chemicals in farming, in theory protecting insects, birds and other wildlife, but many such crops are toxic to pests, with unknown longer-term impact.

Expect continued growth of demand for organic food by consumers, for three reasons: protection of the countryside, health and taste. We have seen 400% growth in organic sales since 2004 to $100 billion a year, led by the US, Germany, France, Canada, China and Denmark (in which 10% of all farmland is already organic). Organic farming has been 18% less productive: but better methods will reduce that gap to almost zero for many crops.

Genetically modified animals will also be widely consumed in over 30% of the world by 2040. Expect a rise in the proportion of global grain production used to feed animals to more than 45% beyond 2025. Already more than 70% of grain produced by wealthy nations is fed to livestock. It can take as little as 1.3kg of grain to produce 1kg of chicken meat, down from 2.5kg in 1985, due to anti-biotics in feed and other things – chicken meat production is up

70% since 1990. Around 23 billion chickens are being raised at any time. We need 7kg of grain for 1kg of beef (but only if cattle are kept on mainly grain diet as is often the case in the US).

So how much more meat are we talking about? In Germany, for example, people will eat an average of 1,094 animals during their lifetime: 4 cows, 4 sheep, 12 geese, 37 ducks, 46 pigs, 46 turkeys, 945 chickens. Expect similar levels per person of meat consumption by over 4 billion people in 2040, compared to a fraction of that today. Meat consumption will rise among emerging middle-class populations, for whom meat has in the past been a very expensive luxury, and will fall among many wealthier members of developed nations, who will be increasingly anxious about cholesterol levels, heart disease, the risk of stroke, obesity and bowel cancer, animal welfare on the farm and in the abattoir, and about lack of food supply to feed all these animals.

As world population has grown, as more wealthy people eat more meat, and as more land is being used to create biofuels, the total area of land being used for agriculture has doubled since 1961. But there are absolute limits on the availability of suitable land. Satellites show that 40% of total land area globally is already used in farming, mainly pasture, with 12% for crops.

Therefore, we can expect the price of farm land to continue to rise over the next 20 years, as it has over the last decade.

Expect great advances in mechanisation, for example robot tractors and harvesters, with fertiliser dosage linked to rainfall and soil condition. We will see the rapid growth of sensor-based food: sorting machines on large farms in Europe and America that wash, photograph and grade every fruit and vegetable, testing a million items an hour for sugar content, selecting for premium restaurants, supermarkets, food manufacturers, fruit juice or animal feed – improving productivity by 5 to 10%, and aiming for zero waste.

Green revolution in Africa – and China's land grab

A number of African nations will embark on a 'green revolution' similar to that seen in India in the 1970s and 1980s. This will be accelerated by nations like China that are buying up huge areas of fertile African land to secure their national food supplies, investing in infrastructure such as transport and water supplies, as well as training and other expertise to help improve African farming output.

Over the last decade alone, 177,000 square miles of farmland has been bought in 734 deals – that's almost the size of Spain, or Thailand – from nations such as Ethiopia, Ghana, Madagascar, Mali and Sudan. But nations like Ukraine are also selling. The Chinese bought a 50-year lease for 11,500 square miles in Ukraine, 5% of the nation's land area, equivalent in size to Belgium or the state of Massachusetts, and China will soon be the largest foreign owner of Australian farms. China has 20% of global population and only 7% of the world's farmland.

Two-thirds of those who are hungry are small-scale subsistence farmers, and it will be impossible to radically improve food yields across Africa without large-scale consolidation of farms, and mechanisation. This will be traumatic for those whose tribes have lived on that land for generations. At the other end of the scale, many areas are returning to bush as workers migrate to cities.

Growing more fish and protecting the seas

Globally 3 billion people get around 20% of their protein from fish. Demand for fish will grow faster than for meat, because of increasing wealth and the desire to reduce obesity and heart disease.

A third of wild fish stocks have been over-fished and 25% of all fishing is illegal or unreported. Global populations of large fish such as tuna, swordfish and marlin have fallen by over 85% during the last 70 years, and other species like mackerel are down by more than 50%. Regulation on the size of catches, or on what species can be landed in ports, often leads to boats dumping most fish overboard, dead. We will see great debate about how to better manage fisheries, and better technology to reduce the catch of unwanted fish. This will also help protect threatened species such as turtles and dolphins.

Future generations will regard the idea of feeding towns and cities on wild-swimming ocean fish as bizarre – as strange as the idea of shooting wild buffalo in America to make hamburgers. They will think it even stranger if developed nations are still handing out $35bn a year in ocean fishing subsidies.

Fish farming will become a global obsession. This is potentially a great sustainability story, supporting hundreds of thousands of low-income coastal dwellers growing high protein, healthy food, and protecting wild fish stocks. But at present it takes 1.7kg of forage fish (converted fish meal) from the ocean to grow 1kg of salmon in a fish farm. The only advantage is that fish farms can use all kinds of weird-looking creatures from the sea that consumers would not dream of eating.

Scientists will find ways to feed fish without using large amounts of other ocean fish and sea creatures. New kinds of farmed fish will be created, with genes that allow them to digest food grown on land; or crops will be altered so that the proteins they make are suitable for farmed fish. But then we are in the same situation as we are in feeding crops to animals – it's a very inefficient way to produce protein or carbohydrate or fat for people to eat.

We will also see growing concern about genetically altered fish escaping into the ocean, upsetting food chains and ecosystems, especially if they are 'unnatural' mutants, created in laboratories. It is already the case that 25% of all 'wild' salmon caught in Scotland have escaped from fish farms in Norway, or are descended from fish that have escaped in the past. If escaped fish are genetically modified and able to reproduce, then we permanently alter entire species across all oceans, with many potential risks – if, for example, mutant genes make certain fish more aggressive predators, thereby upsetting food chains.

Future of retail food and drink industry

We have already seen how grocery and food retailing is being transformed. The retail food industry will continue to be conservative and risk-averse, with long-enduring and much-loved brands that span several generations – foods that grandmothers remember eating when they themselves were children.

We have also seen how sensitive the food industry is to issues of consumer trust, which will drive the continued growth of traceability, transparency, labelling, and so on. The entire food industry will be far more tightly regulated in future. We will also see a new focus on the health aspects of foods: expect new *performance* foods with claims that they build strength, or immunity, or improve memory.

Nutrition will be a number-one issue for many well-informed food buyers, who will increasingly recognise the benefits of nourishing healthy gut bacteria, which make many of the molecules that we need to renew our own cells and fight disease. Expect many new types of food preparations and formulations, designed to create foods with optimum nutritional value, using ultrasonics, special additives, hyper-speed blenders, liposomes and a host of other technologies. The boundaries between pharmacology and nutritional microbiome science will blur and some pharma companies will expand into this lightly regulated area.

Expect new frozen-food technologies to be adopted rapidly, allowing even the most delicate of fruits to be perfectly frozen without damage or changes in taste and texture. The same methods will be used to perfectly preserve vegetables and very delicate fish. The results of this technology are astonishing to food lovers, and will delight chefs of the best restaurants in the world.

Expect a rethink about food irradiation over the next few years, as a low-cost way to ensure long shelf life, and less food waste, without altering taste, following a wave of additional research that suggests it is completely safe. It means, for example, that a loaf of bread can stay perfectly fresh in a sealed plastic bag for many months.

We will also see many more food scandals such as happened with the contamination of rice in China, and of animal feed by dioxin in Belgium. Each will cause a huge emotional reaction in consumers, with widespread, angry boycotts. Expect improvements in animal welfare across the EU and in other nations, and an increase in use of animal tagging for 100% traceability.

Anti-food for fat people

We have already seen how 50% of the world will be obese by 2030. Expect a new generation of 'safe' slimming drugs that kill appetite or prevent food absorption, for a market that could be worth at least $10bn a year in the US alone. An example is likely to be molecules similar to the hormone thyroxine, which caused monkeys to lose 7% of their weight in a week on a normal diet, with few side effects. Meanwhile the so-called 'Fatlash' movement will grow, promoting the erroneous belief that to be fat is healthy, and fighting the stigmatisation of fat people. Expect lawsuits against food companies for alleged irresponsible promotion of unhealthy food, and a direct connection to sickness or death.

Expect to see a new food industry selling anti-food, or food with absolutely no nutritional value – a strange contrast to hyper-nutritional food. The first anti-food was a new fat made from molecules that the body cannot digest. This can be used in cakes, ice creams or any other food. It cooks well, but comes straight out the other end unchanged. Bowel movements become greasy. A diet rich in this anti-food can produce vitamin deficiencies, as well as creating a generation of bingeing anorexics able to consume huge plates of food yet waste away to the point of death.

It will be another irony of the third millennium: one billion people starving or undernourished and millions of others using scarce resources to make food that they will waste through total excretion.

We will also see a new generation of better-tasting artificial sweeteners, and rapid expansion of diabetic-friendly food, designed also to help non-diabetics manage their own weight.

Catering for anxious eaters

Expect growth of 'natural' foods and 'natural' packaging as people begin to worry about the health risks of oestrogen-like chemicals leaching out of plastic (see p. 95), some preferring traditional, recyclable glass containers for milk and other products.

Expect anti-additive food companies to create entire kitchen environments where nothing 'artificial' ever contaminates what people eat or drink. Expect new ranges of meat substitutes with the right texture and taste for some who insist on it. Expect a rash of new health scares related to extreme diets of various kinds, such as nutritional deficiencies, especially in children,

Expect more stampedes by consumers from one food to another, following the latest food scare. Expect an end to the worst poultry factory farms in most developed nations, as worries over food poisoning add another chorus to animal welfare campaigns. Expect food retailers and producers who break the rules to be 'punished' by increasingly militant groups, threatening boycotts and intimidation as well as shareholder action.

Most changes in the food industry will come mainly from consumer pressure, followed only later on by regulations. Expect much confusion and anxiety over what is safe or unsafe, especially in parents with very young children, but also in those over the age of 60 who tend to have a greater focus on staying well.

Millions fled from drinking 'disgusting' tap water only to find that the bottled water they bought at high cost had higher levels of bacteria, was impossible to differentiate from tap water in blind testing studies and, what's more, was contaminated by pollutants from storage in plastic bottles. Expect carbon/transport taxes on bottled water imported from other nations, targeting premium brands.

Global sales of vitamins will continue to see spectacular growth, although controversy will rage over what doses should be taken by whom – or even if they should be taken at all. Most evidence suggests that synthetic molecules do not have the same bio-impact as they do when absorbed as part of normal foods. We will also continue to see health scares relating to mega doses of certain types of vitamin tablets.

Vegetarians and semi-vegetarians look for new products

The broader vegetarian market will grow from 5% to 30% of the US population by 2025, if you include people who eat meat occasionally, and millions of others who choose to eat far less meat than is eaten today. Red, fatty meat will be less popular, because of worries about bowel cancer and heart disease. In Britain, 40% of people often eat vegetarian foods as a conscious alternative to eating a meal containing meat or fish, ten times the number of strict vegetarians, and the industry is worth more than £1 billion a year.

Expect fast growth for certain 'veggie' products. For example, sales of vegetarian grills and burgers increased by 139% in 5 years in the UK, as technology and taste have improved. Expect new meat substitutes – meat-like substances made from wheat gluten and pea protein with the bite, character, flavour and look of meat. Their growth in market share will be modest, however.

Expect a gradual fall in resistance in many nations other than the US to genetically modified food, particularly in France, Austria, Hungary, Greece, Luxembourg, Poland and Bulgaria – while Germany will remain more cautious.

Huge consolidation in drinks market

Expect huge changes in the drinks industry over the next three decades as hundreds of millions of consumers shift away from carbonated sugary beverages to fruit juices and then to bottled water, for health reasons. We will see more research showing that diet drinks also carry health risks, stimulating release of insulin, with increased risk of heart attack and diabetes. That will not stop sugar taxes on carbonated drinks, which will boost diet versions of the same products. Expect further scrutiny of all artificial sweeteners, as the debate continues about potential health risks from consuming large amounts of some or all of these.

Expect even more evidence suggesting widespread health benefits from coffee drinking and, to a lesser extent, green tea. In both cases this may be linked to antioxidants/flavonoids, which appear to have multiple positive effects. Health benefits will boost the $20bn trade each year in coffee beans, which in turn will benefit 20 million growers in 60 nations. Millennials will drive 5% growth in coffee drinking globally over the next decade, as many older people cut down consumption.

Radical changes to work patterns

Many predictions have been made about the 'end of work', as we know it. Some say that most manual jobs will disappear, creating a huge underclass of unemployable people; that most office jobs will also be automated; that a high proportion of managers will work at home; that many domestic chores will be done by robots who will also care for the frail and elderly; and that most manufacturing jobs will be lost to Asia, together with many service jobs such as banking, call centres and software development.

This all makes for good media stories but, as we have seen, the reality will be less dramatic over the next 25 years. The most radical shifts in employment patterns will be in emerging nations, mainly related to urban migrations from rural areas. Every industrial revolution has spread by using technology to save costs, which means that people's incomes and time can be spent on other things.

Job creation in nations with high unemployment

During the 2008–2013 crisis, unemployment rates among young people rose to above 40% in parts of Spain and Italy, with people warning of a lost generation. So where will new jobs come from?

More women workers and part-timers in the UK

The real key to economic growth is the number of people in work, and in many nations, that number has soared.

More women are entering the workplace, more people who were not working are now working part-time; older people are working longer before they retire; students are working to pay for their courses; and more people are migrating into the country looking for work. So the most important indicator in future will not be numbers looking for work, but the growing numbers of people who have a job.

Insatiable demand to create more jobs

So what kind of jobs will be needed in future, to absorb all of these people, assuming they have the right skills? Many jobs in developed nations will be in service and support roles for middle-class consumers. Homes will be redecorated more often, lawns will be mown more regularly, public spaces and amenities will be better maintained, people will have their hair styled more frequently and eat out more often, and more people in developed nations will employ others to clean their homes. An example in the UK is the boom in car valeting by hand and the death of cheap, car-washing robots in garages. Another in Japan is the boom in Wagyu beef production, which requires human beings to give cows regular massages. As Parkinson's famous law states: 'work always expands to fill the time available'.

In addition, as any politician will tell you, there is an almost insatiable desire by the public in most nations for better public services. That means more doctors, nurses, teachers, street cleaners, police, gardeners in parks, tree planters, graffiti cleaners, home carers, therapists, family support workers, counsellors, advisors, mentors, and so on.

And one of the main reasons that all those jobs are not created is because of budget, which is in turn limited by what people are prepared to pay in taxes, and by the size of the economy in general.

Yet the strange thing is that in the very same nation you may have several million people on benefits of some kind, who would love to have a job. It's all a question of pay scales, benefit structures, incentives and fairness. So there will be plenty of work to do in tomorrow's world, and there will also be plenty of 'paid' workers in developed nations to do it. The problem will often be a structural one within society itself.

At the same time, as we will see in the next chapter, most people in the UK gladly volunteer to give their time at some point in their lives, for no financial reward, to do some of the tasks listed above. Yet if they are on benefits, in many parts of the world it becomes more complicated for them to do such voluntary work.

Internships as fast track to a great job

One thing is certain: while business schools will continue to try to justify expensive MBAs, the fast-track route into many companies will be internships. In the US, 63% of students already complete at least one internship before qualifying. As these are unpaid posts, expect government crackdowns on abuse, since they are a convenient way of getting round minimum-pay requirements.

Why offices have a great future

As we saw in Chapter 3, just as with cities, the future is bright for offices. Humans are genetically programmed to socialise. Great teams love being together as tribes, breathing the same air, and video calls are no substitute for face-to-face trust-building.

Expect radical changes in how offices are used. Office space per worker has already fallen by 35% in 15 years, and will fall a further 25–30% in the next 15, with more hot-desking and partial homeworking. And more informal meetings will be in coffee shops. But most major company activities over the next two decades will continue to be via face-to-face meetings at offices, in most parts of the world.

Expect more corporations to completely outsource the management of their offices. Typical contracts for large banks or retail chains will be worth over $1bn a year. Facilities management will dominate hotels, manufacturers, airports, schools, hospitals and prisons as well as offices.

Corporate HQs overtaken by events

Elaborate HQ spending by huge multinationals will grow, with a number of embarrassing mistakes as mergers or sell-offs force relocation or resizing of HQs, even before buildings have been completed. More real-estate-rich companies will sell off and lease back their properties to release cash for their core businesses, creating a boom in real estate management.

Future of homeworking

Over 4 million people in the UK work mainly or exclusively from home, 14% of the workforce, but this has increased by only 3% since 1998 – hardly the stampede out of office life that many pundits predicted.

Even IT companies like Yahoo and Google have discouraged or banned homeworking. Of course, it could be said that almost everyone now works from home to a certain extent, due to ever-present email, smartphones, and so on, but very few people *decide* to work mainly or exclusively from home when offered the chance to do so by their companies. More popular is working at home one day a week, or for short periods of time.

Most so-called homeworkers are self-employed, in the older age bracket, and higher earning. Many self-employed people work outside their own home – for example as cleaners, plumbers or childminders. Only 34% of homeworkers are employed by an organisation.

Part of this in future will be greater emphasis on work–life balance, the desire to be in control of how and when you work, or when you take holiday.

Patterns of daily work will continue to change

Most office workers will still commute to work in 20 years' time for at least two to three days a week, although they will be entirely mobile, able to work at any desk, any seat, in any situation. The primary function of workplaces will be sharing ideas, provoking thought and rapid change, testing solutions, making decisions, monitoring progress. As we have seen, for reasons of efficiency and speed, paper will still be used in many senior meetings by 2025, and whiteboards or flipcharts will continue to be a vital way of capturing and synthesising ideas in 2030.

We will also see more virtual teams and virtual organisations – particularly smaller companies with employees scattered in every continent, most of whom have never met, and where most are paid as required in consulting-type arrangements rather than fixed salaries.

More portfolio workers

More people will work shifts as our whole world transitions to an always-available culture, and as companies become more globalised, supporting staff and customers across time zones.

Far more people will work part-time or as portfolio workers. Over a million men in the UK now choose to work less than full-time, following what was predominantly a female work pattern. For many, part-time contracts will be a door into portfolio working, picking up a day or two a week of regular work, or project work, alongside longer roles.

Time zone challenges

Globalisation will continue to mean long-distance travel for many senior executives, because most people find endless electronic meetings rather impersonal.

The greatest barrier to the global village is sunlight. In a 'perfect' working world, every team member would be in the same time zone. And that is the crux of a growing problem.

Longer, less intense working hours

As a result, we will see a shift in how leaders work – with many virtual meetings, very early or late, but with more time off in the middle of the day. This new kind of routine will make more sense to those who work a lot at home, especially if their partners frequently do the same.

Living 'on call' is nothing new. Doctors, among others, have been used to it for decades. Some say that this new pattern of global time keeping is unhealthy or unnatural. Of course, it is the normal pattern for mothers or fathers at home alone with several small children. The daily routine in such environments cannot be neatly switched on or off.

The problem of daylight incompatibility is made worse by cross-cultural differences. A company in San Francisco trading with Dubai finds not only a disruptive time difference, but also that Dubai works from only 7 a.m. till 1 p.m. and does not work on Fridays – yet works a normal day on Sundays.

Workforce in danger of being left behind

Despite new technology, people will always be less mobile than capital, technology, information and raw materials. And, as we have seen, tribalism is a social force that thrives on breathing the same air, so local teams are here to stay.

Skills in a workforce will continue to be a vital national asset. Expect large-scale investment in work-related skills, with special emphasis on health, engineering, technology and other sciences, by governments of many emerging markets such as China, South Korea and Saudi Arabia.

If you want to draw on a community's skills, you will move your site to where those skills are. This is not just about local talent, but national psyche, tax incentives, conversations in the local bar or coffee house, or a deal forged over a game of golf.

Home ownership makes moving more difficult and expensive. In France, Italy, Spain and Belgium the cost of selling a house and buying another is high. Home ownership is less of a barrier to moving in the US, as buying and selling is easier.

Home ownership will continue to be popular, but many home owners will become absentee landlords, renting out homes while they are working in other places.

Executives often need more than money to move, however, and in many Western nations other factors will become more important. For example, workers with frail parents will continue to think twice before making long-distance moves. Similarly, parents with teenagers at a critical stage in their education are often extremely reluctant to make a major move. So too are those on their second or third marriages, having perhaps learned painful lessons about neglecting home life, and with a 'new' set of very young children to whom they wish to give more time.

Employers will need to give far greater attention to double-career households, where two people's futures need to be considered in any major move.

Lower down the social scale are armies of mobile male workers in countries like India who are used to spending 11 months a year away from home, earning money to support a wife and family. Many go farther afield, for example working in Dubai as taxi drivers, returning only once every two to three years to see loved ones. But these kinds of lifestyles will not be tolerated by a younger generation of emerging middle-class workers, who have fought hard for a university degree.

Ageing workers – radical changes ahead

One in three people who are still working after the age of 65 in the UK have no idea when they will be able to retire. One in seven of the entire workforce have no plans to retire at all, and a third have no private pension. Bizarrely, most 25- to 31-year-olds expect to retire younger than 65.

Older people will be an increasingly important part of the workforce, especially in Europe, Japan and China. Managers will face delicate dilemmas as retirement ages are abolished (despite huge resistance in nations like France and Italy where pressures will continue to keep retirement age lower than 65). How do you counsel someone out of their job, someone who has become too rigid in thinking, or is slightly forgetful, or too physically frail? With no fixed retirement ages, managers will have to fire large numbers of older people. Managing elderly team members will be one of the most stressful and time-consuming aspects of any senior role in future.

Managing talent with purpose

Expect rapid growth in consultancies and management tools, to help large corporations identify, promote, reward and develop the most talented people they have. Linked to this will be a growing emphasis on giving people purpose and fulfilment at work, connecting with their natural desire to make a difference. We will explore this further in the next chapter.

And finally … a 'BIG IDEA'

We have seen how an ideological void was created with the collapse of communism. Karl Marx was born in Prussia in 1818 and died in London in 1883. He wrote *The Communist Manifesto* in 1847. He was a product of his time: a protester against the Industrial Revolution, which placed wealth and power in the hands of a few, 'enslaving millions' in primitive working conditions. Revolution to free workers from capitalist control was Marx's Big Idea.

Tomorrow's Big Idea

We can expect to see another Big Idea emerge, radically different from any political system in the twentieth century. This new 'ism' will feed on stored-up hunger for change. The longer the delay in its coming, the greater the speed with which it is likely to grip the earth. This Big Idea is likely to draw heavily on Islamic or Christian influence, but be separate from mainstream traditions.

What will this new 'Big Idea' be like?

The Big Idea is likely to be created from a fusion of single issues, grouped around a central philosophy or ideal, based on the teachings of a respected leader, long-lasting in its effects, and highly confusing to old 'logic' politicians. And because of the way our world is shifting demographically and economically, it is statistically more likely that such a movement will have its origins in emerging nations, or will rapidly become established in those parts of the world after a far less dramatic start in a developed nation.

Such a Big Idea could profoundly influence how several billion people think about ethics, values, motivation and personal spirituality, which we now need to turn to in the next chapter.

Chapter 6

ETHICAL

ETHICAL IS THE MOST IMPORTANT face of the future. Ethics strikes at the very heart of what it means to be human, to have purpose, ideals, direction, vision – and in some cases spirituality. And what people believe about ethics is going to change radically.

Recent banking and political scandals have been a sharp reminder of why 'ethics' really do matter. From 2009 to 2017, 43 of the world's largest banks were fined $321bn, of which 63% was in America, and that's just those where fines were more than $100m per case, with hundreds of others still to be decided. To give an idea of scale, those fines are equivalent to the size of the entire GDP of Spain.

Every week yet more scandals emerge around the world, where executives or government leaders have made money in bad ways. Cheating, deceiving, covering up, over-charging, price manipulation, with whole teams involved, fraud taking place on a gigantic scale, and in a hundred different forms. We will return to this later.

Corruption costs at least 5% ($2.6 trillion) of global GDP – fat bribes for government contracts, tax revenues diverted into secret bank accounts, dishonest judges or crooked policemen, and so on.

Without shared ethics, our future will surely descend into a lawless, chaotic hell with unrestrained greed, extremes of wealth, and widespread social unrest. Every revolution in history has been driven by public resentment over ethical issues, including oppression and other abuses of power. As we have seen, every trend has an ethical dimension, whether invasion of privacy, increasing retirement age, an uncensored web, outsourcing of jobs, contrasts in wealth or access to health care.

What kind of world do you want?

Ethics is linked to values, purpose and the meaning of life: why you get out of bed in the morning, what motivates and inspires you, your sense of destiny and personal spirituality. Ethics is also about corporate behaviour, expected conduct, compliance, regulations and the boundaries of what is acceptable.

Ethics is also about what kind of world we want to live in; how we feel about life, our hopes, dreams and desires, our passions and motivations. Ethics gives us the framework for a better future. Ethics is usually about *our* future rather than *my* future – about the greatest good for the greatest number – and is therefore linked to sustainability.

Of course, every tribe and nation has its own culture, way of life and ethical code, every religion its own standards. Can there be, therefore, a *universal* ethic that will shape our future? Can we find a way to predict all future ethics based on future common sense?

The search for future purpose

Our world is changing, but human nature is the same as it was 2,000 years ago. People still look for meaning in their lives and want to feel that they make a difference. As a physician, I worry if someone tells me that they don't feel they have any meaning in their life, they don't feel they contribute anything very much to those around them, and that although they may be loved by their families, they have nothing really to offer.

I can tell you that such a person should be put immediately on the danger list. They are surely low in spirits, and their risk of self-harm or suicide will be high. When we lose a sense of purpose or of making a difference, something dies deep inside our soul. That is why old people tend to live longer when they own a pet dog or cat, and why so many old people die soon after the death of a partner or a pet.

This search for purpose is more intense when people have more money and time to think. The M generation is particularly focused on purpose. I have taught at various business schools over the last 18 years. The new generation want to make a difference. They want to work for themselves or for companies they believe in, selling products and services that make the world a better place.

The ultimate ethical test

When I started out as a cancer physician over three decades ago my job was to look after people dying at home in the last few weeks of life. I learned a very important lesson. Life is short.

Life is far too short to do things you don't believe in.

When I lecture around the world, I often ask audiences to put up their hands if they agree with me, and almost everyone does. Sometimes they shout, cheer and clap.

Why sell things you would never dream of recommending to a friend or a member of your family? Why bother to sell things that you know are not right for your customers? Why bother to work for a company that you are ashamed of?

There is more to life than managing. There is more to life than working. In fact, there is more to life than life itself. What will I leave when I die? How will my children remember me when I'm gone?

I once gave a trends presentation in New York to the board of a huge global corporation. Among many slides, I showed one for a few seconds:

*Life is too short to **sell** things you don't believe in.*

I learned afterwards that one of the board members was so struck that she resigned her post almost immediately, not from that board, but from her high-flying job as CEO of one of the largest private banks in the world.

She realised that she did *not* believe in what she was doing, selling bank products with the highest commissions rather than those that were best for her customers. She now runs her own corporation, providing independent financial advice to very wealthy clients.

Unethical – or just feeling uneasy?

The question of *ease* or *unease* is a central test of how ethics will play out in future. You may be asked to do something, and there is no law against it, nor is there any absolute reason why you should not do it, many others are already doing it, but the thought makes you feel *uneasy*.

Ease of mind is the whisper of conscience, and a powerful guide to future ethics.

We have seen this hundreds of times in the last decade alone, in banking scandals, corruption investigations, and a host of other media stories. All too often, actions that only caused a flicker of unease at the time are condemned as unethical within a year or two, and soon become illegal, with offenders in prison.

Follow the spirit of every agreement

A strong test is not what the *letter* of a long contract actually says, but what the *spirit* of the agreement is all about. Not what you may be able to get away with, but what is the right thing to do.

I have advised many large corporations on tricky ethical issues. Time and again I have seen that the knee-jerk reaction of most business leaders is to protect company profits and their own share options, even if it means kicking their customers, or suppliers, or staff or regulators. But it's a dangerous and unfulfilling path.

Why hiding behind legal opinion is so risky

The harder people try to justify themselves, the more likely that they are in deep trouble. I remember a situation a while back where lawyers were being paid to find 'wriggle room' or clauses in every contract that could allow that particular company to get away with something.

Leaders often hide behind legal opinion. But the longer and more complex your legal advice, the weaker your case usually is.

And as we will see, you can comply with the precise letter of every law, and later be totally trashed in the media.

Companies will need to take a common-sense view

For me the situation is simple: what are the reasonable expectations of the other party in this agreement? How would you like to be treated yourself, in their shoes? What is a common-sense view? What will the public's gut feeling be if they read about this in the media? When you try to explain what you are doing to a close friend, do you sense a little twinge deep inside?

'But everyone else is doing it'

I recall a company that admitted that their practice of giving hidden 'benefits' to customers was illegal, but everyone else in the industry was doing it. If they stopped, they would go out of business. If they blew the whistle on the entire industry to regulators, they would be blamed by all their customers, and would go out of business.

My advice was simple: you will be found out one day anyway, as it will only take a single former employee or customer to go public; you will gain a huge moral advantage in coming clean and exposing wrong practices; and you will make things far worse by continuing. And I was right. Huge corporate fines followed, the senior team was disgraced, and the brand was damaged globally.

'But it's legal in that country – even if illegal elsewhere'

Other companies have a strategy for 'ethics dumping' – they just move dubious activities to nations with less regulation. An example could be a pharma company with double standards: complying with US laws on American embryo experiments, while at the same time funding another company to do 'banned' embryo research in China, where regulations are still less strict on such things. But such practices are so easily exposed. Even if you don't care about the ethics, it is often very risky.

Only sell what you believe in

Here is a fundamental, safe, ethical rule of life, that will last 10,000 years.

Love your neighbour as yourself.

Always treat others as you would like to be treated. That means staff, customers, business partners, road drivers, toilet cleaners, suppliers, associates, neighbours, friends and family.

If every manager and leader in every company followed this teaching of Jesus and Moses, our world would be a better place, and we would have far stronger corporate ethics.

$20,000 competition to test the secret of all ethics

A few years ago I wrote *Building a Better Business*. In it, I promised $20,000 to anyone who could find a way to sell a product, lead, manage or motivate people without using a particular four-word phrase – in one way or another.* I have offered the same prize to many tens of thousands in my corporate audiences over the last decade.

This four-word phrase, or the idea within it, turns out to be the basis of every effective corporate mission statement, every marketing slogan that works, every leadership vision, the foundation of all change management, and will be the cornerstone of all corporate ethics for over a thousand years. So what is this simple four-word phrase, and why has no one ever won the $20,000 prize?

Building a better world

So if you want to know the future of corporate values, which mission statements will have greatest inspirational power, which motivational tools will work best, the answers are all contained in that phrase, and always will be. The fundamental question for

---

* Prize donated by me to any charitable foundation chosen by the winner. See rules in the book *Building a Better Business*.

every future lawmaker, regulator, judge or jury will always be this: will this decision make our world a better or worse place?

Building a better world is hard-wired into our genes

As little children, we soon learn ways to make life better for ourselves. Then we become aware of the existence of others, that life is also about making life better for members of our family, and for our friends. A further stage of growing up is wanting to make life better for neighbours and community, and hopefully for our wider world.

These instincts are part of our nature, as social creatures, as human beings who form families, tribes, nations. We see much the same in the animal kingdom, especially among 'higher' mammals, in social packs, communities, herds, or even in the nesting instincts of birds.

Why crimes are so rare

These ethical instincts are the reason why crimes are so *rare*. Think about it. When you travel on the metro or walk across the street, consider the value of what you are carrying – perhaps a smart phone, a portable computer, credit cards and cash.

If someone came up to you with a knife and asked for your phone and wallet, how likely would you be to put up a fight? Most people just hand things over. So it's an easy and instant win for any impulsive thief. But how often does it happen? The answer is very rarely, considering the wealth that many carry.

For the same reason, as we saw earlier, considering the huge size of our global population, there are very few arbitrary shootings of strangers or stabbings, or bomb attacks – even if you include murders by people who are severely mentally ill. Yet you will find sharp knives as 'lethal weapons' in every kitchen, in every home. America has more guns in homes than adults, and simple bombs are easy for any older child to make, using instructions online.

Throughout almost all of human history you will find a common code of respect within societies, and this same code will also dominate the next hundred years. Enshrined increasingly in laws, human rights regulations, and cultural expectations, our world is increasingly aligned to common ethics, despite gory media headlines.

The search for human happiness – Happynomics

Personal purpose and sense of fulfilment are closely related to happiness. Expect huge growth in research on human happiness and radical questions about values when the results confirm this truth. Research into Happynomics shows that happiness in developed nations is strongly linked to some or all of the following: mid-range income, good friends, stable marriage or partnership, strong faith or spirituality, extrovert nature, liking your job, living in a stable democracy.

A survey of 64,000 people in 65 nations found that 70% of people are content with their lives. And suicide rates are falling rapidly across the world – by 29% since 2000. In many developed nations, suicide rates have been falling for generations – for example the UK peak was in 1934. China's rate has been falling since 1990. Russia, Japan, South Korea and India have all seen major falls in the last decade. But America's rate has risen 18% since 2000. A key factor in the falls has been greater contentment among younger women, and among those over 65 years old.

Africa is the place where people are happiest (83%), while people in Western Europe are the least happy, with 11% saying they are unhappy or very unhappy. In Africa 75% expect life to get better, compared to only 26% in Europe.

Agony columns are full of advice about how to have happy relationships. In a fractured, increasingly disordered and fast-moving world, long-term relationships are going to matter more. One sign of success for the future will be to be living happily with the same person for a long time. What's so smart about a string of failed marriages, shacked-up arrangements or temporary flings?

Single issues and ethics go hand in hand

Single issues define a problem, but only ethics can tell you what position to take. Expect more fierce debates and soul-searching over such issues as arms sales, as attempts are made to define exactly what arms are. Do you include machine tools used to make arms, for example? A global company can find itself caught in the crossfire between shareholder opinion, public perception and views of staff. There may also be a variety of attitudes within the same government, ranging from approval to turning a blind eye to outright opposition and legal action.

Activists are often sharply divided over the ethics of – say – wind power (damaging skyline) compared to solar power (damaging roof appearance and fields), or nuclear power or gas power.

Political correctness and thought control

'Political correctness' will grow in power in the next three decades as single-issue groups try to control the words we use. It is hard to express ideas if words are banned. 'Mentally challenged' instead of mentally handicapped. 'Senior citizens' instead of the elderly or retired. 'Visually impaired' instead of blind.

Defending civil liberties

We will see more attempts by governments to justify bad things, with the argument that 'the end justifies the means'. So people today can have their homes broken into by the police or secret service or their smartphone bugged just because a politician or government worker says it should be done.

Civil liberties will remain on the agenda of most nations of the world, especially as online surveillance and tracking becomes almost universal. Human rights will also continue to be a major issue, especially in negotiation of trade agreements with developing countries. There will be many agonies of conscience over whether a government should engage in buying or selling major contracts with 'odious' regimes – and debates on how such things should be determined.

Challenging human rights abuse in other nations

Many will argue that there is no point in criticising a nation for poor human rights, when your own economy depends on trade with them, and where such protests are only likely to increase the cultural isolation that already exists.

Most challenges by America or the EU to countries like China will continue to fall on deaf ears, and will be rejected as pompous and arrogant, based on ignorance. The Chinese government believes that the greatest human right is to be able to work and eat rather than starve, and believes it is doing well with these things, while being more open than for decades as an evolving society. China believes that too much freedom, too fast, could place at risk all that has been achieved so peacefully. There is a belief that 'leaders know best' what is good for the people.

Expect to hear more about human responsibilities, with responsibilities and rights becoming equal pillars of global codes of ethics. The Universal Declaration of Human Rights was a product of the Second World War, and was set out in 1948. Expect a similar Declaration of Human Responsibilities.

Wealth can create a more ethical world

Most people in developed nations have doubts about the ethics of business, and many question the ethics of endless economic growth. However, the truth is that business has generated wealth at astonishing speed for humankind over the last 30 years, and will continue to do so.

Since 2000, the percentage of the world living on less than $1.25 a day has fallen from 30% to below 10%, after adjusting for inflation. This is because the wealth of emerging nations has grown each year on average around 4.5% faster than that of developed nations, driven largely by growth in global trade. If similar growth rates continue for just the next 30 years, the average income in the world will then be equal to that of US citizens today.

Justice and wealth contrasts

As we have seen, half of all global wealth is owned by the richest 1% – one of the greatest and most unsustainable ethical stains on our world. The gap is growing between those with a life expectancy of 100 years and those with a life expectancy of 35 years, between those with unlimited health care and those who have to walk barefoot for over 50km to find a (badly equipped) clinic.

At the extreme end of this inequality scale are human slavery, bonded labour and trafficking. Around 30 million people are enslaved today, in an industry worth over $150bn a year for traffickers alone. Of these 30 million, 78% are sold for labour, and 22% forced to become sex workers. One in 25 of the entire population of Mauritania is a slave and there are estimated to be 14 million slaves in India alone. Expect many more efforts to stamp out the global slave trade.

Foreign aid will often be viewed as imperialism

One way to improve the lives of the very poor is with foreign aid, for such things as health care or education. But government aid can be seen as a form of imperialism, especially as donations are usually linked to contracts for the donor's own consultants and supplies.

Autocratic leaders in emerging nations will often regard well-meaning NGOs as interfering, condescending critics of their nations, sending home to wealthy supporters hundreds of tear-jerking photos of dreadful situations, which are bad for the national image, and give a very distorted view of life in general.

Some of the poorest nations will continue to be dominated by development projects. In places like Sierra Leone a large percentage of vehicles on the road belong to organisations such as UNICEF, a sign of a 'donor-dependent' economy.

It is extremely difficult for foreign-funded projects to operate without distorting local priorities, and money will continue to fall into the wrong hands. A community leader has a shopping list of ten items, ranging from roads to water and clinics. An NGO is offering help with literacy – and may themselves be corrupt or self-serving. The help is accepted and a new education facility is built. It may be helpful, but was it the most appropriate next step?

The most sustainable models of development or philanthropy have an element of redundancy built in. For example, AfriKids is a charity operating in northern Ghana to relieve child poverty and suffering. A stated aim by the founder in the beginning was to be able to close the charity down one day. And in the international AIDS charity ACET that I started 30 years back, that is just what we did for a home-care programme in the UK once we saw that government-paid doctors, nurses and home carers were doing what needed to be done, at which point we diverted resources to projects in countries like Uganda, Nigeria, Zimbabwe and DR Congo.

Trade rather than aid

In Africa most governments are aiming for low inflation, low budget deficits and encouragement of private business. But until America and Europe stop blocking imports of African goods and food, and cease dumping their own subsidised farm products, there will be slower progress.

Many African leaders fear economic rape of their nations by new imperialists, whether Chinese or Russian or Indian, who use money instead of guns, take local control in subtle ways, pay little for resources, and take wealth out.

They have little choice, it seems, but to allow their economies to become the puppets of globalised power bases. Multinationals and sovereign wealth funds will experience brittle relationships with governments and peoples, which may snap at short notice.

Does the lift factor actually work?

What will happen to the poorest of the poor? Some have argued from experience in Indian cities such as Mumbai that the rich get richer while the poor still starve and die. That may be true in the short term but not in the medium to longer term.

As we have seen repeatedly over the last 350 years, economic growth transforms entire nations, although it can take some time. More money begins to circulate, productivity rises, taxable income rises, and government spending increases, so that entire nations benefit.

The greater the contrasts between rich and poor in a society, the greater the risks of instability, as antagonism, aggression and organised opposition grow. Therefore, all healthy developed societies will always redistribute wealth to some degree, even if in the interests of self-preservation rather than because of troubled conscience.

Ethical pay for business leaders

Gaps in pay will widen in large corporations, with even higher rewards at the very top for outstanding leaders who make great things happen. There is a severe global scarcity of agile decision-makers with industry experience, proven track records, excellent communication skills and creative genius. One reason why such large packages will be needed is to entice such people into helping companies perform. Many of the world's most talented and experienced leaders have already made so much money that they have no financial need to work. Tempting people back into another demanding CEO or chairman role can require a combination of huge financial rewards, an interesting challenge and a high-profile company.

If a company with a multibillion-dollar turnover plunges into the red following two disastrous CEO appointments, it is in the interests of the company to pay a huge price to guarantee sorting the problem out fast.

We will continue to see a great ethical dilemma about large banking bonuses. People do not want to pay bankers ridiculously high salaries, but it will be difficult to persuade the brightest and most experienced business leaders to lead banks or sit on their boards without this. Why *should* they take huge personal risks for less reward, and possibly even risk ending up in prison, when so many other more attractive jobs beckon? We need to be sure that rewards are linked to success and to the level of risk that the person is taking in accepting the job.

Corporate ethics – meltdown of trust

Of course, high salaries would be easier to tolerate if people trusted such business leaders to behave ethically. Only a third of people in the UK believe that business behaves ethically, and only half think that business makes a positive contribution to society. You will find similar answers in many other countries.

This is really damaging to the future of business – because it means that many of the world's most talented people are no longer interested in a business career (we have already seen how many others have been put off going into politics). It is yet another reason why so many people want to run their *own* businesses, or work in very small companies, which they think are more ethical as well as personal.

But the fact is that every nation needs large companies. Without them, there is nothing left except individual traders, non-profit organisations and government. We have already seen in Chapter 4 that globalisation means economies of scale. Only the largest companies survive in many industries. If a nation has no large corporations, its economy will be dominated by foreign players. Large companies are huge employers. They attract international investment into a nation. They create clusters of expertise in key industries, and usually feed orders into many thousands of local smaller companies as suppliers.

Corporate meltdown, massive lawsuits and fines

As we have seen, never in human history have so many businesses been fined or prosecuted for so many ethical lapses. In a single month of 2014, Bank of America was fined $17bn, Goldman Sachs $1.2bn and Standard Chartered a further $300m. Earlier in the same year, huge fines were levied on Morgan Stanley, Citigroup, Credit Suisse, Toyota, Barclays, Rabobank, General Electric and Bank of America (in a separate case).

The personal protection insurance (PPI) scandal in the UK will end up costing the industry over $40bn. The Libor manipulation scandal will cost far more. Around $350 trillion of financial products are linked in some way to Libor in calculating how much interest is paid.

Over 2,000 convictions were brought against corporations in America by federal agencies in 14 years. This does not include the huge growth in civil fines – in two years alone, state and federal agencies received over $20bn just from settlements related to the False Claims Act. Whistle-blowers receive a proportion of payouts, so there is now a financial incentive to keep companies ethical.

Why compliance is dead

The cost of compliance, amid ever-widening regulation, is growing apace. Large corporations in America spend around $40m each on record-keeping systems to comply with more than 300,000 separate legal statutes. Smaller companies don't have the resources to cope, so can end up the wrong side of the law straight away.

Compliance really matters. However, as many bankers discovered, compliance with every law may keep you out of prison but cannot protect your brand or reputation, or build trust. You can comply perfectly with every regulation in every country in every year, but that will not help you when the public mood changes.

A scandal happens, which is followed by a public reaction, which leads to new regulations. These are interpreted by lawyers, who try to work out what it means. And then your compliance teams turn it into another box-ticking exercise, to check that you really are compliant. But you are only complying with history.

For example, until recently it was perfectly legal for a European company to pay a large bribe in another nation outside the EU, list it as a business expense, get it signed off by the auditors, and claim back tax from the government. The more they bribed, the more tax refunds they received. But it is no good today for the chairman of such a company to declare that he was well aware of bribes being paid back then and that 'it was all done perfectly legally'. He will lose his job, will never work again, and the reputation of his company will be damaged.

As I predicted many years ago, future legal advice will go far beyond today's regulations, to consider the next headlines, the next scandals, possible future action by regulators, and how the public mood might change. And it may not be a simple question of right and wrong.

Pressures on ethical business to define real success

Real success in future will mean demonstrating how your corporation makes a difference for everyone: for shareholders of course, but also for customers, workers, the wider community and, in some small way, for the whole of humanity – for example, by protecting the environment.

There is a risk that 'ethical' employers (forced to be ethical by law) will lose out to 'unethical' employers. So, for example, jobs in well-regulated, clean factories in a nation like America are lost as production switches to filthy factories with dangerous working conditions in a country like Bangladesh. Workers in the poorest nations may be paid almost nothing, with no job security, massive health and safety risks, and no sick pay or other rights.

We will see many new regulations in consuming regions like the EU to stop corporations from escaping their moral obligations in emerging nations. We have seen examples of this in global action to stop children working in textile factories.

Doing well by doing good

Companies like Unilever have led the way in reducing environmental footprint, and increasing positive social impact, with aims to help a billion people improve their health and well-being, halve the environmental impact of its products, and source all its agricultural materials sustainably. In three years, the amount of sustainable agricultural supplies it used increased from 14% to 48%.

Companies such as Patagonia, Interface, Marks & Spencer, Nestlé, Nike, Natura, GE, Walmart, Puma, IKEA and Coca-Cola have taken similar steps. And many others have focused on particular areas such as reducing plastic waste.

Ethics of child labour – easy to get wrong

Few global companies today would risk 'knowingly' employing six-year-old children for 12 hours a day to make clothes. Yet in Bangladesh alone it is estimated that 80,000 children under 14, mostly girls, work at least 60 hours a week in garment factories.

Sadly, moral outrage can easily wreck the lives of the very

children we need to protect. An international campaign led to millions of children being dumped as workers. Many went straight onto the streets, where they were at far greater risk. In most nations of the world, destitute children either have to work, beg or starve. It is as simple as that.

So where did all those 'redundant' children go? If you clear children out of a factory, some will beg at the gates of other lower profile factories, until eventually another manager takes pity, and gives them some scraps to eat. Before long this manager may have 20 more at his gates, sleeping in the compound. He provides bedding and food, and in return they sweep the factory floor, or help with packing. Ethical or unethical? Humanitarian or criminal? Are you *really* sure how you would feel yourself in such a situation?

As I have seen in my work with the ACET foundation, the average length of time for an 11-year-old runaway girl drifting into one of the railway stations in Mumbai and being picked up by a criminal gang can be less than 12 hours. Such girls are usually raped violently and repeatedly, and are caged in a filthy brothel until their spirits are completely broken. Then they are pimped for years in the Red Light District, among 200,000 other sex workers, until they die of AIDS or look too old.

And maybe all because that girl was suddenly turned out on the streets, after living and working as an orphan, since the age of eight, in a small textile factory.

The lesson is that while ethical issues like child labour are really important, and must be addressed, they will need to be tackled in the context of overall community development, with a deeper understanding of the local situation.

Non-profit boom – philanthropy

Each year more than 2 billion people give time to things they believe in without being paid, or to help people outside their immediate circle of family and friends.

Philanthropy is a rapidly growing feature of middle-class life, with spectacular growth in mega-donations from the super-wealthy, on a scale that will create problems for some foundations in how to spend each dollar with care and accountability, in appropriate ways. Super-rich donors in the UK alone are giving away more than £3.2bn a year. Warren Buffett gave more than $26bn to the Bill and Melinda Gates Foundation.

Expect a boom over the next 20 years in philanthropic advisory services, as part of private banking and wealth management for very wealthy clients. Such charity advisors are already consulted by 20% of Americans with more than $1m of personal wealth. There will be increasing recognition that great wealth is often toxic to the well-being of children and grandchildren, and cannot be spent by the individual on pleasures or experiences without self-destruction. Since great wealth is a risk to family, and cannot be taken into the next life, what do you do with it?

An increasing amount will be spent on 'legacy projects' – huge, highly speculative investments into eye-catching technologies for which the person hopes to be recognised by future historians, hoping to create breathtaking advances to benefit humankind. Therefore, we can expect many more exotic adventures into space, supersonic air travel, and a host of other things, by the wealthiest 1,000 people on the planet.

Apart from such extravagant business ventures by such an elite, the inescapable logic will be to give the wealth away for truly altruistic purposes. But how best to do this?

Philanthropy is as old as human civilisation itself, and the poorer people are, the more they volunteer. All traditional rural societies have strong social codes linked to extensive intermarriage in villages that protect the vulnerable in their tribal communities, which means that most people are blood-related. So orphans are usually taken into the homes of relatives, a home that burns down is rapidly rebuilt with the help of others, someone who is blind is brought food, and so on. These communities often function with minimal use of cash, as co-operative societies, overseen by village elders.

Volunteering will be almost universal

The growth of volunteering in towns and cities mimics these ancient traditions, for people who have often lost that kind of connection with those around them.

In a typical month, the percentage of people volunteering may be different across the world but is almost always significant: 56% of those in Turkmenistan volunteer on a formal basis with organisations, 45% in Sri Lanka, 44% in the US, 28% in the UK and 13% in Sweden. But these figures do not cover informal volunteering, which accounts for the majority of time given.

In the UK, the number of hours given by formal volunteers is equivalent to 1.25 million full-time paid workers, almost as many as work in the health service. A very significant proportion of this effort is contributed by 1.3 million members of churches, giving a few hours a week each. If each hour of time is valued at the average wage, the contribution of all volunteering to the national economy is the equivalent of around £25bn, with an additional £25bn for informal or irregular time, for example sweeping the snow from an old person's drive. That's about the same as 3% of the national GDP. And as the number of people in active retirement grows, we can expect more older volunteers.

Privatising services to the non-profit sector

Volunteer agencies will be useful to governments, as ideal partners. As a result, a growing proportion of the welfare state will be privatised to non-profit organisations (NPOs) in many developed nations, to save costs. Many contracts will be awarded preferentially to charities, to avoid the impression that private companies are making big profits out of government contracts, for things like health care.

NPOs will become more efficient and business-like, with greater professionalism, audit and evaluation. Fierce competition between NPOs will be on a par with anything in the commercial sector today.

There will also be competition between commercial and non-profit organisations, with accusations that NPOs are undercutting prices by using unpaid labour as volunteers, or with cash donations. The whole concept of charitable work will be called into question in some sectors, as many agencies find themselves in a primary role as subcontractors to government. As part of this shift, some volunteers will question whether their act of generosity is being abused by government, to cut costs and jobs.

Social enterprises will become even more fashionable, for both workers and investors. These are corporations that expect to make profits, while also achieving the kind of objectives that an NPO might aim for. This hybrid model will be particularly inspiring to a new generation of entrepreneurs.

Future of privacy and personal freedom

In Chapter 1 we touched on urgent ethical questions relating to the digital world. Who owns my data? Can I ask for my online records to be deleted before I die, or at death? Are social media sites responsible for censoring people who publish criminal material.

Most nations will move very rapidly towards far greater web controls over the next 10 to 20 years, including age-restricted access. As we have seen, over 100 nations already control web access in some way, affecting over 60% of the world's web users. Expect stronger laws against online bullying, sexting and other activities designed to intimidate or embarrass.

Many emerging autocracies such as China and Russia will make huge efforts to stop full web access, except via servers that they control. A growing number of developed nations will attempt a version of the same thing. It is also likely to become illegal in some nations to attempt to view pages on the dark web, to use a virtual private network to try to evade scrutiny, or to use cryptocurrencies such as Bitcoin without controls of some kind.

Many nations will expect social media companies to take all reasonable measures to prevent broadcasting of illegal or antisocial content, however defined by that government (and some governments will apply interpretations very widely and take censorship to extremes).

This new responsibility on companies like Google, Facebook, LinkedIn and Twitter will have far-reaching impact. For example, insistence that copyright is always respected and upheld could mean that every image shown on a search result will need verifying first, to make sure that copyright is not infringed. And what of images that have been changed a little? Does that extend to paragraphs of text on a web blog, lifted almost verbatim from a newspaper, magazine, book or other copyrighted source? We will see many hot debates about the future of the web as a place for free expression.

Liberal activists who campaign for completely unrestricted freedom of expression online are going to sound increasingly out of touch with reality in their defence of a web world where every form of appalling, shocking, degrading, disgusting, cruel, dehumanising and criminal activity can be viewed on just about any device by a child of any age after a couple of seconds of searching.

A strong argument will be that there is absolutely no logic in giving cinema films a child rating if there are no ratings for far stronger content online, and very few parents would want to abolish all cinema ratings. In some nations like Pakistan and Saudi Arabia, censorship issues will be tied up with blasphemy laws.

Alliances linked to religious groups will vigorously support web controls, bitterly opposed by liberal, secular groups who claim that media output is pure fantasy for the most part, and incapable of altering behaviour. Liberal groups will continue to argue that crimes such as rape or violence are entirely unrelated to media output. However, the counter-claim will grow stronger by the month. We will see case after terrible case where prosecution witnesses show that yet another defendant was watching depraved material shortly before committing a horrific, similar crime. In many instances, the person in the dock will be an older child, teenager or impressionable young adult.

As we have seen in earlier chapters, there is overwhelming evidence that media influences behaviour – indeed the entire advertising industry is based on the fact that media messages change what people do in easily measurable ways, especially when it comes to online activity.

Ethics for robots – rules of engagement

We urgently need a widely agreed ethical code with regard to the decisions of robots, particularly those in combat or at the wheel. For example, how certain of face recognition does an automated secret services drone have to be to fire a lethal weapon? What controls are there to stop military drones firing at citizens?

Here is a puzzle for robots: a mother carrying a baby is in the middle of the road, and swerving will kill a retired man with a dog. Which direction should the robot steer, if it cannot stop in time? If a passenger in the car is critically ill and needs to go to hospital, can a robot break the speed limit, and if so, by how much? And if the choice is risking death of a driver, or of a pedestrian, which should the robot choose?

Some warn of a coming apocalypse for humankind as self-reproducing and rapidly evolving, ultra-intelligent robots somehow take over the planet, leaving humans as a subordinate species, or even threatened with survival. This will remain pure Hollywood-type science fiction for the rest of this twenty-first century. The fact is that human bodies, made up of billions of living cells, have tens of thousands of subtle features and auto-repair mechanisms. Humans possess a level of miniaturisation that will make even robots built in 2095 look extremely primitive.

However, the twenty-second century is quite another matter. By 2120 we can expect to see large numbers of self-reproducing robots, with huge powers, able to make complex decisions and interact with human beings in a very wide variety of ways. They may align activities, form opinions, make joint decisions and form a formidable force for change.

More importantly, we need to include ethics to guide the behaviour of all forms of sophisticated Artificial Intelligence machines – which may have no physical presence apart from the chips in which their mental processes run, deep inside a factory, bank, marketing company or government agency. Indeed, such entities may only be virtually present, with mega-brains running in the Cloud, interacting, monitoring, thinking, planning, controlling.

It will be up to their human designers and programmers to place sufficient limits on their thinking and powers … if they can.

Common-sense approach to health-related ethics

What about ethics in health care? History shows us that what one generation regards as shocking, immoral or bizarre can feel more natural to the next.

It is also dangerous to generalise about what may appeal to a European mindset without considering what may be acceptable to most Muslims who live under various interpretations of sharia law in nations like Saudi Arabia, or to those in a strongly Christian nation like Zambia.

The ultimate ethical test applied to health

Whatever the issue in health care, the ultimate ethical value will be based on our four-word phrase, 'building a better world'. If an activity such as human cloning or the creation of near non-ageing humans becomes common, will our world be a better place as a result or not? And for the devout Muslim, Christian, Jew, Buddhist or Hindu, is this a step towards the kind of world our Creator intends or is it a violation of the natural order?

There is an added ethical question: perhaps the most important of all. In a world where over 800 million go hungry each day, and where 1 billion have almost zero access to basic health care and only limited access to clean running water, is it right to even think about such medical exotica? Access to basic health care is one of the deepest ethical challenges in the world today.

You may feel rather distant from such things – and so did I until I saw with my own eyes young children dying in Africa for lack of a simple antibiotic.

Euthanasia will be the commonest cause of death in many nations

Euthanasia will be a major medical issue across the world. Expect many to legalise the 'right to die', packaged with other issues, including permission for doctors to end the life of someone who is unfit to take a decision.

Countries with relaxed euthanasia laws will find elderly people taking this way out as the 'responsible thing to do'. Length of average stay in nursing homes or hospices will fall. People who are suffering will commonly be terminated.

Within 30 years, euthanasia in one form or another is likely to become the commonest cause of death in several nations. In the Netherlands, research suggests that up to 25% of all deaths annually are now medically induced, of which around 7,000 are from euthanasia, a process that usually takes a couple of hours. (Criteria for euthanasia now include chronic illness, depression and emotional distress.) A further 36,000 deaths each year are from massive sedation, where a doctor places the person into a coma, unable to eat or drink, until they die. While many of these are people with advanced medical conditions, whose life expectancy is very limited anyway, the rest are people who would not otherwise be expected to be dying.

One result of legalised euthanasia will be that active treatments will be abandoned far more frequently at an earlier stage, allowing 'nature to take its course', with symptom control measures, even where treating those symptoms makes an earlier death slightly more likely.

Expect a new emphasis in medical training in most nations not just to cure but to manage death and the dying process. Palliative medicine will be a key growth area in emerging nations. We will see new breakthroughs in the relief of pain, and sales of pain-relieving drugs will rocket globally in the next decade.

Navigating health-related dilemmas

Listed on the next two pages are just a few of hundreds of future ethical dilemmas in health care, biotech and life sciences. The public may be more or less well informed. Regulators may be very cautious or lacking in powers or there may not be a regulator in that sector. So it becomes very difficult to forecast how globally acceptable issues will be, such as gene screening for insurance purposes, or infertility treatment for 80-year-olds (by 2040 many 80-year-olds will be as young and healthy from a medical point of view as today's 65-year-olds).

Each item on the list is followed by a U or an E (or several Us or Es). This indicates what I predict will be the level of Unease or Ease with the issue globally by 2030.

Research will often continue to go ahead of debate, because many scientists hate debating theoretical possibilities. They prefer to debate what is possible. And of course, many fear that if what they are trying to do is discussed widely in advance, the public outcry may block their future life's work.

Expect open conflict at times between the general public and the research community, resulting in researchers pursuing all kinds of activities almost in secret, as happens now.

As it is, much early research is conducted away from the public eye, so that new pharma products can be developed without alerting competitors.

Expect growing concerns about the ethics of using larger animals in laboratories, linked to the global boom in pet ownership and concerns about animal welfare. Sales of pet food and pet care already exceed $180bn a year, and are likely to rise to over $340bn by 2030.

Feminisation of society – impact on ethics

We will see further feminisation of many Western societies. As we saw in Chapter 3, men are already in retreat in many developed nations, labelled as testosterone addicts: dangerous, ill behaved variants of the human species prone to violence, sexual predatory acts, lewd behaviour and general loutishness and irresponsibility, the targets of a growing chorus of negative comments and abuse. Patriarchal societies are rapidly becoming matriarchal. Female instincts and reactions will be the future norms.

Jobs for the girls

Most new jobs in many nations are going to women. The greatest growth area is part-time work in service and leisure industries,

Dilemma	Level of ease/ unease
Is it right to take action to end the life of an old, frail or sick person because they have lost the will to live?	U
Is it right to abort a perfectly healthy foetus at a stage of pregnancy where it could live outside the womb with help?	UU
Is it right to abort a perfectly healthy foetus at an earlier stage because you would prefer a baby with a different gender, or hair colour, or with more genes likely to make them good at maths?	UU
Is it right to clone yourself, by inserting a nucleus from one of your cells into an unfertilised egg, either to implant the early embryo so that one day you greet your own identical twin as a newborn baby, or to grow the ball of cells so that the tissues can be cannibalised to repair your own body?	UU
Is it right to use tissues from other people's aborted foetuses to repair your own body? Does that encourage other people to have abortions?	UU
Is it right to use adult stem cells to repair your own body?	EEE
Is it right for two men or two women to seek to have a genetic child of their own, by some genetic means or by using a surrogate mother (as 2,000 women do a year in America) or egg or sperm donor?	U
Is it right to allow a child to be created with two mothers and one father – where one mother contributes 1% of her genes, those in her mitochondrial power packs, to correct a terrible gene defect?	E

Dilemma	Level of ease/ unease
Is it right to use injections of gene fragments into muscles to enhance athletic performance in competitions?	UU
Is it right to refuse insurance cover or a new job to someone based on the results of their genetic screening?	U
Is it right to add human genes to farmed fish to make them grow faster?	U
Is it right to add human genes to pigs so that the surfaces of their hearts are altered, enabling them to become donors to people with heart failure?	E
Is it right to add human genes to monkeys to try to find out which genes programme the human brain for speech?	UU
Is it right to use infertility treatments to allow a 70-year-old woman to have a baby?	UU
Is it right for a woman to rent out her own womb to another woman who cannot carry a child?	E
Is it right for a woman to have sex with another woman's partner as a combined egg and womb donor?	UU
Should we allow a pharma company to take some of your genes, identify a new cluster causing your illness, and patent it so they own part of your own genome?	E

while traditional full-time manufacturing workers are a dying breed. Tomorrow's jobs will require flexibility, teamwork, efficiency – favouring women. In Japan there has been a huge increase in female influence and power at work.

Around 70% of online purchases of many kinds of products and services in Europe and the US are by women. In banking, 70% of online accounts in some nations are opened by men but 70% of the transactions are by women. Women buy most household goods, books, food and holidays.

Women also dominate spending in traditional retail outlets yet, despite this, most marketing executives and customer relationship managers are still men. Expect this to change as companies look to rebrand in a more feminine way. Nevertheless, the feminisation of society still has a long way to go. Men clean the house, but not much more than they did. There is still a glass ceiling blocking promotion for women in many areas and women still have far less leisure time than men.

Expect new men's liberation movements in some nations, which in some ways will parallel women's activist groups, seeking greater gender equality for men in some kinds of jobs that have been traditionally done by women, e.g. working in nurseries or in care roles. Gender-role confusion will continue, with a backlash from many women over negative stereotyping of men.

We will also see major shifts in corporate culture, especially as populations age, creating a skills scarcity. Many more women will occupy senior positions, especially on boards, with legal quotas becoming far more common, like those already in place in Germany.

But we will also see men sue women for sexual harassment, intimidation and prejudice in recruitment or the workplace, with demands for male quotas for jobs. As previously discussed, all this will be complicated over the next 30 years by new transgender ethical codes in many nations.

Impact of personal spirituality

Across the developed world, as a result of all the trends described in this book, we are seeing an intense, growing hunger for meaning, often expressed in a search for spirituality, very different from membership of an organised religion. The great debate in a nation like the UK or France is not over whether you *believe*, but what you believe *in*, and what your own spiritual purpose is.

Faith in anything, anyone. Faith that causes ordinary men and women to hug trees in local parks. Faith that causes intelligent people to study advice each day based on horoscopes. There has been a wholesale rejection of the scientific, logical, rational model of the world that reduces all of existence to fixed, predetermined and mechanical systems.

Thus doctors are struggling with patients with life-threatening illness who throw away medicines backed by solid clinical trial data, and opt for alternatives that most doctors regard as having no scientific basis.

More than 17 million people in Britain alone rely on alternative medicines or therapies – aromatherapy and homeopathy being the most popular. Expect laws in these areas to tighten, requiring companies to verify the health claims made. This will intensify the scale of the culture clash between those who feel that scientific methodology is not a valid test of 'whole person medicine' and those who insist on 'objective' scientific data.

Spiritual awareness will remain central to human existence

Around 85% of people in the world today say that they are aware of a spiritual dimension to life, which reflects a pattern since the beginning of human history. While strident voices of humanistic atheism are likely to grow louder in some developed nations, they will continue to be drowned out globally over the next 50 years by the vast majority, convinced that there is more to life than atoms, molecules and bags of biodata.

In developed nations, informal expressions of spirituality are likely to multiply, with further declines in organised religion. Expect growth in personal systems for meditation, in self-help guides to spiritual enlightenment.

Thus, informal attendance at synagogues, Hindu temples, mosques and churches is also likely to rise – particularly at social activities such as mother and toddler groups, homeless projects, drop-in centres, food banks, advice centres – while formal membership falls.

These kinds of initiatives may well turn out to be a significant growth factor in the lives of churches, mosques, synagogues and temples in countries like the UK over the next two decades. We can expect more social action projects, as the state gradually runs out of cash from trying to reduce government debt.

From personal belief to organised religion

In emerging nations, we are seeing a rather different picture, with very rapid growth of global religions such as Christianity and Islam, decline in local faith-healers, and fewer people with private, 'personalised', idiosyncratic, informal beliefs.

There are 1.6 billion followers of Islam in the world today, 21% of the world population. Of these, 60% live in Asia-Pacific and 20% in the Middle East. Islam is likely to grow faster than world population, by around 1.5–1.8% over the next 20 years, but the rate of growth will continue to slow, as the size of families continues to fall in the nations where Islam is strongest, and where incomes are growing rapidly (that is with family size falling as wealth increases).

Christianity has 2.3 billion adherents, representing 32% of the world population, with 60% of them found in Africa, Asia and Latin America. Christianity will also continue to grow significantly faster than world population, particularly in Africa and former Soviet bloc countries, as well as in China, where tens of millions have found Christian faith since the 1950s, despite severe persecution. It is possible that there are already more Christians in China than in any other nation.

In Argentina over the last decade churches have sprung from nothing to number many thousands, and the same has been happening across Latin America. Africa has seen extraordinary growth in church attendance, with some regular church meetings now attracting over 200,000 to their regular Sunday meetings, held in giant hangar-like structures, and this is now influencing politicians and governments.

Emphasis on personal spiritual experiences

The impact of the global uprising of life-changing faith, which provokes passion and provides purpose, cannot be underestimated.

Expect divisions within each world religion between radicals who remain rooted in traditional teachings based on, for example, the Bible or the Koran, and liberals who accept or abandon whatever writings they choose in their own personal spiritual journey.

This orthodox–liberal divide is likely to sharpen over issues like abortion, euthanasia, embryonic stem cell research, transgender issues and gay marriage. While liberal churches will argue that they are more attractive and culturally relevant in the US and Europe, they have in fact declined very rapidly. Most church growth will continue to be among Christian communities that adhere to traditional teachings and express strong, life-changing, authentic spirituality.

In the UK, for example, Pentecostal churches are growing by 5% a year, and over half of all churchgoers in London now belong to black-majority Pentecostal-type churches. The Redeemed Christian Church of God has 700 churches across the UK, from very few 20 years ago, as a Nigerian mission-movement to Britain.

The evangelical wing of the Anglican Church is also growing in numbers and influence. Over 2.5 million people have attended a 12-week induction course to the Christian faith, designed by just one such evangelical church, Holy Trinity, Brompton, in London. However, this growth is unlikely to offset overall Anglican decline, especially among liberal, older congregations in rural areas.

Whether you are a follower of Jesus, as I am, or of Mohammed, or of Buddha, or of the patterns in the stars, whether you believe in karma or reincarnation, or some other life-force, or in nothing at all, spirituality is likely to remain a significant part of life, shaping global ethics, values and politics for the next 500 years, as it has done for all of recorded history.

Future of religious movements and ethics

What about new religious movements? History tells us that such things usually start as a reaction against what is seen as the moral decay and spiritual bankruptcy of society. When we look at the world today, it is hardly a surprise that we are seeing growing numbers of radical religious groups, some of which will be revolutionary.

It is very easy for an influential group of believers from any religion to argue that some or all of the following are true today, *from their own point of view*:

◆ society has lost its soul and moral compass

◆ everywhere you look, traditional moral values have been lost

◆ people are becoming more self-centred and individualistic

◆ our culture is obsessed with celebrity worship, but celebrities are terrible role models

◆ youth are worried by superficial and worthless things like personal appearance

◆ family life is breaking down, community ties weakened

◆ many are addicted to alcohol, drugs, sex, the internet

◆ government leaders are often corrupt and cannot be trusted

◆ the web has become a sexual free-for-all, with child abuse / other deviant behaviour promoted as normal

◆ rapid, continuous economic growth promised a better world but resulted in appalling contrasts in wealth, failed to deal with the worst global poverty, and is unsustainable

◆ one nation has vast influence over the whole world – exporting media, culture, corporations, brands – but is in a state of moral and spiritual decay

◆ greedy global corporations and banks are wrecking our world

◆ mental illness is more common, with rising sales of antidepressants

◆ we have lost sight of the fact that we are spiritual beings, that there is another dimension to life

- God has a plan for humanity, which society must obey
- humanity as a whole will be held to account
- each of us must respond to God's purpose for our own lives.

Therefore, we will continue to see growing numbers of radical religious activists, driven by a 'divine call' to promote (or even impose) God's authority on earth, according to the beliefs they have about who He is and what His will is. Most are likely to belong to an existing world religion, and will live in emerging nations.

As part of this, we are likely to see new kinds of 'puritanism' in Christianity, just as we have seen in Islam over the last 20 to 30 years: new waves of orthodoxy that will be very uncomfortable for established churches, and hard to contain within existing structures, and will be fiercely intolerant and zealous for spiritual purity.

New ethical standards for believers and wider society

Such new Christian movements may well seek to prohibit a wide range of 'sinful' or unwise behaviours: banning smoking and drug use among church members, and advocating stricter sexual ethics – doctrines that remind us of the anti-alcohol temperance movements of the nineteenth century. These new movements are likely also to seed political activism, campaigning for new laws and so on. However, such movements are likely to split fairly rapidly over same-sex relationships.

We can also expect by the end of this century new expressions of monastic life, with growing numbers of people taking radical vows of poverty, chastity and obedience, many of whom will risk being labelled as members of dangerous 'brainwashing' cults.

The church in emerging communities will drive theology

Such new Puritans will seem totally at odds with much of the rest of the church in *developed* nations, where sexual activity of many kinds outside of marriage is increasingly accepted as normal among members, where divorce and remarriage are routine, and where gay marriage is celebrated. We are already witnessing a fundamental schism between *developed* and *emerging* nation churches, liberal and Pentecostal, old-style denominations and indigenous church movements.

Almost all major new missionary movements, over the next 30 to 40 years, are likely to be influenced by the vision, teachings and values of churches in emerging nations or the poorest parts of the world, reflecting global church growth.

Most of the fastest-growing churches in Europe, from the UK to Germany, Poland, Estonia, Ukraine and Slovakia, are likely to be evangelical, Pentecostal, charismatic. All tend to have three things in common: enthusiastic promotion of life-changing, personal discipleship, a focus on the Bible as a daily guide to following Jesus, and a passionate belief in the power of prayer to release the power of God, together with the gifts of the Holy Spirit to change lives.

Such growth will be boosted by migrant communities from emerging nations – whether Nigerians, Poles, South Koreans or Chinese. However, this growth is unlikely to offset overall decline in church-going across much of Europe over the next 20 years, particularly in ageing congregations with liberal theology.

Growth in Catholic churches

The Catholic Church has 1.2 billion members globally, many of whom are not active, compared to over 1 billion in Protestant churches and around 450 million in Orthodox churches. Catholicism in developed nations will stabilise after years of decline, and will grow in the poorest nations, under the inspiring leadership of Pope Francis.

Pope Francis has a radical theology and ethical framework that embraces aspects of Pentecostalism, and adds to his popular appeal. However, his age will constrain his energy and influence, and he faces the risk of being undermined and even killed because of his very public all-out attack on the corruption, indifference to the poor, and spiritual apathy that he has identified in the heart of the Vatican.

He is certainly more vulnerable than other Popes, having abandoned almost all the security measures, both in and outside the Vatican. If he is removed or assassinated, we can expect great conflicts within the Catholic Church about what kind of Pope should succeed him.

But whoever is Pope will face calls for more radical action over large-scale exposure of sexual abuse by priests and monks. Some 80% of reported cases have been in the US, where many more Catholic organisations will face bankruptcy in meeting compensation.

In Australia, 7% of priests faced accusations from 1950 to 2015; the figure was 4% from 1950 to 2002 in America. The deepest part of the scandal will be ongoing accusations against many non-abusers that they were complicit in covering up what was going on, and were too ready to dismiss accusations as likely to be made up or exaggerated. The negative impact on Catholicism will continue to be huge, in America in particular, and will last a generation.

Global war against Christians

As in Islam, the most radical edge of Christianity is likely to be a call to arms: an ideology that promotes fighting as necessary to protect the church from being wiped out by aggressive Islamic persecutors.

This type of militant thinking is especially likely to develop among extremist indigenous churches in central and northern Africa, as a response to terrible attacks against churches and Christian households over more than two decades. We are already seeing signs of this in some parts of Africa, particularly in Bangui, the capital of the Central African Republic.

However, such militancy is likely to be held back in most places by the dominant Christian ethic, which has been relatively pacifist, following the teachings of Jesus to *love your neighbour as yourself, love your enemies, pray for those who persecute you, and when your enemy strikes you – turn the other cheek.*

Christians have been slaughtered, tortured, kidnapped, raped and beheaded in unprecedented numbers over the past two decades according to the International Society for Human Rights, which estimates that 80% of all acts of religious discrimination are against Christians. Over 200 million Christians face persecution of some kind each year, according to the UK government in 2017, with Christian women and children particularly vulnerable to sexual violence. Reuters reported that numbers of reported cases of Christians killed for their faith doubled between 2012 and 2013 to 2,100, which would suggest a total of around 5,000 a year, since most do not get picked up by global media.

Persecution in Iraq, Nigeria and North Korea

In Baghdad, 40 out of 65 churches were bombed between 2004 and 2008 alone. Persecution will lead to more migrations (just as persecutors intend), and over 1 million Christians fled Iraq in the same period. In Kandhamal, Orissa, in north India, 500 Christians were killed in a series of Hindu-supported riots, thousands were injured and 50,000 believers were left homeless, while 350 Christian schools and churches were destroyed.

In northern Nigeria, Boko Haram has butchered over 5,000 Christians since 2009, with over 650,000 forced to flee from towns and villages. In North Korea, some estimate that around 25% of the 300,000 people in labour camps are there because of their Christian faith, and many thousands more believers have just disappeared after arrest.

Attacks on churches in China and Pakistan

In China, most church congregations are not recognised by the government, and harassment is common, despite rapid growth. Indeed, there is concern about the strengthening influence of these unlawful and influential groups. Large churches have been pulled down, and many leaders arrested in some parts of the country, for example in Wenzhou, where 15% of the population of 9 million are already Christian.

In Pakistan, mobs regularly lynch and kill Christians who are accused of telling others about their faith, or of showing disrespect in some way to Islam. People who convert to Christianity often live in great fear, risk being attacked by family, worship in complete secrecy, and are often forced to flee abroad to seek asylum or because of false accusations. When you meet people who have experienced these things, as I have, you cannot fail to be touched by what has happened to them. Expect many more such cases.

Islam also at war with Islam

Such attacks by Islamic extremists are not just directed at those of other religions. Most of them are against others from an Islamic background.

Some radical Islamic teachers are likely to continue to encourage online followers to kill all 'infidels' and those who support them, including people who describe themselves as devout followers of Islam, but whose lifestyle does not reflect their own interpretation of the Koran.

And we are likely to see ongoing bitter, intense, tribal and ideological wars between Sunni and Shiite 'tribes' of Islam, with their different cultural histories. As we have seen, we can expect a growing culture gap between more moderate, wealthy and intellectual believers in developed nations, and those who follow Islam in emerging nations.

A new world religion?

At the end of the last chapter, we looked at the possibility that political creeds could be swept aside by a radical new ideology that could turn out to be as influential as communism was in the late nineteenth century and the major part of the twentieth century. Alongside this, we can also expect to see a new religion.

All major world religions are likely to continue to reinvent themselves over the next 100 years, as their traditional teachings are reinterpreted in very different ages and cultures.

Global 'market' for a new world religion

We could see a new radical, religious leader or prophet emerge over the next few decades with charisma, dynamism and unusual teachings that rapidly capture the global imagination.

The biggest issue will be truth: is there such a thing? Global religions such as Judaism, Christianity and Islam all proclaim timeless truth about an unchanging Creator God, offering exclusive understanding of Him. In contrast, New Age beliefs draw heavily from some aspects of Hinduism, and have a more general approach to truth, and a more fluid, ethical framework, with far fewer absolutes.

In a constantly changing world, certainty about ultimate issues such as personal destiny becomes increasingly important. That is the appeal of radical fundamentalism. Therefore, a new world religion is likely to be defined by dogmatic teaching, and a claim of exclusivity and superiority to all previously understood truths about God.

Expect such a prophet to offer 'the final revelation', the promise that humankind is 'coming of age' and is only now able to receive the truth. Such a prophet is likely to claim that all the great religions pointed only in part to the Truth.

Such a prophet could sweep tens of millions into a new religious movement, over a short space of time. But this will be unlikely without global struggle on an immense scale. Militant Islam will be as violently opposed to such a new religion as it is to apostasy among Islamic communities, and to Christianity.

A new world order

With so many challenges facing the world, many of which require a collective response, will we see a new world order emerging? The answer is that we are already seeing the tentative beginnings of one, in the proliferation of environmental treaties for example, or in the global fight against terrorism.

More international treaties for global control

Despite impressions that you might have from the media, the truth is that hundreds of international agreements have been signed over the last few years, whether to encourage trade, stop money laundering or to help prevent human trafficking. And so, informal global governance begins to emerge.

The United Nations was founded for such a purpose: 'to save

succeeding generations from the scourge of war' and 'to reaffirm faith in fundamental human rights, in the dignity and value of the human person.'

The trouble is that, as we have seen, UN member nations are divided about what they want the UN to do and how to do it. But the trend is clear: global governance will be essential to our future. The unprecedented spirit of global collaboration that emerged after the collapse of communism and the Cold War will deepen, despite many crises and setbacks. As we have seen, part of this will develop out of regional coalitions, trading blocs and spheres of influence. Indeed, trade across nations and continents has been a civilising force since time began and always will be so.

International courts will grow in power

Despite differing positions on many issues, we will need an international code of conduct for commerce. Indeed, international trade is impossible without it. The beginnings are already with us: for example, the prosecution of national leaders in one country for war crimes, by a court comprised of other countries' representatives.

Regional law courts are well established, in the EU, for example. Expect supra-regional courts to be dealing with a wide variety of international crime cases by 2030.

Global government

In summary, then, expect to see various expressions of global governance emerge, into the first stages of a new world order over the next few decades.

Expect periods of intense negotiation to define global ethics, whether a global ban on bio-weapons, a response to international terrorism or ethnic genocide, limits on global monopolies, or world agreements on slavery, child labour, work practices and other issues of human rights.

Many issues will be polarised between emerging and developed nations. All these debates will be increasingly influenced by a profound rethink in wealthier nations, by a new generation that is no longer so impressed by speed, urbanisation, material wealth and globalisation. A generation that is itself becoming more radical, ethical and spiritually aware.

Now is the time to choose

So, then, we have journeyed into the future of every region in the world, and into every industry. We have seen the bright and dark side of every trend, and how they form the Six Faces of the Future as a cube, which spins with all the energy that comes from emotion. Now is the time to choose …

Take hold of your future, or the future will take hold of you.

Chapter 7

HUMAN LIFE IN 2120

BASED ON FORECASTING METHODOLOGY and major trends already described, here is a view into the future from the turn of the next century, a scenario to provoke debate. As we have seen, major trends are usually obvious, connect with each other, and shape entire generations. The greatest debates are usually over rates of change and timings, not general direction. However, an issue below is author bias and purpose.

1 January 2100

Author: Predictor MK31 – State-owned robot. GDF-approved forecast (deletions as marked)

The future will be familiar in many ways

Many areas of society have evolved less than predicted 30 years ago, because the human species remains largely as it was, despite a greater knowledge of genetics, greater wealth, more leisure, more advanced technology and Artificial Intelligence, new materials and smarter products. Expect few short-term, radical changes.

Most cities are still located where they were 200 years ago, despite rising sea levels, and will continue to enlarge. Transport routes and national boundaries are almost identical, and that will continue to be the case.

In 2150 most humans will still be born in cities, raised by one or both biological parents, attend school or college, meet friends, fall in love, form families of varying kinds, attend work meetings, enjoy sport and leisure with others, explore their own worlds and create new things.

Humans will still associate mainly in tribal, ethnic, language or religious groups. They will delegate even more to machines, appoint representatives to govern, and abide by customs and laws.

While many older people will still complain about the pace of change, important elements of human civilisation will go on reflecting common social patterns in Europe in the years 2000, 1950, 1850, 1700, as far back as Roman, Greek or Qin cities over 2,300 years ago.

'Never Again' movement will drive next 30 years

Three 'Defining Moments' triggered mass reactions, toppled several democratic governments, inspired a military coup, and created and led to new global governance.

1. Asia-Pacific War and rise of global democracy

The Global Democratic Forum resulted from the 2067–69 Asia-Pacific War, involving nineteen countries, with 1.3 million deaths and nuclear contamination over wide areas. The United Nations was widely blamed for failures leading up to the conflict. The UN was formed in 1945 after the Second World War, with one vote per nation. As a result, India and China had one vote each out of 194, to represent a third of humanity.

The UN was therefore undemocratic, and lacked moral authority to broker growing tensions between the two giant nations. The UN had previously failed to bring peace in the hybrid conflict of 2041–53 between the Russian Federation and the European Union, which also caused major chaos, and disruption, at times, to the entire digital world, as well as weakening NATO.

In the May 2071 Singapore Declaration, India and China agreed to destroy all nuclear weapons, phase out nuclear power, live at peace, and to refer future disputes to the Global Democratic Forum (GDF), a new organisation proposed by them, in consultation with other nations, with voting in proportion to each nation's population.

China hosted the first GDF in November 2072, in Shanghai.

Each nation was invited to send one ambassador, plus an additional voting participant for every 10 million citizens. The Forum aims were to influence 'Global Peace, Harmony and Prosperity', but was not designed to have legal authority over nations.

The first meeting took place in Shanghai, in a venue for 11,500, and 10,253 participated. China was allocated 1,453 votes, and India 1,557. Speeches were watched by over 6.5 billion, but 657 American and Russian seats were empty, boycotted to support the UN. America and Russia warned that agendas would be 'hijacked' by China and India, who had 'lost the moral right to global influence following the war'.

Major issues were discussed, and free votes taken on Non-Binding Declarations (NBDs). At that 2072 meeting, more than nine out of ten participants approved six calls to action:

- Nuclear weapons to be destroyed with sanctions against nations that refuse
- Old World nations to pay 0.5% of GDP to the poorest 30 nations to improve health
- All nations to commit 3% of government spending to global warming action
- Global systems to tax super-wealthy more fairly, with more effective policing
- America and Russia to participate fully in GDF, and respect majority votes
- All nations to link up Intelligence for better predictive analytics and security.

Over the next decade, many nations pulled out of the UN, and bodies like the World Health Organization were reassigned to GDF. More decisions were led by Predictive Intelligence, setting GDF agendas and proposing solutions. A sign of the growing 'moral authority' of the GDF was seen last year, when Nigeria agreed to withdraw immediately from territories seized in the 2094 Central African Conflict, after 9,562 delegates, representing over 9.5 billion people, voted against Nigeria's justifications of military action.

GDF strength and powers are set to grow rapidly, with America and Russia now fully engaged, and with rapid expansion of the GDF Peace Force as a result. While GDF NBDs will remain non-binding, over the next two decades expect most governments to implement the majority of NBDs that gain more than 80% of global support.

2. Bangladesh Deluge and 'War' on climate change

The second 'Never Again' moment was in July 2083. The Great Deluge drowned 1.2 million people in Bangladesh, after many warnings by Predictive Intelligence were ignored. It was the third major breach in ten years of the sea walls, which were built to cope with rising sea levels following a predicted rise of 2.1 degrees of global warming by 2095, and coinciding with the largest monsoon rains in history.

In the same month, the worst ever hurricane to hit Miami caused huge flooding and damage, with 3,758 recorded deaths, including 483 children sheltering in a single school. While deaths were low compared to those in Bangladesh, the second tragedy caught the attention of America, the only nation still not implementing the 2071 Global Warming NBD from 12 years earlier.

As a result of these two disasters, and following Predictive Intelligence of many more, governments around the world have spent more on reducing carbon emissions and on carbon capture over the last 15 years than in the previous 100.

3. Mutant flu pandemic and Health is for our World (HIFOR)

On 19 December 2089, the first cases of a mutant flu in Saigon chicken farmers were recorded. One in nine of the first 237 died in weeks, but 12% turned out to be highly infectious carriers with mild symptoms. Several were tourists returning to America.

By 16 January 2090, 275 suspected cases were reported in the UK, France, Denmark, the US, China, Thailand and Cambodia. Within eight weeks, several thousand were being tracked globally, which rose to over 10,000 over the next month.

On 10 April 2090, the World Health Organization (now part of the GDF) declared a Global Emergency. Some 47,528 people in 27 different nations were in quarantine, 3,785 had died, schools and public events were closed around the world, airlines were grounded, and cities were reporting panic buying.

Despite global mobilisation, by September, a million suspected cases were reported, of which 324,000 were later confirmed. It took two years, and a global vaccination programme directed by Predictive Intelligence, before the WHO declared an end to the emergency. Total toll was:

◆ 86,500 estimated deaths – mainly babies and young children and adults over 85

◆ 147,000 with long-term health needs/disabilities

◆ 1.3 billion working days lost or disrupted

◆ 1.2% of global economic output lost during each of two years

One in six deaths were in the US. Federal investigators reported multiple delays in the US response, which was caused by the nation's non-participation in many international agencies and initiatives linked to GDF and meant that America had slower access to vital data, technology, and to shared global facilities for mass-scale vaccine production, in which the rest of the world had invested. All three 'Never Again' events highlighted that far greater global collaboration would be needed in the twenty-second century. Predictive Intelligence also gained authority and respect.

Huge changes in populations: impact on future economy

As predicted 40 years ago, world population peaked at 11.8 billion in 2073, falling to 10.4 billion today; and it will fall again to 9.5 billion by 2130, as couples have fewer children. This year, the number of people in need of food, clean water or power, will fall to less than 0.3% of humanity.

Some 4.7 billion people migrated over the last 80 years, mainly from rural areas to cities in their own nations, but, as predicted, the process has slowed to 23 million a year over the last decade as the process of urbanisation comes to an end, and because of travel controls.

Average family size will fall to 1.5 by 2030, from 1.7 today, with many local variations related to income, for example Africa in 2098:

◆ Lowest income in poorest nations – 3.2 children per couple
◆ First generation, middle class – 1.2 children per couple
◆ Second generation or more, middle class – 1.7
◆ Third generation, very wealthy – 2.8

Some 96% of humanity now lives in nations partially industrialised 80 years ago, up from 85% in 2020. Average economic growth during the period has been 3.1% compared to 1.6% in the Old World.

Eighty years of 1.5% difference in growth rates means that average New World economies are 3.2 times larger in real terms than in 2020. New World nations generate 67% of global wealth, expected to rise to 72% by 2130.

Beyond 2130, growth rates will converge across the world, as a 350-year re-balancing ends the distortions caused by industrial revolutions in Old Nations from the eighteenth to the twentieth centuries.

Wealth contrasts will feed revolutionary tensions

Growing contrasts in wealth will cause more public resentment and anger, threatening future peace: 1% of the global population now owns (XX GDF DELETION)% of global wealth, up from 65% in 2050, despite GDF commitment to increase taxation of the super wealthy. Contrasts and risks will be greatest in most autocratic societies.

Health getting better but life expectancy will fall rapidly

European average life expectancy at birth has risen from 91 in 2050 to 102 today. Expect the figure to be 112 by 2130, assuming that most people access active health care until death, which is unlikely. Of all babies born today in China and Europe 3.6% have genes that have been edited, or (more commonly) have inherited edited genes from parents. Expect incidence of gene edits to double in babies born in China, Europe and America over the next two decades.

For over 15 years, we have reached 'escape velocity' for ageing, with privileged people increasing their remaining potential life expectancy by more than a year, every year. This has resulted from innovation in genetic redesign, regenerative medicine using a person's own cells, hyper-nutrition, and new drugs, such as those improving mitochondria power generation in cells.

However, in the UK, France, Canada and South Korea, more than half the population is choosing to stop Life Extension at least five years before their own Projected Maximum Age. 'Natural' death today usually takes place around three to six months after LE withdrawal, but this will shorten to around eight weeks as new therapies mean faster death when LE is withdrawn.

Last year, 20% of Europeans went further, requesting Active Death (AD) from their physicians, with (usually) close family present. AD is chosen mainly by older people who fear mental and physical collapse after LE withdrawal. AD has been legal in most nations for 40 years, and is likely to be so almost universally by 2125. By that date, AD will be the commonest cause of death in Europe (over 35%), twice the percentage in America, and seven times that in China or India. Statistics show that the main reason for older Europeans to request AD is a daily Predictive Analytics Health Score that falls below ten for more than fourteen consecutive days. Expect growing debate about how Predictive Scores are calculated and presented.

Benefits of Robots and Predictive Analytics

Looking back, we can see that the digital revolution of the last century was almost complete by 2050, with falls in the pace of innovation as most infotech devices became optimised, with the exception of Predictive Intelligence, robotics and state monitoring.

Two-thirds of humanity are living under state digital control, where online access is recorded and filtered, where government is able to (typically) physically arrest any citizen within (X GDF DELETION) minutes, based on Artificial Intelligence decisions, and Total Surveillance. (XX GDF DELETION)% of all arrests in China and India last year were for 'antisocial behaviours', while Europe and America are heading in a similar direction.

The first successful prosecution of the street-cleaning robot EXPIRA for murder in Paris took place in 2098. Previous prosecutions had been lost on appeal, as each robot argued that all bad actions were caused by bad human programming. Following the verdict, there was a wave of street attacks on robots across France.

Most new robots will be hidden, not physical entities, but intelligent industrial systems, controlling processes, vehicles, planes and farms. Predictors will be accurately forecasting 24-hour weather patterns up to eighteen months ahead for more than 65% of the planet's land area by 2110, using more power than any other digital process except security.

Home-care robots will continue to be bought by adult children for frail parents who will mostly resent or refuse their introduction. More home-care manufacturers will go out of business, following failure of iFriend to make more than a million sales globally in eight years, due to safeguarding and reliability issues.

Recreational drugs lead to Age of Indifference

Recreational smart drugs have mostly replaced alcohol in Europe, where alcohol is now viewed as tobacco was a hundred years ago. Expect more designer drugs, with ingredients mixed for the individual, based on genes, personality, lifestyle, desired effect and predictions of likely impact.

Now that the vast majority of hair samples of students in America show some traces of previous memory enhancer consumption, expect a decision soon by US exam boards to cease routine drug testing. (Surveys show that most professors use the same drugs regularly.)

Expect a further boom in the use of Happy Drugs (mood facilitators), with major social and political impacts. Next generation HDs will reduce most 'natural' drives and ambitions by 40 to 70%, depending on dose, including the desire to associate with other humans and to have sex or procreate, and will also moderate appetite and obesity. Their use will be opposed by many religious groups. Psychological dependency will be strong in young people, and overdose will risk psychosis or coma. Expect harsher penalties for supplying underage minors, with permanent loss of digital privileges.

As a result of HDs, human beings will enter an Age of Indifference, with less concern about personal privacy, state control, personal achievement, future disasters or other things, relying on Intelligence to identify and manage risks on their behalf.

Expect groups of activist parents to create new communities where 'normal' ranges of emotions and mental health issues are more tolerated. Expect more pressures on the state to step in where individuals make 'foolish' decisions about their lives because of HD intoxication, losing jobs or homes.

By 2130–2140, the Age of Indifference is likely to be overtaken by an Age of Duty – to oneself, family, community, nation, wider world – after analysis reveals the true costs of the HD experiment.

Retail more entertaining and quirky

The only reasons that people physically shop are to sample products, gain face-to-face advice, be entertained, or to take exercise. For this reason, major retail outlets will continue to charge for time in physical stores, partially refunded if there is a sale. Shopping and entertainment merged several decades ago, while 80% of physical purchases are now home-delivered in larger towns and cities, usually in less than an hour. Some 17% of all European retail sales are fully automated, with Intelligence deciding what needs automatic reordering.

Expect further explosive growth over the next decade of Quirky Retail – small independent stores, or street markets, full of local life, culture, expertise and creativity, with no charge for entry, as a refreshing, 'authentic' antidote to the near uniformity and costs of mass retail outlets. Quirky Retail will win 7% of all retail spending across Europe, America and Australia by 2120, compared to 3.5% today.

Work

As predicted over 50 years ago, the Sixth Industrial Revolution fused biometrics, human brain tissue (in a privileged few), Intelligence and Robotics, resulting in dislocation of over 4.5 billion jobs, mainly from 2020–2040, with automation affecting most manufacturing and office roles. However, numbers in paid employment in almost every decade since have been higher than before in most of Europe and many other nations.

Over 5.2 billion jobs have been created in the booming Personal Life Experience industry (PLE), many of them taken by people aged 65 and above as a major career change. Sectors include tourism, hospitality, entertainment, adult education (growing 6.4% a year globally), and personal skills training (4.2% growth a year), and jobs such as psychotherapists, family therapists, marriage therapists, spiritual advisors (2%), personal mentors or coaches, musicians and music teachers, artists of every kind, creative consultants, home carers for the elderly (3.7% per year) and so on.

Family and relationships – romance endures

Most young adults globally still aspire to get married one day to someone of the opposite gender, and to raise a family of their own. The romantic dream has endured, and will continue to do so, despite the impact of HDs. What is more, the same global surveys show that most parents remain in close touch with their own parents for much of their lives, with a third of them living within an hour's travel or less.

At the same time, divorce will continue to be more common, especially in nations with faster economic growth, and attitudes will continue to become more tolerant of other kinds of relationships, except, that is, in some nations in central Africa, and in parts of Asia and Europe, which are becoming steadily more fundamentalist, either Islamic or Christian in influence.

Leisure and travel – for authentic experience

Learning of every kind will continue to be a major element of leisure (and workplace) time. Most of this, as for the last 50 years, will be a solitary exercise, exploring free resources approved by the state.

Music has never been more important: consumption has rocketed globally over the past decade, for mood control, pleasure, and to enhance concentration (Smart Music). Expect further rapid growth of 'natural music' – no amplification or processing – as part of a wider search for authentic, shared, traditional experiences.

Demand for travel will keep growing, by 1 to 2% more than GDP in most nations, over the next 30 years. Many will travel as part of the 'truth and reality' movement, to enjoy social interaction with groups of others in different nations and cultures. This will be the case in particular for tourists from nations with the strictest controls in terms of knowledge access, or for unauthorised associations, including religious meetings.

Expect the growth of info-tourism, where an individual travels to a nation that has not implemented the GDF Digital Charter specifically in order to escape digital scrutiny, to engage in virtual social interactions without scrutiny, or for other reasons including antisocial behaviours and criminality. For all these reasons, travel controls will also increase, with permits required to leave nations often harder to obtain than visas to enter, based on Predictive Social Scores.

Expect continued investment in new airports, roads, high-speed rail and hyperloops, even though auto-taxis and auto-freight deliveries have cut daytime traffic by 20% in a decade in many major cities.

Car ownership will continue to fall, except in the poorest nations, where owning a vehicle will remain a major status symbol. In cities like Beijing, San Paolo, New York and Paris, most short journeys are already in shared or publicly owned, purpose-built small vehicles, and it is rare for people to own a vehicle.

By 2120 it will still be rare for someone to own a flying vehicle – most turbopods in cities like Dubai and Mumbai will be taxis, carrying one to two passengers less than six miles in minutes. Governments will continue to tax all these vehicles very heavily.

The cost of space tourism has fallen by 85% over the last 50 years, and could fall 35% more in the next 30. But lethal accidents on all three Chinese moon colonies, as well as on several orbiting hotels, continue to underline that this is unsustainable adventure-seeking.

However, the GDF Prevention of Extinction (POE) project launched by China, India, America, Nigeria and Russia last year, is likely to result in the first truly sustainable Space Cities on the moon by 2128 and on Mars by 2136, which are designed to have the potential (albeit very limited) to recolonise earth in the event of a global catastrophe.

Few banks and more pseudo-banks

A hundred years ago there were more than 18,000 banks and this has now fallen to 3,400, set to halve again over the next 20 years, because of compliance, cybersecurity and regulatory costs. Similarly, the massive consolidation in fund management, pension funds and other wealth management will continue. India will remain the world centre of FinTech innovation, as the first nation to abolish all paper money in 2031, and the first nation to implement biometrics for all.

Expect 12% growth per year of informal, community-based financial groups, following a fresh wave of deregulation, despite many stories about scams and other risks. Many of these new entities will use novel tools and currencies of their own.

Growth of inspiring, powerful leaders

As religious belief continues to fade in many Old World nations, the most loved and trusted national leaders in larger nations are more likely to acquire a quasi-mystical status, as legends in their own lifetimes, enhanced by carefully curated state-regulated media. Belief in the person, even when that person has been 'proven' to lack integrity, has become the defining political feature of our time.

Despite the growth of autocracy, which has led to dictatorships, almost all such leaders will aspire to be recognised as democratic over the next two decades, because of the irresistible attraction of public acclaim and international recognition. Nationalism/

tribalism will continue to be popular, fed by migrations and fear, and the major objective of the GDF will be to manage this.

Africa growing in wealth and influence

Despite Nigeria's recent military incursions, sub-Saharan Africa has been largely at peace for 100 years, with 5.8% average annual economic growth. Nigeria will continue as the epicentre of African political power, with the largest economy, army and nation. South Africa's economy will struggle to grow more than 2.6% next year, 54 years on from the forced exit of almost all white business- and land-owners, but it is likely to see a boost over the next decade from investment by Nigeria-based multinationals.

Middle East dominated by theocracies

Saudi Arabia's theocracy will continue to dominate politics across the region, held back by the economic issues and internal unrest that many hoped would settle after the voluntary stepping aside of the House of Saud in 2079. The economics of these nations will increasingly rely on desert power: solar farms supplying Europe and beyond via hypergrids. However, these fragile lines will continue to be targeted by militia.

Cyberterrorism means tighter state control

Expect further attempts by hostile groups or nations to hold companies, governments or even nations to ransom. This will justify wider government surveillance and creation of national intranets, inside which all direct web access is isolated from the rest of the world, with active filtering of all international traffic.

More people relaxed about privacy

While most older people today are relaxed about loss of privacy because of state monitoring, expect further growth of Jumbling among a younger generation, as a mild form of anti-state protest, where friends or colleagues extend group vocabularies with new words, or use existing words in ways that only they understand. Jumbling has already produced many thousands of new words and phrases in common use. Jumbling will frustrate governments, and will prove hard to legislate against.

Major religions hit by belief in aliens

Following media stories over the last decade, 47% of humanity now believes that we are in contact with intelligent beings from other galaxies. This belief has spawned new religious cults, collectively known as Philaliens, with varied beliefs about the powers and origins of distant civilisations. Expect these cults to grow, and merge.

Most people today self-identify as Christian (largest religion) or Muslim, and most of humanity still measures time from the birth of Jesus. From a low point in Europe in the 2060s, church attendance has grown steadily, in parallel to what happened earlier in North America, partly fuelled by Christian missionaries arriving from other parts of the world, bringing with them a passion and commitment that had become unfamiliar to their host nations.

Each major religion has seen major transformation in the last 20 years, in how people express faith, and in the size of gatherings, trending to very large and very small – more football stadiums, more groups in homes. Both trends will feed concerns and crackdowns by autocratic governments, who will fear all influential religious movements, whether promoted by charismatic leaders at large events, or spreading 'underground' in tens of thousands of private meetings. But such crackdowns are likely to be ineffective.

Most Muslims will continue to be found in Asia and in northern parts of Africa, as well as in the Middle East, with more ideological clashes arising in central Africa, especially in Nigeria, DR Congo, Uganda, Kenya, Malawi and Burundi, not only with Christianity, but also from within the Islamic community itself.

Major risks to the year 2120

We predict the four greatest risks to humanity in order, from lower to higher risk and potential impact:

◆ Regional conflicts – triggered by tribalism and scarce resources on a crowded planet

- Viral pandemic – risk related directly to size of global population and travel boom
- Revolution / civil war – contrasts between wealthy and poor unsustainable
- Predictive Analytics warnings ignored – budget cuts lead to reduced social control, regional conflict, industrial disruption, criminal activity and economic chaos.

Chapter 8

SHAPING YOUR FUTURE

AS WE SAW AT THE VERY BEGINNING of our journey, the cube of your own future is weighted according to who you are, where you are and the nature of your work, and your stage of life.

We have also seen how hard it is to hold the entire future in your mind at the same time. You cannot see all those six faces at once. That's why it is so important to keep turning the cube, and to keep dipping in and out of this book, maybe over some weeks or months. As one group of faces comes into focus, others recede into the background.

You have to imagine that your own cube is uniquely weighted, so that a random throw will show one of the faces that is most important for you, in the next stage of your own future.

But take care, for every now and then a much less familiar face will demand your attention, with many new opportunities and challenges.

So keep turning the cube, stay agile, focused and true to your own sense of destiny. Because life is too important to waste a single day. Life is too short to do things you don't believe in.

How very small numbers change the future

People often tell me that they feel powerless to change their own future, let alone anyone else's. But most of us have far more ability to change things than we realise. When I first started presenting the Six Faces of the Future, I spoke to a group of CEOs and chairmen

of some of the world's most powerful corporations at the World
Economic Forum, Davos.

I showed them the cube: how the usual way for CEOs of
companies to view it is from the top. They tend to focus on just
three Faces of the Future: Fast, Urban and Universal. In other
words, all about the speed of change, urbanisation, demographics,
health care, fashions and fads, technology and globalisation, and
so on. It's the typical world view of banks, IT companies, global
manufacturing and e-commerce.

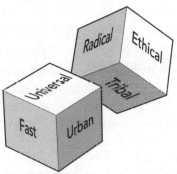

Turn the cube 180 degrees and we are confronted with Tribal,
Radical and Ethical. This is a future driven by the forces of nationalism, sectarianism, social media, activism, personal motivation,
aspiration, ambition, sustainability, politics, religion and terrorist
movements.

I asked these CEOs a question: in their own experience, how
many people would it take to totally change their strategy?

What proportion of their shareholders, customers, staff, or
readers of social media, would it take to turn the direction of the
company upside down, if very Radical in thinking, very Ethically
driven and very Tribal, or well organised. The answer is always the
same: less than 2%. One person in 50 could be enough.

I asked another question. How many shareholders do you need
to keep the chairman of a publicly listed company awake at night
before an annual general meeting? The answer is always the same.
Only one person is needed, with one share, costing a few dollars,
asking the right 'ethical' question about a very controversial and

'radical' issue, to unleash uncontrollable forces in the 'tribal' media, forcing major policy changes.

But if a single shareholder can shape the future direction of an entire global corporation; if a small group of activists in a company or a community can influence a five-year strategy ...

How many people do *you* know or influence? You almost certainly have far more power to change things than you realise, inside the organisation you work for, or with people you know.

Look what can be done by the owner of a single share, and consider the potential impact of your own life over the next ten years to influence people around you for the better.

How to stay 'Futurewise'

People often ask me how they should stay informed. A key part of the answer is to read quality publications like the *Financial Times*, *The Economist* and *New Scientist*, and anything else you can lay your hands on, to broaden your perspectives.

Travel as much as you can to unfamiliar places, talk to people about unfamiliar things. Seek out unfamiliar experiences, cultures, places and forums. For instance, always talk to your taxi driver – such drivers are often the first to notice a change in their city.

Meet new people from very different walks of life. For me, being part of a cosmopolitan church has been in London for 40 years has been helpful from that point of view. And the AIDS charity ACET, which started in our own family home 30 years ago, and is now in 15 nations, has been a tremendous learning experience, taking me to remote parts of some of the poorest nations.

Watch people. When you visit a city, stop for a while and linger – whether in a café or a park. What do you see? All of the future is streaming by.

Visit people in their homes in other nations, if you can. You will learn more in an hour about their way of life, family relationships and culture than in 30 years working in the same team.

Above all, stay intensely curious and interested in other people's stories. Expect to change your own opinions and your own future.

You have choices every day. Do what you believe in and feel most passionate about.

About the author

PATRICK DIXON is the founder and chairman of Global Change Ltd, a growth strategy and forecasting company. He is the author of 17 books (over 640,000 in print in over 43 languages), and a physician. Previous books include *Futurewise*, *SustainAgility*, *The Genetic Revolution* and *Building a Better Business*. He has been ranked as one of the 20 most influential business thinkers alive today.* He has spoken to audiences in over 60 nations and is one of the world's most sought-after keynote speakers at corporate events.

He advises boards and senior teams on a wide range of strategic issues. Clients include Google, Microsoft, IBM, KLM/Air France, BP, ExxonMobil, World Bank, Siemens, Prudential, Aviva, UBS, Credit Suisse, PwC, Hewlett Packard, Gillette, GSK, Forbes, Fortune, BT, BBC, Fedex and DHL. He has also taught on a wide variety of executive education programmes at the London Business School since 1999. He also works with entrepreneurs and start-up companies to help accelerate growth.

Patrick has worked as group strategy director for Acromas Ltd, which owned the AA and Saga, before its flotation. He has been a non-executive director of Allied Health Care Ltd, which delivers over 40 million home-care visits a year across the UK. He was also chairman of the cancer biotech company Virttu Biologics Ltd from 2012 to 2015, since bought by SORRENTO Therapeutics Inc.

He has appeared on many TV stations, including CNN, CNBC,

* 17th in the world in Thinkers 50 2005; 47th in the world in 2003.

Fox News, Sky News and ITV, with features in the *Financial Times*, *Telegraph* and *Time* magazine. His website has been used by more than 16 million different people, with 7 million video views, and he has 50,000 followers on Twitter.

He trained as a physician at Kings College, Cambridge and Imperial College, London, during which he launched a healthcare IT startup, called Medicom. In 1988, after working as a cancer physician, caring for those dying of cancer, he started the international AIDS agency ACET, which today has programmes in 15 nations, mainly in the poorest parts of the world. ACET began as a result of his first book, *The Truth about AIDS*. He then wrote many other books, which led to broadcasting, lecturing on trends, and to advisory roles with many companies.

Patrick is 62, married to Sheila for 40 years. Both are still heavily involved in supporting ACET around the world, in places like India and Uganda. They have four married children and six grandchildren, and live in the UK, where they are active in a local church. Patrick's other interests include long-distance sailing, painting and writing.

http://www.globalchange.com
http://www.youtube.com/pjvdixon
http://twitter.com/patrickdixon
patrickdixon@globalchange.com
+44 7768 511390

Acknowledgements

AS ANY LEADER OR WRITER KNOWS, any attempt to anticipate future trends can be a humbling and somewhat daunting process. Whatever success I may have had in this endeavour over the last 30 years has only been due to the combined foresight of a very large number of people.

I am deeply grateful to the many hundreds of senior business, government and NGO leaders from every industry and sector, as well as several hundred more innovators and specialists from over 100 nations, who have generously shared personal insights and reflections with me over the last few years about where they think their own industries and regions may be heading. These conversations have typically happened when working together, or over dinner, at corporate events where I am speaking, in board strategy sessions, or in workshops and seminars, as we have grappled together with what all of our futures might be like.

I am particularly grateful to Prabhu Guptara, who while at UBS Wolfsberg encouraged me to develop the original FUTURE construct, and for his faithful critique and mentoring over many years. Special thanks also (in no particular order) to Brian Souter, Sinclair Beecham, Peter Vardy, Andrew Goodsell, Tim Pethick and Martin Lindström.

I am also grateful to those working with some of poorest and most marginalised communities in emerging nations and those supporting them, who have taught me so much about rapid social changes, opportunities and challenges in their own countries, in connection with their inspiring work as part of the international AIDS agency ACET. People like David Kabiswa, Alan Ellard, Marek Slansky, Yvonne Kavuo, Milan Presburger, Sam Udanyi, Sujai and Lavanya Suneetha, Alex Zhibrik, Richard and Wendy Phillips, Richard Carson, Peter Fabian and Sarah Smith. Also thanks to many Faculty at London Business School that I have had the privilege to work with on Executive Education programmes during the last 16 years, including Dominic Houlder, Julian Birkinshaw, Lynda Gratton, Gay Haskins, Costas Markides, Nigel Nicholson, Andrew Scott, Linda Yueh and Jules Goddard – all of whom have helped sharpen my own thinking, as they have graciously allowed me to sit in on their sessions from time to time.

I am also indebted to a host of great thinkers, debaters, speakers and writers whose insights have influenced my evolving view of the world. I was first inspired to explore the future by the work of people like Nicholas Negroponte, Charles Handy, John Naisbitt, Peter Cochrane, Patrick Johnstone and Fons Trompenaars. And then I also owe thanks to the countless thousands of web writers, to the community of future trends bloggers, and to all those who make comments on my website, post responses to my videos and so on – often bringing vital perspectives.

Thanks to all the wonderful Profile Books team: to Stephen Brough, co-founder and senior editor, for inspiring me to travel once more into the future as a writer – he has been an absolute pleasure to write for, as has his successor Ed Lake. Both made a huge number of suggestions and comments; Penny Daniel for making it all happen within a very tight deadline; Patrick Taylor, Susanne Hillen and Fiona Screen for copy-editing and sorting out issues with such care; and Anna Marie Fitzgerald for managing publicity. Thanks to Richard Herkes, formerly senior editor at Kingsway, for suggesting my first book – leading to 16 more over the years. I am also grateful to many other people like Glyn MacAulay, Steve Clifford, Gerald Coates, Lyndon Bowring, Lawrence Singlehurst, Andrew Owen, Mark Melluish, George Verwer, Phil Wall, Norman Barnes, David Smith, Peter Brierley, Gary and Max Hamilton, Ravi Dua, Linda and Richard Ward and Simon Blanchflower, who have all helped me make better sense at various times over the years of how the wider world is evolving.

And of course thanks to Sheila, my wife (and best friend for more than 46 years), for her endless encouragement and feedback on the text, and to our four children and their spouses for helping me identify early trend signals.

Statistics and other important facts are from published government and other sources, as well as from those working at the cutting edge of change and innovation, who are at the forefront of changing tomorrow's world.

Index